THE Qur'anic System OF Sustenance

G.A. Parwez

Translated and edited by
Saleena Karim & Fazal Karim

ISLAMIC DAWN SOCIETY

The Qur'anic System of Sustenance

ISBN: 978-0-9571416-4-3

Translation: Fazal Karim & Saleena Karim
Editor: Saleena Karim
Cover design: Saleena Karim

Published by Islamic Dawn Society, London
in association with Tolu-e-Islam Trust, Lahore
and Libredux Publishing, Nottingham

www.toluislam.com

I am but a humble student of the Qur'an, and disseminating the teachings of the Qur'an through lectures, speeches, broadcasts and publications is my life's work. Along with presenting the Qur'an's recommended system of life, I have also stressed its methodology. I myself follow the Qur'an's call and instruct others to do the same. And since I have full conviction in the Qur'an's guidance, I do not wish to ever budge an inch from it, regardless of any external pressures.

- G.A. Parwez

CONTENTS

ABOUT THE AUTHOR

Ghulam Ahmad Parwez was born at Batala, Punjab, British India in 1903. He studied the Qur'an and the classics of Islam under the tutelage of his grandfather, a celebrated scholar and eminent *Sufi* (Muslim mystic). Parwez gained a thorough understanding of the traditions, beliefs and practices of conventional Islam including the discipline of *tusawwuf* (Muslim mysticism) with its arduous meditation and spiritual exercises. His study of the history of Islam, beliefs and practices of pre-Islamic religions and wider knowledge of human thought throughout the ages inspired him to question the prevailing beliefs of Muslims. He moved away from the religious ideas that have accumulated around Islam over the centuries and turned his attention to the pristine beliefs expounded by the Qur'an.

Parwez's immense philosophical work is the result of his deep study of Islam not as a religion but as *deen* – a word that has no parallel in Western languages. It can best be described as a 'Way of Life' and in the Islamic context, a social system based on Qur'anic values and its immutable principles. The exploration of the meaning of *deen* forms the core of more than forty-five books and innumerable essays, articles and lectures. His most famous books in Urdu include:

- *Mafhoom-ul-Qur'an* (Exposition of the Qur'an) in three volumes
- *Lughaat-ul-Qur'an* (Dictionary and concepts of Qur'anic words) in four volumes
- *Matalib-ul-Furqan* (Exegesis - *Tafseer* - of the Holy Qur'an) in six volumes (the seventh volume was printed posthumously)
- *Tabweeb-ul-Qur'an* (Classification of the Holy Qur'an) in three volumes

- *Miraaj-e-Insaaniat* (Biography of Messenger Muhammad)
- *Nizam-e-Rabbubiyyat* (System of Universal Sustenance)

His writings have inspired widespread awakening in intelligentsia and the public alike in many parts of the world.

Aside from being an author and scholar, Parwez was the founder of *Tolu-e-Islam*, a monthly magazine, which he launched in 1938 at the instance of Dr Sir Muhammad Iqbal and under the guidance of Quaid-e-Azam ('Great Leader') Mahomed Ali Jinnah, founder of Pakistan. This magazine continues to be published from Lahore regularly to this day.

He also took an active part in the Pakistan movement, and as a counsel of Jinnah on matters pertaining to Islam, Parwez was one of the few people who was allowed to visit Jinnah without an appointment. He received the *Tehrik-e-Pakistan* (Pakistan Movement) Gold Medal posthumously for his services to the nation on 14 August 1989 (Pakistan Independence Day).

Maqbool Mahmood Farhat, Essex, UK

ACKNOWLEDGEMENTS

After publishing his book *Nizam-e-Rabbubiyat*, Ghulam Ahmad Parwez had a burning desire to have this work translated into English so the world could know what Islam offers as a solution for the economic issues that continue to plague modern society.

It was fortunate that Maqbool Mahmood Farhat of Bazm Tolu-e-Islam London found Saleena Karim, author of the well-known book *Secular Jinnah & Pakistan*, and her father Fazal Karim, both of Nottingham, UK for this project.

With a sense of solemn responsibility they have produced the English version in the shortest possible time and have also helped to put it into print in the UK. Both deserve my deep appreciation. I can truly say that the completion of the translation of the Urdu book presented a great challenge and it was possible only with the hard work and commitment of father and daughter.

A final note of thanks must go to Bazm Tolu-e-Islam London whose guidance and support made this work possible; and with special thanks to Mohammad Aslam of Elm Park, UK, who met the entire cost of the project.

Dr Zahida Durrani
Executive Head
Tolu-e-Islam Trust
Lahore, Pakistan

1 October 2012

FOREWORD
(editor)

Ghulam Ahmad Parwez was without doubt one of the greatest minds of the last century. In his time he was misunderstood and deemed a heretic in his own country, and his essentially rationalist approach was viewed with much suspicion in the Muslim world. Since his death in 1985 however, his popularity has steadily grown both in Pakistan and across the world. The full impact of his work has yet to be properly assessed and appreciated.

My father (Fazal Karim) and I feel honoured to have had the opportunity to translate Parwez's seminal work, *Nizam-e-Rabbubiyat*, into English. The Urdu title literally translates to *System of (Universal) Sustenance*, but over the years among those discussing his work in English it has wrongly been referred to as the 'Qur'anic Economic System', which is not only a misnomer, but also exposes a gross misinterpretation of Parwez's thought. Although this book discusses communism and capitalism in light of Qur'anic principles, and, notwithstanding the fact that Parwez describes this book as a 'monograph on the subject of economics'[1], it is fair to say that it does not, as such, present a purely *economic* system with the mere aim of meeting material needs. Whereas the very word 'economy' implies an acceptance of the scarcity principle, the Divine principles of sustenance cannot be characterised together as 'economy', being based on the Qur'an's self-attested principle of 'abundance'. Nor should the Urdu word *nizam* (system) in the title be taken to mean a closed system. On the subject of the word *deen* (usually translated as 'religion'), Parwez has stated elsewhere that whilst 'way of life' (or 'system') is the closest meaning of the Arabic, even this is insufficient.

---

[1] See Parwez's Preface to the 1978 edition. In fact it seems he wrote this line only because he had added three appendices on economic subjects.

Deen certainly is a systemic word, but it does not literally translate to 'system'. Since (to paraphrase Parwez) Islam as a *deen* equates to the Divine process of sustenance (*Rabbubiya*) at work throughout the universe,[2] his chosen Urdu word *nizam* likewise does not point to a fixed system, but to a set of principles taken together as a whole.

Moreover, this book is really an attempt to delineate the Qur'anic method of meeting human needs in their entirety – both material and 'spiritual'. Parwez himself remarks in Chapter 4: 'Meeting our physical needs is a means to an end, and not an end in itself'. Again in Chapter 8, he writes: 'The higher purpose of the Divine system of sustenance is not just to meet the physical needs of people. Indeed, meeting physical needs is only a rudimentary and superficial aim. From the Qur'anic perspective this is only a step in the direction of life's true purpose, which is to develop and perfect the self, and this can be achieved only by enacting the principle of universal sustenance'.

In short, Parwez has tried to show that the Divine system of sustenance not only serves to rewrite the generally accepted rules of economy, but also those of human society, and by extension, of reality. While there are those who would view Parwez's views as utopian and unrealistic, he was inspired by the Qur'anic line that it is all 'easy for God' (as mentioned in Chapter 8 of this book) – suggesting that what may seem difficult in view of humanity's present mindset would in fact be very easy for a nation that understands the Divine Message.

The translation

This is a translation of the 1978 edition with minor editorial revisions and additions made by the translators solely for the purpose of clarifying the content of the main text. We have also added footnotes (all marked *Translators' note*), again to either expand upon or clarify statements made in the original Urdu text.

The chief difference between the original 1955 and 1978 editions was the addition of some appendices by Parwez, namely: *Islami Socialism* (*Islamic Socialism*), *Jahaan Marx Na-Kaam Reh Geya* (*Where Marx Failed*), *Mao Tse Tung aur Qur'an* (*Mao Tse Tung and the Qur'an: A Comparison*) and *Riba ke Behs* (*The Debate Over Interest*). As these titles suggest, Parwez wrote these appendices mainly to address communism, which was still operational in both Russia and China at the time. Since then communism has essentially failed worldwide

---

[2] See end of Chapter 1.

(even China, while technically remaining a communist state, is behaving increasingly like a modern capitalist state in practice), and so the content of these appendices is no longer relevant to the present economic climate. For this reason we have not reproduced them. However we have translated two important sections on *zakaat* and *riba* from the third of Parwez's appendices, *Riba ke Behs*, and included it as a short additional chapter, inserted before the Afterword.

When it comes to quotes from the Qur'an, we have taken the liberty of inserting well-known English translations (slightly edited to modernise the English) wherever Parwez has referred to particular verses and reproduced the Arabic. Parwez's approach (as he explains in his Preface to the 1978 edition, also reproduced in this book) was to translate meaning for meaning (exposition) rather than translate literally word for word. This is because literal translations sometimes fail to convey the full meaning of the Qur'anic text – a fact universally acknowledged by all translators of the Qur'an. Nevertheless, wherever the meaning of Parwez's expositional translation is close to a traditional version, we have seamlessly combined the two. This has the added benefit of showing the reader how to better understand literal translations. At other times, Parwez's expositional text is either included in the main text immediately following the traditional quotations, or occasionally part of it appears in footnotes.

We would like to express our heartfelt thanks to Mr Maqbool Mahmood Farhat of Ilford, Essex, who went to a great deal of trouble in locating the vast majority of the references in this book. Some of the works were not fully referenced in the original Urdu text, which made the task of locating them that much more difficult. To Mr Farhat goes the credit of saving us much time in this area.

Finally, it goes without saying that no translation is ever truly perfect, and so we end by saying that any deficiency in this translation is ours and ours alone.

Saleena Karim, Nottingham, UK
15 July 2012

INTRODUCTION
to the first edition (1955)

Every Muslim from a cleric to a layman proudly proclaims that Islamic teachings are without parallel anywhere in the world; and that even the combined efforts of the world's scholars, lawmakers and diplomats could not hope to create a constitution like the Islamic Code. They provide solutions to every aspect of human life, be it socioeconomic, political, public or personal. No doubt this is true, and it is accepted universally amongst Muslims. Surprisingly however, if we ask anyone what is so exceptional about Islam that the world's greatest thinkers couldn't match its teachings, no one will be able to offer a satisfactory answer. At best we will get the reply that Islam teaches us to be honest, to not steal, not be unjust, not exploit others, to always be courteous, to treat your fellow man as your brother and as your equal, etc. Alternatively, Muslims may say that God instructs us to pray, fast, and perform the Hajj pilgrimage, and then they will proceed to explain the merits of such ritual acts. But leaving aside the rituals, the question is: Which of these moral teachings are unique to Islam, and which cannot be found anywhere else? It might be argued that these teachings can be found in every major religion, as well as amongst agnostics and atheists. No one ever says that dishonesty is a good thing, or that theft is acceptable, or oppression is a virtue, or deceit is honourable. Thus it is hardly true to say that the teachings of Islam have no parallel. Therefore, all that remains to distinguish between Islam and other faiths is the ritual aspect, i.e. prayer, etc.

Spiritual advancement

At this point an outsider may object that regardless of their dedication to their faith, it is no secret that the Muslim world is presently in a poor state of affairs. And in truth we will be unable to offer a response to this objection. At best Muslims might reply that notwithstanding our status in the modern world, we are ahead *spiritually* and so we will be the victors in the life to come. Of course such a statement is impossible to corroborate with hard evidence. 'Spiritual advancement' (being related to the noumenal, the non-physical) can neither be quantitatively measured nor weighed. Every religion of the world claims to offer the means for spiritual advancement, yet there is no empirical standard by which to determine which of our belief systems actually offers what it claims, and which does not. Then there is the question of salvation for the afterlife. Producing evidence for this is even more difficult than for spiritual advancement. Again, every religion equally claims to be the means to salvation, but no religion provides either any physical proof or rational argument to verify it. Indeed, if we stop to consider all that we blindly learn about spirituality and pass onto others throughout our lives, we soon realise that we have no rational basis for doing so. This is not to say that our beliefs are wrong in themselves; there is no doubt that they are legitimate in their own right. But however hard we search we fail to find a rational basis for the truth, and so ultimately we have to take it from an alternative source.

Before the revelation of the Qur'an, all the world's religions chose to focus solely on spiritual advancement and salvation, and dissociated themselves from earthly affairs. They left the worldly kingdom to Caesar, and sought the Heavenly Kingdom for themselves. Eventually the pious learned to hate the material so much that they wouldn't even speak of it. In their view the allure of material things was an obstacle in the way of spiritual advancement. Since they never felt a need to verify for themselves whether or not their beliefs were correct, the religious elite felt self-assured that they were on the path of truth, and that everyone else was on the path of falsehood. Later I will show how the Qur'an challenges this idea. Suffice it to say for now that Muslims have failed to adhere to Qur'anic teachings and have reverted to religious beliefs instead. They have let despots of every kind rule the earth, whilst spiritual advancement and salvation have become the sole domain of religion. Consequently conventional Islam can hardly be distinguished from any other religion, and so it is futile to try and contrast between it and them.

The Qur'anic approach

The Qur'an states with regards to the story of Adam:[3]

> You will have to live on earth for a long time and will need a means of subsistence. 2:36

And so we must remember that:

> Whoever believes in God's law of *mukafat* (i.e. 'law of requital'[4], or the Last Day), and leads his life accordingly, will be duly compensated by his Sustainer; and no fear need they have, and neither shall they grieve. 2:62

The Qur'an makes its warning clear to those who fail to abide by this guidance:

> On the other hand, those who reject Our Guidance will lead a life of constant torment in this world and beyond. 2:39

Hence the Qur'an provides guidance for humanity's earthly existence. It offers solutions to fundamental questions of the kind that humans have grappled with throughout history and have failed to resolve for themselves. In short, Qur'anic teachings enable humanity to succeed both on earth and in the hereafter. We can thus see that the Qur'an's principles and laws are essential to resolving all human issues, and this is where the uniqueness and veracity of Islam lies.

Leaving the Qur'an aside for the moment, we might ask why humanity has failed to resolve these fundamental issues. In my book *Insaan ne kya socha?* (*What has Man Thought?*) I have discussed the history of human thought. After the publication of this book I came across Dr. Reinhold Niebuhr's *Moral Man and Immoral Society*. The first chapter of his book opens with the following words:

---

[3] The meaning of the story of Adam is explored in my book *Iblees-o- Adam* (*Satan and Adam*) (1945).

[4] **Translators' note:** Law of requital (Parwez's own English term as taken from *Islam: A Challenge to Religion* (1968)) – i.e. every action in this universe has a reaction which will in turn be ongoing, with the final results manifesting themselves in full sooner or later.

Though human society has roots which lie deeper in history than the beginning of human life, men have made comparatively but little progress in solving the problem of their aggregate existence. Each century originates a new complexity and each new generation faces a new vexation in it. For all the centuries of experience, men have not yet learned how to live together without compounding their vices and covering each other "with mud and with blood." The society in which each man lives is at once the basis for, and the nemesis of, that fullness of life which each man seeks. However much human ingenuity may increase the treasures which nature provides for the satisfaction of human needs, they can never be sufficient to satisfy all human wants; for man, unlike other creatures, is gifted and cursed with an imagination which extends his appetites beyond the requirements of subsistence. Human society will never escape the problem of the equitable distribution of the physical and cultural goods which provide for the preservation and fulfilment of human life.[5]

Selfishness

The greatest challenge before human beings is how to fairly distribute all in nature that has been freely[6] provided by God for their physical development, and thus enable humanity to unlock its hidden potential for its intellectual development. To date however, humans have not come up with a viable solution to their problems. The Qur'an has summed up the reason in the following few words:

[You will be] enemies to one another. 2:36

(In other words: Humanity was divided by race, culture and nationality, leading to enmity, and the more powerful groups and individuals took control of the resources that God had provided freely for the benefit of all humanity.)

With the birth of selfishness and inequality, bloodshed and chaos was bound to ensue:

---

[5] Niebuhr, Reinhold (1932) *Moral Man and Immoral Society: A Study in Ethics and Politics* 2005 reprint, London: Continuum International Publishing Group, p.3

[6] 'Freely' meaning resources that are freely available and for which no human effort was required to attain it, e.g. water

> [The *Malaika* [7] said] O God! What kind of creature is this
> who is now being settled upon the earth? This creature will
> rebel against Your Law and, thereby, cause bloodshed and
> disorder. 2:30

Hence human society is in a perpetual struggle, and although throughout history we have endeavoured to find peaceful solutions to our problems, we have failed time and again. The nineteenth-century philosopher and social reformer Jeremy Bentham spent his life studying different societies to see if he could find a way to put an end to the trait of selfishness. He even began movements in pursuit of this end, but his attempts all ended in failure. Eventually he became so disillusioned that he wrote:

> Now, for some years past, all inconsistencies, all surprises,
> have vanished: everything that has served to make the field of
> politics a labyrinth, has vanished. A clue to the interior of the
> labyrinth has been found: it is the principle of self-preference.
> Man, from the very constitution of his nature, prefers his own
> happiness to that of all other sensitive beings put together: but
> for this self-preference, the species could not have had
> existence. Place the chief care of each man in any other breast
> or breasts than his own, (the case of infancy and other cases of
> intrinsic helplessness excepted,) a few years, not to say a few
> months or weeks, would suffice to sweep the whole species
> from the earth. [8]

Niehbur was of the same opinion, but he has also added that 'self-deception and hypocrisy is an unvarying element in the moral life of all human beings'.[9] To his mind, if a single individual is corrupt, he will inevitably corrupt his nation with him. Hence, as Bentham discovered, a few corrupt individuals may be responsible for the given condition of an entire nation. In fact the underlying reason for this injustice is that different people have varying earning capabilities. Animals don't encounter this issue and hence no animal has to worry about earning its keep. Similarly, the simple class structure within primitive human

---

[7] *Malaika* – usually translated as 'angels', but is obviously a metaphoric reference to the forces of nature that have no free will.

[8] Bentham, Jeremy (1838-43) *The Works of Jeremy Bentham, published under the Superintendence of his Executor, John Bowring* Edinburgh: William Tait Vol. X p.80

[9] Niebuhr, op. cit. p.63

tribes is based solely on physical prowess rather than on intellectual difference and hence here also we won't find a complex socioeconomic hierarchy. But as we move up in societal types and the emphasis moves to intellectual difference, socioeconomic class division becomes increasingly acute and so we see more conflict in the cause of self-interest. James Madison has written:

> The diversity in the faculties of men, from which the rights of property originate, is not less an insuperable obstacle to a uniformity of interests. The protection of these faculties is the first object of government. From the protection of different and unequal faculties of acquiring property, the possession of different degrees and kinds of property immediately results; and from the influence of these on the sentiments and views of the respective proprietors ensues a division of the society into different interests and parties.[10]

This is exactly what the Qur'an has succinctly described in verse 2:36 cited earlier.

The failure of reason

The question is: Can a viable solution be found by intellectual means? We have seen that Bentham denounced humanity and declared that selfishness is in our nature and can never be eliminated. Dr. Niebuhr has likewise written:

> While it is possible for intelligence to increase the range of benevolent impulse, and thus prompt a human being to consider the needs and rights of other than those to whom he is bound by organic and physical relationship, there are definite limits in the capacity of ordinary mortals which makes it impossible for them to grant to others what they claim for themselves. ... it will never be possible to insure moral antidotes sufficiently potent to destroy the deleterious effects of the poison of power upon character. ... So difficult is it to avoid the Scylla of despotism and the Charybdis of anarchy that it is safe to hazard the prophecy that the dream of perpetual peace and brotherhood for human society is one which will never be fully realised. ... While rapid means of communication have increased the breadth of knowledge about world affairs among

---

[10] As cited in Niebuhr (Ibid. p.76)

citizens of various nations, and the general advance of education has ostensibly promoted the capacity to think rationally and justly upon the inevitable conflicts of interest between nations, there is nevertheless little hope of arriving at a perceptible increase of international morality through the growth of intelligence and the perfection of means of communication.[11]

So our thinkers up to the present day have concluded that the problem cannot be resolved by the use of reason. Nevertheless, one intellectual solution being considered at present is communism. As such this political ideology contains nothing truly new; thinkers have long been aware that the issue revolves around 'private ownership'. If private ownership could somehow be abolished, then the problem would solve itself. Communism therefore seems an attractive proposition. But it is also true that the abolishment of private ownership has never been broadly adopted within any social system. The reason for this is simple: if people are not allowed to keep the surplus of their earnings, irrespective of how hard they work, then the incentive to work hard is greatly diminished. But if people are subsequently permitted to retain private capital, then our original problem of inequality returns. Karl Marx introduced the idea of communism and the experiment is presently being tried in Russia. As to the result of this experiment, there is a wealth of literature both for and against it. But one thing all are agreed upon is that Russia has lowered its iron curtain, and no one is allowed to see what is behind it. Obviously if communists are giving their all to portray their ideology as a potential paradise on earth, and yet they are hiding their experiment from the eyes of the world, then surely the communist system is not as rosy as it seems.

The truth is that communism doesn't a have a solid ethical basis for a society in which people work day and night, only to give their earnings away for the benefit of others. As a result there is no option but to keep people working by force and to provide them with just enough subsistence to keep them able to work. The communist experiment taking place in Russia is detrimental to humanity. In the first place, human life is deemed to be no different to animal life, revolving purely around the physical and ending with death. In other words, it is assumed that there are no human needs beyond the

---

[11] Niebuhr op. cit. p.4, 15, 16, 57.

material. Secondly, once their material needs are met, their individuality is lost.

As part of my own search for a rational solution to the socioeconomic problem, I have closely studied the communist movement for a long time, and have concluded that this movement poses a grave danger to humanity. My heart trembles at the thought of what might happen to humanity if communism is adopted worldwide.[12] In fact it was my apprehension that compelled me to return to the Qur'an for a solution to the socioeconomic question. I am only a student of the Qur'an, and I have spent much of my life studying it closely. In seeking its guidance I have approached it without any preconceptions. I open its pages with an empty mind and then try to find the answer to my question. I accept whatever guidance I find in the Qur'an, even if it goes against the view of the whole world, and even if it goes against my personal opinion. This is the reason why my own people as well as outsiders are generally critical of my findings. I have even looked to the Qur'an for guidance on this matter, and am including its solution in this book.[13] The Qur'an is Revelation (*Wahi*), in which there is no possibility of error. But I don't claim that my own understanding is immutable like *Wahi*; I acknowledge that there is always a possibility of error on my part and that what I have understood should not be taken to be the last word. Certainly I must insist that you, the reader, examine what I have written in light of the Qur'an, and wherever you spot a flaw, you must show me the error of my logic with Qur'anic support.

Islam, not communism

From what I have learned the Qur'an doesn't allow people to hoard their surplus, and it doesn't allow the means of production (whether natural or manmade) to be privately owned, whether at the individual or social level. The layman may think that this is no different to

---

[12] I originally made this statement in 1955. Since that time the world has witnessed the complete failure of communism in Russia. After Russia, China also took up communism but the troubles following Mao Tse Tung's death suggest that communism will soon fail there as well. – G.A. Parwez, February 1978

[13] **Translators' note:** The solution that Parwez is referring to is to be found within the programme of the Qur'anic 'establishment of *salaat*' – i.e. the preliminary educational movement designed to expound the true meaning of the Qur'an. For details, see Chapter 8.

communism. He may think it strange that on the one hand I call communism a great danger to humanity and on the other hand I call Islam (which appears to operate on similar principles) a panacea. Some people have taken this criticism further, going so far as to say that whatever I have written is in fact communism in the guise of Islam. But as we will later show in this book, people who make such criticisms know neither enough about communism nor about Islam. Similarly, there are some people who have coined the term 'Islamic socialism'. This term is as absurd as saying 'Qur'anic atheist'. There is no doubt that communism rejects private ownership as does Islam, but it is also true that communism is opposed to Islam on ideological grounds. The fact that the two share a similar principle does not make communism Islamic in of itself. It's like saying that Aryan society rejects idolism as does Islam, and thus the two are one and the same. Communism is not only an economic system, but also a philosophy based on principles that are in stark contrast to Islam. According to Qur'anic teachings the whole universe is created by the Supreme and all-Knowing, and it operates under His inviolable laws. There is a purpose to creation. Humanity likewise has come into being as part of this Divine programme. The Almighty has provided guidance called *Wahi* (Revelation), and its purpose is to enable humanity to reach its full potential. This *Wahi* comprises permanent values and immutable laws for the whole of humankind. When we conduct ourselves in accordance with this code, we will achieve material success and happiness on earth and this will enable us to advance after death also. Any society that follows this code of life can thus be called a Qur'anic society. Such a society aims to provide for all, so that not a single person goes without the basic necessities of life, leaving all citizens free to develop their hidden potential to the full. This makes for a collective of free, stable and completely developed egos.[14] These results come about naturally and not by compulsion. All citizens are wholehearted participants in the system, and this is down to their conviction in God's law of requital, according to which even our thoughts must have a consequence. When our intention and actions are in accordance with God's Revelation (i.e. permanent values), then we see the best possible results at the individual as well as collective level. This is in fact the secret to attaining true human dignity. Conversely, every intention and action that violates these same values

---

[14] **Translators' note:** 'Ego' here means the 'self' (*nafs*, sometimes translated as 'soul').

diminishes human dignity. In this system every person works at full capacity and takes only what he/she needs in return for the labour. He wholeheartedly leaves the rest of his earnings open for the benefit of society because of his conviction that this is good for the betterment of his self and for making him worthy of everlasting happiness. Hence neither does anyone possess a surplus, nor does the question arise of who owns the means of production.

Can we see any similarity between the values described above and those of communism? Communism neither accepts the existence of God, nor the higher purpose of the universe and human life, nor Revelation, nor the permanent values, nor in the self, nor the hereafter, nor God's immutable law of *mukafat* (law of requital). Now if such a way of life rejects all these things, can it justly be identified with Islam? Communism and Islam are diametrically opposed and the two can never meet. In light of the Qur'an, no Muslim can also be a communist. In fact, communism is the first social movement to confront Islam as a *deen* (way of life). Islam at present is in a battle of ideas, and it is of the utmost importance that it should defeat communism and reveal the truth to the world. But this is only possible if the Qur'an's *nizam-e-Rabbubiya* (Divine system of universal sustenance)[15] is presented as the alternative.

Traditionalist opposition

To the best of my research, this is the first attempt (since the first Islamic century in which the Qur'anic system was first established in accordance with the needs of its time) to compile and present the socioeconomic system of the Qur'an in a written form. Our conservative class is likely to raise strong objections to this work, since they believe that whatever our ancestors have practised is true and correct and any attempt to bring change in our traditions is heresy. For centuries they have accepted the concept of private ownership in controlling the means of production, and subsequently they consider it to be part and parcel of Islam. Hence they will not be prepared to consider the idea of abolishing private ownership. When shown what the Qur'an has to say on the subject, their first response will be: 'our forefathers understood the Qur'an better than we', and their second

---

[15] *Rabb* – usually (and inaccurately) translated as 'Lord', the word is a reference to God's attribute of 'nourishing' or 'sustaining' the universe at every stage of its existence, from initiation to completion.

reply will be: 'if, in any given question, there is a contradiction between the Qur'an and the practices of our ancestors, then we must reinterpret the Qur'an in light of those practices, in order to reconcile them'. But in my view these are futile arguments. We know the Qur'an is the final authority, and it is imperative for Muslims to check and confirm whether the practices that are handed down to them are in accordance with the Qur'an or not. If they find that a practice is against the spirit of the Qur'an, they must reform it, not the other way round. As for the argument that our ancestors too understood the Qur'an, I offer this response: The Qur'an has placed an enormous emphasis on the need for *all* humans to utilise their intellect; not to just a section of humanity, but all humans at all times. The Qur'an's guidance for humanity is supposed to last until the Last Day. Hence the Qur'anic instruction to utilise our intellect applies forever. When we ponder over the Qur'an, we are only obeying God's command, and when we don't, we are ignoring His command.

New challenges confront humanity in every period of history. In any given period, there are always certain issues that demand our close attention. The problem of socioeconomic divide is worse today than it has been in the last 1300 years. So we should not be looking to the past for solutions to our present problems. Rather we should be looking to the Qur'an. To reiterate: Our 'conservative class' will not likely be prepared to give due attention to what is presented in this book. They will consistently claim that this book contains a completely 'new' Islam that they have never encountered from any of our ancestors; and so it is heresy. How rigidly they adhere to their viewpoint can be shown from the following historical incident. In Damascus there is a mosque which was built during the Umayyad period. It happens that during its construction there was an error and the mosque did not quite accurately point towards the Ka'bah in Makkah (Mecca) as it ought to have done. The error was not spotted, with the result that for a long time afterwards every mosque was built to face the same wrong direction. A later generation realised the error of their predecessors. It was clear that they should have rectified the error for the building of future mosques. However the nature of the traditionalist mindset makes it difficult to resist; and so the clerics of the age issued the following fatwa (religious edict) instead:

> If any astronomers or any knowledgeable persons say that the mosques are facing the wrong direction, then we will decline to trust their opinion or give their views any attention, because the Umayyad mosque has

existed since the time of the Companions of the final
Messenger and they and those who came after them
have all offered prayers in the same direction. The
Companions were more knowledgeable and trustworthy
than today's specialists. We don't know whether these
experts are right or wrong, but since the Companions
and their descendants certainly used the mosque, this is
sufficient proof that the experts must be wrong. Hence
we should disregard their claims. Remember that
adhering to tradition is better for us.[16]

Subsequently all congregations have continued to pray in the same
direction as the Damascus mosque to this day. When a society takes its
traditionalism to such extremes, we cannot expect them to pay heed to
anything that isn't supported by their traditions.

Islam and property

All that remains is the value placed on the right of private ownership.
In short, this concept originates from the minds of European
philosophers and economists, and it is the very foundation of
capitalism. Bodin, Hobbes, Locke, Voltaire and Hume belong to the
same school of thought. They consider ownership to be a natural right,
and that it is our primary duty to defend this right. But let us look to
the Qur'an. It outlines the ways of the messengers as an example for
humanity. Nowhere does it mention anything privately owned by any
messenger. In fact it is universally accepted that the messengers
neither possessed nor hoarded anything (notwithstanding the things
that they utilised everyday). In the following *hadith*[17] (concurring with
the Qur'anic position) it is written:

> The final Messenger said: 'I have no heirs. What I am
> leaving behind, is being left for the benefit of everyone.'[18]

---

[16] As cited in the classical book of *fiqa* (jurisprudence) titled *Shaami* Vol. I,
p.447 (Publication details are as provided in Parwez's original text. Edition
details unknown)

[17] **Translators' note:** *Hadith* (lit. 'history'): A body of literature pertaining to
the sayings and practices of the Final Messenger, not dissimilar to the oral
traditions of Christianity.

[18] Bukhari Vol. II, p.996 (Publication details are as provided in Parwez's
original text. Edition details unknown)

It is in accordance with this principle that even the Messenger Muhammad's personal plot of land, the *Bagh-e-Fidak*,[19] was not divided up among his family members upon his death, but was left to the *ummah*[20] (community) instead.

Now the question is: If private ownership is forbidden in Islam, why are the laws of inheritance provided for in the Qur'an? Here we must understand that in order to achieve its final objective for humanity, the Qur'an reforms existing society in gradual phases. It provides guidance for each and every stage from first to last. In the early stages it necessarily covers existing issues such as inheritance, lending, trade, alms-giving and aid, etc., all of which must be overcome before society can advance. It must also be borne in mind that Muslims across the world are living as minorities in countries that operate on non-Muslim (manmade) systems. These Muslims are living in relative isolation. Therefore it will only be possible for them to conduct themselves in accordance with the basic principles that we have outlined above as those belonging to the early phase. Ideally in such a situation Muslims ought to migrate to a place where the Qur'anic system has already been established. But as long as this is not possible, they will have to make do with following the Qur'anic laws that apply to them and their particular situation.

It is also true that any society following the Qur'anic programme will eventually reach its destination. In fact the whole of humanity is gradually progressing in this direction, as indicated in the Qur'an itself. Whoever thinks carefully about this will come to realise that the pressing issues of his time cannot be resolved by any means other than by adopting the idealism of the Qur'an, as has already been demonstrated in the life and career of the final Messenger. The crux of the *Nizam-e-Rabbubiya* (Divine system of sustenance) therefore is to reach a state in which humanity constantly works hard for its own betterment but rejects the perceived need to hoard its surplus and privatise property. I have attempted to delineate the Qur'anic system in this book. To those who say that private ownership is a natural right, I respectfully submit that what they call natural is really a product of whatever is handed down to them from their forefathers, their upbringing, their education and their social environment. Man

---

[19] **Translators' note:** *Bagh-e-Fidak*: A plot of land from which the Messenger Muhammad grew what he needed for his subsistence.
[20] **Translators' note:** *Ummah* – 'nation' or community.

has no 'nature'. (I have discussed this in detail in my *Saleem ke Naam Khatoot* (*Letters to Saleem*).

On capitalism

We have already stated that communism is a threat to humanity, but before we discuss the Qur'an's recommendations on restructuring the economy, we must first also comment on western capitalism. Western capitalism is based on the premise that the desire to own property is part of human nature, and therefore any polity that gives individuals the right to control the means of production is only in line with human nature. But this is a falsehood and the supporters of capitalism are deceiving themselves. As long as we don't uncover the flaw of the premise, we can't get to the truth of the matter. Hence the Qur'an makes the rejection of false systems a prerequisite to attaining *eiman* (conviction).[21] In the words of Robert Briffault:

> No resistance to power is possible while the sanctioning lies, which justify that power, are accepted as valid. While that first and chief line of defense is unbroken there can be no revolt. Before any injustice, any abuse or oppression can be resisted, the lie upon which it is founded must be unmasked, must be clearly recognized for what it is.[22]

As a student of the Qur'an I feel duty-bound to expose the un-Qur'anic concepts that have unfortunately come in from external sources and later accepted as completely Islamic, and to reveal the true message of the Qur'an. This is the only way to clear our minds and hearts of our misconceptions, which in turn is the prerequisite to beginning a Qur'anic revolution.

In the words of Iqbal:

> [T]he nations of the East should realise that life can bring about no revolution in its surroundings until a revolution takes

---

[21] **Translators' note:** *Eiman* is usually translated as 'belief', but is more a reference to an informed sense of conviction in the veracity of Qur'anic truth.
[22] Briffault, Robert (1930) *Rational Evolution* (*The Making of Humanity*) New York: Macmillan, p.209-210

place in its inner depths and that no new world can take shape
externally until it is formed in the minds of men.[23]

What makes the Qur'anic revolution special is that it doesn't make
fast and empty promises that can lead to commotion and upheaval.
Instead it focuses on making a gradual and deeper psychological
change, and it appeals to the intellect. At the same time it also directs
our emotional energy productively. In this way the Qur'an brings
about positive change both internally and externally, and so whatever
on the surface seems to be creating disorder is in fact leading to
something more constructive. In this regard Dr. Niebuhr writes on the
last page of his book:

> We are, at least, rid of some of our illusions. We can no
> longer buy the highest satisfactions of the individual life [sic] at
> the expense of social injustice. We cannot build our individual
> ladders to heaven and leave the total human enterprise
> unredeemed of its excesses and corruptions.
> In the task of that redemption the most effective agents will
> be men who have substituted some new illusions for the
> abandoned ones. The most important of these illusions is that
> the collective life of mankind can achieve perfect justice.[24]

This combination of reason and passion, which neither breeds
religious fanaticism nor extinguishes the spark of passion through cold
logic, cannot be found anywhere but the Qur'an. People whose heads
and hearts are in harmony are described in the Qur'an as follows:

> [They are the ones] who remember God when they stand,
> and when they sit, and when they lie down to sleep, and reflect
> on the creation of the heavens and the earth. 3:191

These are the people who envision absolute justice and are also
capable of bringing it about. And the time for this change is not far
away. In the preface to his 1923 work, *Payam-e-Mashriq* (*Message from
the East*) Dr. Iqbal has written:

---

[23] Iqbal, Muhammad (1977) *A Message from the East: A translation of Iqbal's
Payam-i Mashriq into English verse* (trans. M. Hadi Hussain) Lahore: Iqbal
Academy Pakistan, xviii
[24] Niebuhr op. cit. p.181

Nature is building up in the depths of life a new Adam and a new world for him to live in, of which we get a faint sketch in the writings of Einstein and Bergson.[25]

Around a decade later he also wrote in verse:

The fact concealed in words so far,
'Spend what is surplus and is spare,'[26]
May come to light in modern age
And make the meanings clear and bare[27]

The secret in the word *Kulil-Afo*[28]
Perhaps in this period that reality might appear.

After this he wrote in his final book of verse (in Persian), *Armaghan-e-Hijaz* (*The Gift of Hijaz*) using Satan's tongue:

Not   Mazdakism,[29]   but   Islam   is   to   be   the trouble of tomorrow.[30]

I believe the time is fast approaching for the Divine revolution that Dr. Iqbal has envisioned. Therefore it is imperative that I present all that I have learned from the Qur'an in clear language to the

---

[25] Iqbal, op.cit. xvii

[26] *Kulil-Afo* (rendered above as 'spend what is surplus and is spare'): Arabic term for 'provision in full.' (See also Qur'an 2:219)

[27] Iqbal, Muhammad (1936) *Zarb-e-Kaleem* (*The Rod of Moses*). Translation   online: http://www.allamaiqbal.com/works/poetry/urdu/zarb/translation/07rod.pdf Last retrieved 21 May 2012

[28] See fn 26 above

[29] **Translators' note:** Mazdakism is a Persian religion (with no known followers today) with dualistic teachings similar to Zoroastrianism. Due to its emphasis on social justice, and the reports that its founder Mazdak may have planned revolutionary reforms to abolish poverty, the religion is sometimes called an early form of communism. This also explains why, in his original Urdu manuscript of this book, Parwez translated the above verse of Iqbal as: '*Socialism* is not 'tomorrow's chaos'; it is Islam' – i.e. changing 'Mazdakism' to 'socialism'.

[30] Iqbal, Muhammad (1938) *Armaghaan-e-Hijaz* (*The Gift of Hijaz*). Translation online (minimally edited): http://www.allamaiqbal.com/works/poetry/persian/aramghan/translation/09gift.pdf Last retrieved 21 May 2012

intelligentsia of the *millat*,[31] and not only in order that they might understand the Qur'anic position. Humanity is presently passing through a crucial period and is fast approaching a crossroads, at which point it will have to decide which way to turn. If at that time we take the wrong turn, then goodness knows how many centuries we will have to wait, and how much bloodshed and destruction we will have to witness, before we begin to return again to the right path. Today humanity is tired of capitalism's stranglehold. If it cannot find its way out of this quagmire soon, then the world will have little choice but to take on communism, and this will surely prove suicidal. I believe that whichever nation claims to uphold Qur'anic values is duty-bound to guide the rest of humanity to the right path during this critical period. By 'right path', I mean resolving the socioeconomic problem that human intellect has hitherto failed to resolve on its own, as well as putting humanity on the path to 'salvation'. Any system that focuses either solely on the economic (material) and denies the concept of life after death, or conversely abandons the material world in pursuit of the 'spiritual', is not in keeping with the Qur'anic way of life. The Qur'an opens the door both to humanity's worldly and other-worldly success at once. This is why we can say that Islam has no parallel in the world. Every aspect of human life, from its code of ethics to its rites and rituals, as well as mundane aspects such as politics and economy, are all included in the Qur'anic programme.

Finally, I request that my writing on this subject should not be given a superficial reading, but must be studied closely. Consider every word carefully and ask yourself whether or not I have properly understood the Qur'an's message. And if you agree that my interpretation is correct, then is it not your duty to save humanity from capitalism and communism?

Parwez, March 1955

---

[31] *Millat* – an Urdu word for the Muslim community.

PREFACE
to the 1978 edition

The first edition of this book (1955) was sold out within a few days and received national attention. The public soon demanded the release of a second edition. Meanwhile the subject of economy and its problems were at the forefront of debate in the country. The advocates of communism and socialism were keen to put forward their views, and the conservative elements wrote and spoke much in favour of their own respective views. A third group tried to compromise between these two schools of thought by introducing 'Islamic socialism', but since it was neither Islam nor socialism, their efforts failed. They had taken their own interpretation of Islam and tried unsuccessfully to combine it with socialism.[32] During these debates whenever I heard something that was opposed to the spirit of the Qur'an, I always tried to openly criticise it and I also endeavoured to present the Qur'anic economic system in detail through my articles and lectures. During this period I was involved in some intense debate and spent much time answering others' questions, so it was impossible to print a second edition of *Nizam-e-Rabbubiyat*. Now that the atmosphere is calmer I feel the time is right to release the second edition. But the book before you is more than a mere reprint. It has been revised to account for the questions raised during the debate of the 1950s. Otherwise all that I wrote on the Qur'anic system has been preserved from the original edition. The Qur'an's laws are immutable and not subject to change.

---

[32] **Translators' note:** Here Parwez is clearly referring to what Saleena Karim describes as 'secular-Islam synthesis' in her *Secular Jinnah & Pakistan* (2010). Whilst Parwez opposes this philosophical position, ironically some scholarship has erroneously attributed it to him (and others, particularly Iqbal).

Other than making the aforementioned revisions, I have also added a number of appendices comprising some pertinent lectures and articles that I have produced on this subject.[33] They relate to some extra topics which couldn't be covered in the main text. The first is a lecture comparing socialism, 'Islamic socialism', and the Qur'anic system. The second is a lecture on Marx and Marxism, its true implications and what has led to its failure. The third is an article on the philosophy of Mao Tse-Tung. Through these appendices the Qur'anic economic system is clearly distinguished from the communism of Russia and China, and important issues such as *riba* (interest) and *zakaat* ('tax')[34] are also briefly visited. Hence I have attempted to compile what may be described as a monograph on the subject of economics.

A number of Qur'anic terms appear regularly in this book. A comprehensive explanation of these terms can be found in my *Lughat-al-Qur'an* (*Lexicon of the Qur'an*). As far as Qur'anic verses are concerned, I have opted to provide the exposition rather than literal translations. It will benefit the reader if he/she also consults with my *Mafhoom-ul-Qur'an* (*Exposition of the Qur'an*).

For the last fifty years I have been busy in my mission of seeking knowledge from the Qur'an, and broadcasting and publishing all that I have learned. But not once have I ever claimed that my findings are free of errors, or that they represent the final word on the subject. I am of the opinion that no individual can justly make such a claim. It follows that this is very much a human effort to present the philosophy of the Qur'an. If you find yourself in agreement with what I have written, then all is well. If however you find any error on my part, I would be grateful if you would let me know, on the condition that you provide Qur'anic support for your view.

Finally, I bow my head in gratitude to the One Who has enabled me to spend most of my lifetime learning and disseminating the message of the Qur'an. I am indeed fortunate.

Parwez, 1st November 1978   25/B Gulberg No.2, Lahore.

---

[33] **Translators' note:** These appendices are not included in this book for reasons explained in the Editor's Foreword, though we have reproduced part of the appendix relating to *riba* and *zakaat*. See Chapter 11.

[34] **Translators' note:** *Zakaat* in traditional Islam refers to a type of 'charity', and, like the Christian concept of 'tithe', it is given as a set percentage of one's income. However, as shown later in this book, this interpretation of *zakaat* is not in keeping with the true Qur'anic concept.

CHAPTER 1
What is Islam?

The universe as it exists today is starkly different to how it was at the very beginning. The sun, the moon, the stars, the earth, land, seas, mountains and deserts, did not yet exist; it took many billions of years for them to become what they are today. The same is true for all living things. According to evolutionary theory all life began from water. The earliest forms of life evolved from the combination of water and clay. These single-celled organisms soon began evolving into many different types, dividing and subdividing like the branches of a tree, and over a period of many billions of years they evolved into ever more complex and advanced life forms. Humanity too came into being after countless evolutionary stages.

Everything in the universe passes through thousands of stages of evolution between its initiation and its completion; and even each individual stage may take thousands or even tens of thousands of years to manifest.[35] The Qur'an explains this process as follows:

> He governs all that exists, from the celestial space to the earth; and in the end all shall ascend unto Him [for judgment] on a Day the length whereof will be [like] a thousand years of your reckoning. 32:5

(In other words, when God plans a scheme, He initiates it from the lowest level and then it slowly and steadily develops to its destination. The duration of these evolutionary stages, according to the human count, may be a thousand years.)

---

[35] See Qur'an 70:4, in which it is written that this stage can take 'fifties' of thousands of years.

[He] knows all that is beyond the reach of a created being's perception, as well as all that can be witnessed by a creature's senses or mind. All this happens as per the Divine Law, which has the 'power' to take everything to its destination, through proper development ('Grace').[36] 32:6

For a seed to become a tree, for a droplet to form a pearl and for a speck of dust to become a human being, all must pass through stages of development. But let us consider how finely-tuned these processes are. If a seed becomes damaged, then no matter how many times you put it through the cultivating process it will never grow. Similarly you cannot get an acacia tree to grow grapes. Neither can a damaged seed become a tree, nor can one type of seed produce another type of fruit.

The purpose of evolution

What, then, is the point of these stages of development as outlined above? Clearly it is to bring out the latent potential of the 'seed' and manifest it in its final form. In fact the ongoing expansion of the entire universe seems to be aiming in the same direction, i.e. it is working to bring out the latent potential of all creation.

The meaning of *Rabbubiya*

The Arabic language has a single word for this process. It is *Rabbubiya*, and it means the gradual development of something from its very beginning to its final destination. It can also be described as 'nourishment' (or sustenance), and the word for the one responsible for providing 'nourishment' is *Rabb*.[37] To sum this up in one sentence, we might say that 'the purpose of the struggle of the universe is *Rabbubiya*'. Since (says the Qur'an) everything happens in the universe in accordance with His Laws, it follows that God is responsible for

---

[36] The terms 'power' and 'Grace' refer to God's attributes of *Aziz* and *Raheem* respectively. *Aziz* – usually translated as 'great' (but rendered in the above as 'power') – is a word that means 'to have the means to take something to its destination (and to be the only one who can do so). *Raheem* – usually translated as 'Grace' – refers to the provision of full care and development, like the environment of the womb, in which a foetus is fully sustained and developed.

[37] It follows that the term *Rabb* is exclusively used to denote an attribute of God, since He alone has the power to complete such a process.

sustaining the entire universe from its initiation to its end. This is what is meant by the phrase *Rabb-il-aalameen* (lit. 'Sustainer of the worlds'), and it is in view of this fact that all *hamd* (praise, credit and thanks) is due to God. Hence the Qur'anic phrase: *Alhamdu lillahi Rabbil-'aalameen*: 'All praise to God, the Sustainer of the worlds (universe)'. As far as the process of *Rabbubiya* goes, every action and event must necessarily produce a constructive result. The proof of this can be seen when (for example) a seed first produces a shoot. The appearance of the shoot is a constructive or positive result, and thus it is the earliest indication of the process of *Rabbubiya* at work. However if a shoot fails to appear, then this means a destructive or negative rather than a positive or constructive result. In this case, the process of *Rabbubiya* never began, and whereas normally the seed would eventually become a tree, in this case the seed itself is wasted. The Qur'an uses the term *khabees* to denote this negative result, and its Qur'anic antonym is *tayyab* (lit. 'pleasant', 'wholesome', or 'good').

The exposition of truth and falsehood

In the language of the Qur'an, a constructive result is *haqq* (truth), and a destructive result is *baatil* (falsehood). *Rabbubiya* is based on the principle that its every result must necessarily be constructive (*haqq*), which is why the Qur'an has stated that God created the universe *bil haqq* i.e. 'in truth':

> God has created the heavens and the earth *in truth*: for, behold, in this [very creation] there is a message indeed for all who believe [in Him]. 29:44

Professor Whitehead has said:

> The fact of the instability of evil is the moral order in the world.[38]

However two things are necessary for the process of *Rabbubiya* to produce constructive and positive results. Firstly, all the participating elements in the process must work together harmoniously. For example, a seed's growth depends on soil, water, sunlight and heat,

---

[38] Whitehead, Alfred North (1926) *Religion in the Making: Lowell Lectures, 1926*. 2011 reprint, New York: Cambridge University Press, p.83

and air. But if you take a perfectly good seed and leave it out in the sun, and place a sample of soil and water beside it, then the seed will obviously not sprout despite the presence of all the required elements. Before a seed can grow, the soil, water, air and sun must be combined in a specific process so that they can provide the seed with the nutrition it needs. This is the prerequisite for *Rabbubiya* to occur and unlock the potential of the seed. This is true for everything throughout the universe; the system of *Rabbubiya* demands that every part must work together in harmony.

Secondly, if a planted seed is given too much water, or exposed to too much sunlight, *Rabbubiya* will not occur, and the seed will be destroyed. It is clear from this that aside from the order of the process, the balance and proportion of the elements in the process is also crucial. Wherever there is imbalance, destruction will occur instead of construction, and *baatil* (falsehood) will replace *haqq* (truth); that is, the process of *Rabbubiya* will cease. The Qur'an has in some places used the term *hasnaat*[39] to denote proportion and balance, and conversely it has used the term *sayyiaat* for inequity and imbalance. At times it has also used the term *amaal-e-saaleh* for deeds that create balance and bring out the best in something. As an opposite to *amaal-e-saaleh* the Qur'an uses the term *fasaad* meaning chaos or imbalance, and similarly it also uses *qawaam* which means to 'restore balance' and retain stability. From this latter word (*qawaam*) the Qur'anic *deen-e-qayyam* is derived, referring to a system that is founded on the principles of proportion and balance, and which brings out similar qualities of proportion and balance in society. Likewise *siraat-e-mustaqeem* (literally, 'the straight path') refers to the retention of equilibrium in the system. Since retaining equilibrium is essential to *Rabbubiya* (Divine sustenance), so it is written in the Qur'an:

Indeed, straight is my Sustainer's (*Rabb*'s) way[40] 11:56

In other words, any nation that adopts the law of God will retain equilibrium. The ancient Greek thinkers believed that the universe is in constant motion, but its movement is cyclic and there is no advancement. They believed everything in the universe has already been created and thus neither will it evolve nor will anything new

---

[39] *Hasnaat* is derived from the noun *husn* meaning 'just proportion'.
[40] In Arabic a similar term *qistas mustaqeem* exists, meaning 'scale which keeps the balance'. Hence *siraat-e-mustaqeem* also refers to a 'balanced' way.

come into being. According to this theory all creation revolves about an axis, and there is no opportunity for it to advance. This image of an ever-revolving creation goes against the theory of evolution. In using the term *siraat-e-mustaqeem*, the Qur'an has indicated that the universe is not cyclic, but linear. Everything in the universe is constantly evolving and advancing.

Evolution

Other than advancing in a linear fashion, the universe is also moving upward. In verse 70:3 of the Qur'an God is described as *Zilma'arij* (lit. 'He of the [many] ascents'[41]). The root *ma'arij* (from which *Zilma'arij* is derived) means 'stairs that lead upward', i.e. according to the law of *Rabbubiya*, everything in the universe evolves onward and upward. Even the repetitive aspects of nature such as reproduction are really an evolutionary means to an end. As already quoted earlier, the Qur'an states that God initiates the process of creation from the lowest level and then via the process of *Rabbubiya* takes the subject to the height of its development (32:5). It also states that this development is advancing towards Him:

... they are destined to meet their Sustainer! 32:10

Likewise whichever nation adopts the Way of God will, in accordance with the process of *Rabbubiya*, 'rise towards Him':

Unto Him ascend all good words ... 35:10

And in order to rise, a nation depends on the support of *amaal-e-saaleh*:

... and the righteous deed (*amal-e-saaleh*)[42] does He exalt. 35:10

In other words, according to the law of *Rabbubiya* everything in the natural universe is following an evolutionary programme via which it is taking the constructive steps to advance to its ultimate

---

[41] **Translators' note:** Literal meaning is taken from Asad's footnote at verse 70:3.

[42] *Amal-e-saaleh* – singular form of *amaal-e-saaleh* ('righteous deeds')

destination. Therefore *siraat-e-mustaqeem* is the Qur'anic term that describes this process.

The life journey that is taken from its beginning to its end is called 'destiny'.[43] It follows that according to the law of *Rabbubiya* everything in the universe necessarily exists with a purpose,[44] because (as we have already stated) the whole universe is subordinate to the system of *Rabbubiya*. In other words the entire universe is evolving for a higher purpose. This fact is also widely acknowledged amongst today's thinkers. For example Leslie Paul writes:

> It seems to me unreasonable to expect life to be dynamic, to struggle for survival on the one hand and then go on to argue that this purposive quality cannot possibly exist, and cannot affect the course of evolution, which is no more than a mechanical sorting out of those fit to survive. It is of the same order of logic which makes Julian Huxley write that the 'latest triumph of mechanistic thought – the Darwinian theory of evolution – has at last given man the assurance that there exists outside himself a "power that makes for righteousness"'[45] and at the same time to identify this power which is striving in the same direction as man with 'blind evolutionary forces'. If it is a power striving for righteousness it is in that degree not blind.[46]

And Professor of Anatomy at the University of Manchester, F.W. Jones, writes:

> Now, as we have seen, there is nothing more evident in the whole plan of the universe than the working of what "in human affairs is the effective operation of purpose" ... and at this period of the world's history that the others – if all men could

---

[43] **Translators' note:** Thus the Qur'anic form of 'destiny', alluding to a higher purpose, should not be confused with the general notion of 'fate'.

[44] Note that the following elements are vital to progress: 1) the starting point 2) the path we take 3) what we want to achieve. The meaning of 'progress' or advancement is to move step by step towards a known destination. But if a traveller doesn't know his destination, he can walk all day, but we will not be able to say that he is progressing. Progress is meaningless as long as there is nothing to aim for. Today we are moving towards a future without a predefined goal, and so our 'progress' is meaningless.

[45] Leslie Paul's citation of Huxley taken from Huxley, Julian (1945) *Essays in Popular Science* London: Chatto & Windus, p.186

[46] Paul, Leslie Allen (1949) *The Meaning of Human Existence* London: Faber & Faber, p.72

realize that the whole great scheme of things shows evidence of very definite purpose.[47]

The Qur'an has made positive statements that the universe *has* been created with a purpose, and negative statements that it is *not* without purpose. The Arabic word *l'ab* refers to something that moves but goes nowhere (just as a twig may get stuck going forever round in a whirlpool).

> We have not created the heavens and the earth and all that is between them in mere idle play. / None of this have We created without [an inner] truth: but most of them don't understand. 44:38-9

Summary of the Qur'anic view

From everything we have discussed above, it becomes clear that according to the Qur'an:

1) Everything has some sort of hidden potential
2) The purpose of life is to develop upon this potential and advance to a higher destination
3) The process, law or system according to which something is able to unlock its hidden potential and gradually reach its final form is called the system of *Rabbubiya*, and the one responsible for this process, law or system, is called *Rabb*[48]
4) In the process of *Rabbubiya* every stage of development necessarily aims at a constructive or positive result. If there is no positive result, then this simply means that *Rabbubiya* did not occur. A 'positive' result is termed *haqq* (truth). Hence the Qur'an uses the term *bil-haqq* ('in truth')
5) For the process of *Rabbubiya* it is also necessary that the various components of the universe should all act as the means of one another's *Rabbubiya* in unison. In addition, every component must be present in the correct proportion. If any component is not present in the correct proportion, then there will be imbalance (and by extension

---

[47] Jones, Frederic Wood (1942) *Design and Purpose*, London: Kegan Paul, p.77, 82
[48] Of course the one that is responsible (*Rabb*) can only be God.

Rabbubiya will also cease). The 'balanced/straight path' along which the entire universe travels (in accordance with the law of *Rabbubiya*) is termed *siraat-e-mustaqeem*; and every stage of the process of *Rabbubiya* that they take is termed *husn-e-amal* (a just act) or *amal-e-saaleh* (an act that creates balance and bring out the best)

6) The path of *Rabbubiya* (or the path of the evolutionary process) moves both onward and upward. Hence the outcome of *husn-e-amal* is to advance both onward and upward as well

7) By definition the process of *Rabbubiya* gives all things a final goal, i.e. it takes all things to a stage in which their total latent potential will become manifest. In fact this is the natural aim of all things; the whole universe operates according to the law of *Rabbubiya* and thus the whole universe has a purpose. It has a function and a destination

We have seen that the function of the entire universe is to unlock and develop its every individual part, thus enabling everything to gradually evolve towards its final destination. We can observe this from the ongoing activity of everything in nature. Science corroborates this viewpoint. Here the question arises: Who or what guides each and every thing in nature to its respective destination, how does each thing know the right path to take, and what must it do in order to achieve its goal? In order to try and answer this question, let us take a look at a minor example from nature. If you place some mixed eggs – chicken and duck – under a hen in order to hatch them, in time when the eggs hatch, the ducklings will immediately take to water to find food, but the chicks will stick to dry land and look for food there. As another example, a kitten will know that it can get its milk from its mother. A goat will not so much as look at a plate of meat, whilst a lion might be dying of hunger but will refuse to eat grass. A chick will only have to see a kite's shadow and it will instinctively hide under its mother's wings, and a kitten will instinctively jump on a mouse. Who is responsible for guiding these creatures via the law of *Rabbubiya*? Who gives them this knowledge? We can only come to one conclusion, namely that it is 'in their nature'. In the language of science this is called 'instinct'. Moving away from the animal kingdom, let us now turn our attention to other parts of nature. Water runs as long as it is in liquid form. When it reaches its freezing point it becomes solid. At the other extreme when it reaches its boiling point, it becomes steam and evaporates. Fire always produces heat. A mango stone will only ever produce a mango tree. Science terms these properties the 'laws of nature'. However 'instinct' and 'laws of nature' are just words that we have invented for the sake of reference. Otherwise the fact remains that no one can explain why these things exist and behave as they do, and what provides animals with their innate survival capabilities. At best we can say that all this is inherent in nature.

Creation and guidance from God

The Qur'an tells us that the One who created all things is also the One who has provided the ways and means for their sustenance. Creation and guidance are both from God.

> Our Sustainer is He who gives everything [that exists] its true nature and form and thereupon guides it [towards its fulfilment]. 20:50

At another place the Qur'an also states:

> [He is the One] Who creates [everything], and thereupon forms it in accordance with what it is meant to be / And who determines the nature [of all that exists], and thereupon guides it [towards its fulfilment] 87:2-3

Professor C. Lloyd Morgan, known for his theory of Emergent Evolution, writes (on the self or consciousness):

> ... it is my belief that this evolutionary ascent of mind in living creatures is due to the Creative and Directive Power of God.[49]

Wahi at work in the universe

The Divine 'guidance' that operates throughout the universe is termed *Wahi* in the Qur'an. The Arabic word *wahi* means 'subtle yet fast signal'. According to the Qur'an, God's guidance (*Wahi*) pervades throughout the universe.

---

[49] Morgan, Conwy Lloyd, 'The Ascent of Mind' in Mason, Francis Baker (ed.) (1934) *The Great Design: Order and Progress in Nature* New York: Macmillan, p.115

[And God] imparted unto each heaven its function (*Wahi*) 41:12

Regarding the earth, it states:

As your Sustainer (*Rabb*) will have inspired (*Wahi*) her to do! 99:5

And regarding the honeybee it states:

And [consider how] your Sustainer has inspired the bee: "Make your dwellings in mountains and in the trees, and in what [humans] may build [for you, i.e. bee hives]" 16:68

"And then eat of various fruit and flowers, and follow assiduously the paths ordained for you by your Sustainer." There issues from within these [bees] a fluid of diverse hues, which has health-giving properties for humans. In this [behaviour of the bee], behold, there is a message indeed for people who think. 16:69

'Obedience' of the natural universe

Aside from *Wahi* (God's attribute of Divine 'guidance', or directive force), another important fact is highlighted in the above verses. Everything in the natural universe follows the law assigned to it unfalteringly and without question: Everything from the celestial bodies of the heavens, the moon, the sun, the stars; the earth with its highest mountains, the seas and tides, and its rivers; even down to the microorganisms spread throughout the atmosphere. In short, everything is busy following the law of *Rabbubiya* that is assigned to it. Nothing has the power to defy this 'natural law'.[50] If the sun moved even a tiny fraction slower or faster on its axis; if the earth likewise was to alter a fraction from its axis; if water changed its nature even momentarily; or if the wind changed direction of its own accord – then a chain reaction would occur, and the unity of the universe would collapse. The unity will remain firm as long as *everything* in the universe (without exception) obeys His law.

---

[50] **Translators' note:** The term 'natural law' has been used in this translation for the universal law that governs all existence.

And before God, they prostrate themselves, all [things] that are in the heavens and on earth ... 13:15

All that is in the heavens and on earth extols God's limitless glory [i.e. is busy accomplishing the Divinely ordained programme] 57:1

The meaning of Islam

This 'submission' of the universe to God's law is termed *Islam*. In the words of the Qur'an:

Whatever is in the heavens and on earth *submits to God's Laws* [Islam] by choice or by constraint and follows the way which leads to the goal set for them by God. 3:82

The meaning of 'Islam' in this context becomes clear. Islam is the 'natural law' at work throughout the universe that unlocks the latent potential of each and every thing and takes it to its final destination. The meaning of *salaam* (from which 'Islam' is derived) is 'free of faults or imperfections'. *Mussalam* likewise means 'perfect' and 'complete', without defects. To illustrate the meaning, the Arabic sentence *Istala mazzar-u* refers to a cultivated field that has reached the point at which the crops appear, and we can taste the fruit of our labour, i.e. we have reached the point at which the aim and purpose of the whole process becomes manifest. As another example, the sentence *tasaa la ma til-khai lo* means horses stepping together in a synchronised fashion, so that no single horse overtakes the other(s) or upsets the other(s). 'Synchronisation' of this type is extremely important in the process of *Rabbubiya*. From these examples we can see that:

1) *Islam* means the process of taking a subject and nurturing its hidden potential from the very beginning to take it to its final destination
2) Everything in the universe is actively working to fulfil its divinely ordained destiny without faltering and without question. This is what is meant by taking the 'balanced way', or *siraat-e-mustaqeem*

The difference between humanity and nature

So far we have discussed the natural universe, but have not addressed the human equation. No doubt humankind is also a part of the universe. But a fundamental difference between humanity and the rest of the natural universe sets them apart. Humans have free will. We have already noted that the rest of the universe is busy submitting to 'natural law' without question, and that nothing in the universe has the power to defy this law, or to adopt a law of its own choosing. Water cannot choose to flow uphill or downhill. Fire cannot choose to either produce heat or lose it and become cold. The sun cannot decide at a whim to go backwards after midday. The earth can't choose to stop rotating and rest for a while. A chick is incapable of taking to water. A goat cannot choose to eat meat instead of grass. Even the lion, the king of the jungle, is incapable of rejecting meat and turning to eat grapes instead. But a human child is different. There is no doubt that at birth an infant is drawn to his mother's milk as any mammal. But it is also true that he doesn't know the difference between poison and sugar. He will put his hand into fire, or jump into water; he will rub salt into his eyes or put soap in his mouth. A human child simply has no innate knowledge. Even as he grows older, he will continue to make mistakes. It is only as far as his physical development is concerned that the same natural laws apply as they do for animals. When he needs food he will feel hungry; when he needs water he will feel thirsty; when he is tired he will sleep. In other words, the body is subject to the same law of *Rabbubiya* as is nature. The survival instinct – self-preservation – exists in every living thing. This same instinct exists within humans as well. Humans will do anything to protect their own lives. However humans are also capable of something that no other living thing can do, namely committing suicide.[51] This is because nature is compelled to adhere strictly to the law of *Rabbubiya*, whilst humanity is free to follow or to reject it. In the words of Sheen:

> In order to insure the attainment of its goal, or a sharing in the Divine Goodness, Almighty God has placed in each thing an immanent urge, or striving for

---

[51] **Translators' note:** This is not withstanding some natural exceptions. Lemmings for example are known to kill themselves en masse, but it is believed that this may be tied to an innate population control. Similarly a bee arguably commits 'suicide' when she stings, as using the sting results in her death. But even this is usually a last resort by the bee to protect the bee hive.

law. ... In like manner, things below man tend to their perfection unconsciously, but they do so only because God has interiorly impressed them with His Purpose, which is nothing else than to become God-like, each in its own way. In animate creatures this immanent urge toward God is effected by the laws of nature; in the sensible world by the laws of instinct, and in conscious man by intelligence and will.[52]

It is because of free will that humanity faces an issue that the rest of the universe does not. So how did this issue (namely *Rabbubiya*) which is so straightforward and simple in the natural universe, become so complex and difficult for humanity that we have always struggled to resolve it?

A Law for humans

The rules by which the natural universe operates completely change when it comes to humanity. In the natural universe, the law responsible for nurturing the hidden potential of everything is innate, and so the natural universe is compelled to follow it. But the same law responsible for the development of human potential is neither innate in us,[53] nor are we compelled to obey it.

Now the question arises that when ...

1) God has taken responsibility for guiding everything in the universe;
2) 'Natural law' (*Wahi*, God's guidance or directive force) is innate throughout the natural universe;
3) Humanity is not innately guided;

---

[52] Sheen, Fulton John (1948) *Philosophy of Religion: The Impact of Modern Knowledge on Religion* New York: Appleton-Century-Crofts p.170

[53] The notion that we have an innate ability to differentiate between right and wrong, good and evil, and truth and falsehood, is thus untrue. In fact humans have no nature; only natural things – which have no free will – have any innate or instinctual knowledge. He who is endowed with free will cannot possess any innate knowledge. He decides which way to adopt for himself. He is not compelled to follow any particular path. Humans have various potentials, and the purpose of life is to develop these potentials and put them to good use. I have discussed this in much more detail in my books *Letters to Saleem* (1953) and *Iblees-o-Adam* (1945) (*Satan and Adam*).

... then how will humanity receive its guidance? This guidance will of course come from God, but the method of transmission will be different to that given to the natural universe. As far as the rest of the universe is concerned, the transmission of the guidance (*Wahi*) is automatic. But when it comes to humanity, the same *Wahi* is transmitted via His messengers, each of whom is termed *rasool*[54] (messenger) in the Qur'an. This is the guidance about which the 'children of Adam' (i.e. humanity) were told:

> We shall send you Our guidance: and those who follow My guidance need have no fear, and neither shall they grieve. 2:38

At another place in the Qur'an it is written:

> Whenever Our messengers come to you from among you, conveying Our messages to you, then all who are conscious of Me and live righteously – no fear need they have, and neither shall they grieve. 7:35

The first notable difference between the natural universe and humanity is that in the case of the former, the guidance of God (*Wahi*) is innate, but in the case of the latter, *Wahi* is transmitted via a person chosen by God from among them.

The second difference between the two is that while everything in the natural universe is compelled to obey the law assigned to it, humans have only been shown the way of *Rabbubiya*. Thereafter it is left to them to decide for themselves whether to follow the right path or take another of their choosing.

> [We have] shown him the two highways 90:10

At another place the Qur'an states:

> Indeed We have shown him the way: [and it rests with him to prove himself] either grateful or ungrateful. 76:3

---

[54] **Translators' note:** The terms *rasool* (disseminator of the message) and *nabi* (receiver of the message) are two sides of the same coin. Both together refer to the English word 'prophet', i.e. an individual who received and disseminated Revelation. Most Muslims exclusively use the word *Rasool* with reference to the Messenger Muhammad; but it is universally known that it broadly means any messenger of God.

The One responsible for providing the law of *Rabbubiya* in nature has thus also ordained a constructive programme for humanity. But having provided this guidance, He has not compelled humanity to follow it. We are free to adopt this ideal model as we wish, or we can reject it and adopt a system of our choosing.

> Tell them: "The truth has come from your Lord (*Rabb*); whosoever chooses may accept it and whosoever chooses may reject it ..."18:29

Hence this is the second difference between humanity and the rest of the natural universe. From our discussion above, it is clear that:

1) As far as the 'purpose of life' is concerned, humanity as well as the rest of the universe is advancing towards the same ideal. Every single thing (including humanity) strives to nurture its latent potential and completely develop itself. This is the process of *Rabbubiya*

2) In order to fulfil this purpose God provides guidance, but whilst this guidance is intrinsic in the natural universe, humanity receives this guidance indirectly, i.e. it is transmitted via the messengers of God

3) It follows that to successfully complete this constructive programme is to reach a state of Islam

4) Everything in the universe is compelled to 'submit', i.e. follow Islam. But humanity is expected to submit to the system of *Rabbubiya* by choice

In short, the goal before both humanity and the rest of nature is the same, and the means to reach it is also the same for both; but whilst the natural universe has no choice in the matter, humanity is free to choose. The Qur'an states clearly:

> Do they desire to follow a *deen* (way of life) other than that of God, even though whatever is in the heavens and on earth submits itself to Him, willingly or unwillingly, since all must return to Him (i.e. the goal He sets)? 3:83

In other words, the whole universe has a *deen* (way of life, or mode of existence) by which to develop itself. Humanity of course is also part of this universe. Hence it is only logical to assume that in order to properly develop itself, humanity should also adopt the same *deen*. This is the same *deen* that has been taught to humanity via the messengers. For this reason every thinking person should adopt it.

> Say: "We believe in God, and in that which He has revealed to us, and in that which was revealed to Abraham and Ishmael and Isaac and Jacob and their descendants; and in that which was given by their Sustainer (*Rabb*) to Moses and Jesus and all the [other] prophets: we make no distinction between any of them. And to Him we submit ourselves." 3:84

This is the meaning of Islam, i.e. the law of *Rabbubiya* which is active throughout the universe, which is also the secret to unlocking humanity's hidden potential. Hence this is the only *deen* – and no other – that will enable humanity to achieve this objective.

> For, if one goes in search of a *deen* other than that of submission (Islam), it will never be accepted from him, and in the hereafter he shall be among the losers. 3:85

However attractive a given system may seem in the beginning, if it doesn't accord with the law of *Rabbubiya*, it is guaranteed to fail.

Conclusion

To summarise, *Islam* refers to a way of life in which the potential of everything in the universe is unlocked and fully developed in order to take it to its final destination. The natural universe follows this 'way of life' (*deen*) automatically, but humanity has to adopt it by choice. Therefore as far as humanity is concerned, the meaning of Islam is to establish a society that operates in accordance with Divine law. This universal law is transmitted to human beings by *Wahi* (Revelation), and it can be found intact in the Qur'an today. Thus human society can reach a state of Islam only by organising itself in accordance with the teachings of the Qur'an.

CHAPTER 2
What is a human being?

In the previous chapter we saw that the purpose behind the ongoing activity of the universe is to unlock its hidden potential and take every part of it to its final destination. The same applies to humanity. Clearly if we want to see whether humanity has succeeded in its endeavours, and if so, to what extent, then we need to know what humanity's hidden potential actually is; and in order to determine this, we must first know what a human being is. Two viewpoints on the subject have persisted throughout human history to this day. The first is termed the mechanistic concept of life, also known as materialism.

The materialist way of life

It is not our intent to discuss the history of mechanistic thought in detail, with its beginnings in atomism as introduced by the Greek scholar Democritus (c. 470-370 BC).[55] Suffice it to say that in accordance with this view, human life is confined solely to its physical existence, i.e. the meaning of humanity (as with other animals) is purely physical. The body is a machine operating on physical laws. When the machine stops, human life comes to an end. After death the body disintegrates and that is all. Humans are nothing but flesh, bone and blood, and nothing of them survives after death.

> And yet they say: 'There is nothing beyond our life in this world. We die as we come to life, and nothing but time destroys us.' But of this they have no knowledge whatever: they do nothing but guess. 45:24 (see also 6:29)

---

[55] For a detailed review of the history of materialist thought, see my *Insaan ne Kya Socha?* (1955) (*What has Man Thought?*)

Freud has likewise said:

The goal of all life is death.[56]

According to Freud, neither is there a reason behind the existence of the universe, nor does humanity have a higher purpose. Humanity's struggle revolves solely around physical survival and reproduction. To the materialist therefore, *Rabbubiya* is about physical evolution and nothing else. There is no real difference between humanity and the animal kingdom. In accordance with this viewpoint we come to believe that somehow in the beginning particles and energy came into existence spontaneously, and that thereafter, natural laws were responsible for bringing about changes in these particles and energy. This in turn was responsible for the gradual (and ongoing) development of the universe. When the total energy of the universe dissipates, then everything will die. There is no great personality behind the creation and control of the universe, and no higher entity to guide humanity. Human intellect is sufficient to guide humanity's progress. Indeed, there is no other source of knowledge aside from human intellect in existence. Hence the idea of Revelation from God is false. As Lenin writes:

> To be a materialist is to acknowledge objective truth revealed by our sense-organs. To acknowledge as objective truth, a truth independent of man and mankind, is to recognise in one way or another, absolute truth. ... Human thought then by its nature is capable of giving, and does give, absolute truth ...[57]

In short, according to the materialist view:

1) Human life is confined to physical existence. Nothing exists after death
2) Life's struggle revolves around the issue of bread
3) The solution to this issue can be found through the use of human intellect

---

[56] Freud, Sigmund (1922) *The Pleasure Principle* (Authorised translation from the second German edition by C.J.M. Hubback) London/Vienna: The International Psycho-Analytical Press, p.47. Emphasis in original.
[57] Fineberg, J. (ed.) (1935) *V.I. Lenin: Collected Works Vol. XI: The Theoretical Principles of Marxism* New York: International Publishers, p.195, 197

The mechanical view of life reached its peak in nineteenth-century Europe. Modern Western civilisation is the product of this philosophy. However in the twentieth century, recent discoveries about the universe and human life have led some Western scientists and thinkers to new conclusions:

> 'Life must thus be regarded as something which from the standpoint of biology is objectively real,' JS Haldane has written. 'We cannot describe it in terms of ordinary physical and chemical conceptions because these conceptions apply only to what we regard as isolable phenomena in both space and time, whereas the phenomena which we perceive as life are not isolable from one another, and can only be described as manifestations of the unity which we call life. The real basis of biology as a science is the conception of life, and apart from this conception biology would only be a chaotic collection of imperfectly defined physical and chemical observations – imperfectly defined because they do not express the co-ordinated maintenance.'[58]

As to the origin of life, none other than Darwin (the pioneer of evolutionary theory in the West) has written at the end of his *On the Origin of Species*:

> There is grandeur in this view of life, with its several powers, having been originally breathed by the Creator into a few forms or into one; and that, whilst this planet has gone circling on according to the fixed law of gravity, from so simple a beginning endless forms most beautiful and most wonderful have been, and are being evolved.[59]

W.R. Sorely has also pointed out:

> But the self is not merely a set of qualities, tendencies, or dispositions; it is a new centre of conscious life, a new source of conscious activity; and no approach has been made to a

---

[58] As cited in Paul, *The Meaning of Human Existence*, p.62
[59] Darwin, Charles (1860) *On the Origin of Species by Means of Natural Selection: Or, The Preservation of Favoured Races in the Struggle for Life* (5th printing) London: John Murray, p.490

causal explanation of the core of self-hood which marks it off as the centre of its own world and the source of its own activity.[60]

The human self

What is the source of the human self? On this subject C. Lloyd Morgan, whom we have already mentioned, writes:

> ... I confess my belief that this ascent may be regarded as a manifestation or revelation of a Supreme Mind, conceived as the Creator of all that we are led to interpret as new.
> What I find in evolution is one great scheme from bottom to top, from first to last. What I also believe is that this advance throughout nature is a revelation of Divine Agency. And since mind at its best is the highest term in the course of evolutionary ascent, it may well be said that the evolution of mind reveals the agency of Mind. But it is, as I believe, Mind or Spirit infinite and timeless. Therein the words "first" and "last", "novelty" and "recurrence", are divested of the meaning which attaches to them in discussing the ascent of mind through new products to further novelty. *Spiritus Creator* as eternal and omnipresent is not the outcome of evolution, but that of which evolution is the progressive revelation.[61]

On the subject of 'self' (i.e. soul or personality, or ego) Bergson writes:

> [The soul is] a thing incapable of decomposition because it is simple, incorruptible because it is indivisible, immortal by virtue of its essence.[62]

Many other references from Western thinkers and physicists can be provided on this subject, but we need go no further here. As to the ways and means by which the self can develop itself, we will discuss these in Chapter 4. At this stage we need mention only that Western

---

[60] Sorely, William R. (1921) *Moral Values and the Idea of God: The Gifford lectures delivered in the University of Aberdeen in 1914 and 1915* (second edition) Cambridge: Cambridge University Press, p.433
[61] Morgan, Conwy Lloyd, 'The Ascent of Mind' in Mason, Francis Baker (ed.) (1934), p.132
[62] Bergson, Henri (1935) *The Two Sources of Morality and Religion* (trans. R. Ashley Audra and Cloudesley Brereton) London: Macmillan & Co., p.225

thinkers and scientists are themselves abandoning materialist thought and are coming to a new understanding, according to which:

1) Humans are more than just the sum of their physical parts. They don't simply operate under physical laws like machines to merely disintegrate after death

2) Rather, humans possess something in addition to the body – something indestructible – called the 'self' or personality. As Lloyd Morgan states, it is a shadow of that 'Divine Mind ... [which is] nowise limited by the trammels of space and time'[63]

The Qur'anic concept of life

The Qur'an provides its own definition of the 'self', and has laid it out in clear terms. It states that life has developed and advanced in stages, and that its beginnings were in *teen* (inorganic matter):

> Thus, He begins the creation of man out of clay [*teen*] 32:7

Thus the potential of life was dormant in clay, and it was animated by a sprinkle of water:

> We made every living thing out of water. Will they not, then believe? 21:30

The process of evolution advanced from this point, and life spread out like vegetation in every direction.

> And God has created you from the earth, just like vegetation 71:17

Life eventually evolved to the stage whereby the process of reproduction (via male and female) began:

> [Humanity] has been created out of a seminal fluid / issuing from between the loins [of man] and the pelvic arch [of woman]. 86:6-7

---

[63] Morgan, op. cit. p.115

This marked the stage of the evolution of the animal kingdom. Eventually animal life reached a stage whereby human life came into being, and humanity now differed from the rest of the animal kingdom in a crucial aspect. Hence verse 32:7 continues:

> [God] makes everything that He creates most excellent. And so [as with the rest of life which evolves in stages], He [also] begins the creation of man out of clay. 32:7

Following on from this the Qur'an states:

> Then He causes him to be begotten out of the essence of a humble fluid. 32:8

(In other words, the evolution of life continued through various stages of evolution and reached the point at which human beings came into existence via the process of sexual reproduction.)

And then the early humans became sentient:

> And then He forms him in accordance with what he is meant to be, and breathes into him of His Spirit (Divine Energy): and [thus, O humanity,] He endows you with hearing, and sight, and feelings and minds 32:9

Humans were thus bestowed with 'Divine Energy', which was not given to any other animal. This is what we now call the 'self' or human personality.[64]

The meaning of Divine Energy

It was because of this 'Divine Energy' that humans became thinking or sentient beings. So what is this 'Divine Energy'? And what effect did it have on the human being? But this is a separate subject. For now we need only note that according to the Qur'an there is an aspect of humans that is subject to physical laws just as with animals. Aside from this however, humans have another aspect which is called Divine Energy or soul. The Qur'an terms this the *nafs*. Therefore the human

---

[64] Here I have only cited a few verses which pertain to the process of evolution. For further details on the Qur'an and the theory of evolution, see my book *Iblees-o-Adam*.

being is a combination of body and mind,[65] i.e. the body which is always subject to physical laws, and the self (*khudi*, *anaa*, or *nafs*) which is not subject to these laws.

Western materialists have concluded that the universe is purely physical, and so humans are made up of organised matter. When the body dies and disintegrates, the human being also ceases to be. Therefore in their view, the material is all that exists, and it is the only reality. As we have already mentioned, this idea originates with the ancient Greek thinker Democritus.

Plato's thought

Another Greek thinker, Plato, offered an alternative idea that was also totally repugnant to materialism. Plato said that this whole universe is a figment of the imagination, and that it is illusory, not real. This concept (now known as mysticism) has appeared in various forms from Plato's time to the present day, in many different religious and philosophical schools of thought. In the Hindu Veda scriptures, this idea influenced their concept of the universe as a deception and a mirage. In Buddhist philosophy the physical world is a thing to be detested. St. Paul[66] followed a similar line of thought; he believed that the Heavenly Kingdom is in fact true reality, and he attempted to reject the physical world by donning the monk's robe and leading an ascetic lifestyle. The Platonian idea was also adopted by mystics, who declared that the physical world is impermanent and that we should sever our connection to it.

On the subject of physical (or material) development, it is clear that to materialists (and contrary to the mystic point of view) the process of *Rabbubiya* is purely physical. They believe that human beings comprise only of a physical body and nothing else, and that human intellect (and no other source of guidance) is sufficient to resolve the long-standing issue of bread. Whether or not this concept of life really can lead to positive results for humanity will be discussed

---

[65] **Translators' note:** For *nafs*, we have provided the translation 'mind' here, because generally in English the term 'mind' tends to be paired with 'body' (i.e. as the phrase 'body and mind'). Otherwise, *nafs* is better translated as 'personality' or 'self'.

[66] Note that contemporary Christianity is the creation of St. Paul and his disciples, and it bears no resemblance to the teachings of Christ. For further details, see my *Mazahab-e Aalam ki Aasmaani Kitabe* (*The Divine Books of the Religions of the World*)

later in this book. As for the mystics, it may have occurred to the reader that this group might view *Rabbubiya* purely as 'spiritual development', i.e. a means by which the human soul, born into the temporal world, can develop itself and gain immortality. But we will be surprised to learn that this is not the case. In fact mystics believe that the human 'soul' is a part of the Absolute or Great Spirit (Hindu term: *Brahman*). According to their view, the soul has separated from the Great Spirit and become fettered in the chains of the physical world.

Abandoning the ego

According to mystics the purpose of life is to free the spirit from the physical shackles placed on it, so that it can return to its source. Human desires represent an obstacle to this goal, and therefore we should avoid all physical temptations that would induce such desires. By suppressing our desires, eventually we will succeed in abandoning our ego, the source of desire, and thus the physical shackles on our soul will fall away; and then the soul will be reabsorbed into the Great Spirit. This is the ultimate aim of life according to the mystic. This idea can be found in every religion including Hinduism, Buddhism, Christianity, etc., with only some surface-level differences in their respective terminologies. Unfortunately this mystic concept has also manifested itself in Sufism. According to our mystics, killing our desires and abstaining from pleasure-giving things represent the very best that humans can strive to do. This is because the human soul is imprisoned in this world. By abandoning the ego, the human reaches the point at which the shackles of the physical world break and the soul is free to become reabsorbed in the Great Spirit. Sufis call this *waasal bil haqq*, i.e. 'soul meeting truth (God)'. This is the reason that when a great Sufi (mystic) dies they do not use the term 'death' but rather *wasaal*, which means that the 'small part (soul) has been returned to its reality'. This, according to Sufi thought, is the ultimate goal of the spirit and the true way to its happiness. So it is said in a popular line of verse:

The droplet desires only to be reabsorbed in the river

Thus we can see that the terms *Wahdat-e-wujood* (lit. 'Oneness of body') and *Wedanat* (the Hindu equivalent) both represent the same concept. Both have their origins in ancient Greece, the source of the quagmire in which humanity is stuck and cannot find its way out.

Summary

In light of the above discussion:

1) According to the materialist, *Rabbubiya* refers purely to physical development, and thus we can utilise our intellect to meet all our physical needs

2) According to the mystic, the aim of life is not to *develop* the soul (via the law of *Rabbubiya*), but rather to *abandon* the ego, and the soul's ultimate goal is to become reabsorbed into the Great Spirit

There is no further need for us to critique the spiritual concept of life in light of the Qur'anic concept of *Rabbubiya*, but the materialist school of thought needs further discussion. We will do so over the following chapters.

CHAPTER 3
The materialist view

L et us begin by briefly reiterating the materialist viewpoint:

1) The human being is merely the sum of his physical parts, and thus *Rabbubiya* is likewise confined to the physical, i.e. meeting food, shelter and other material needs.
2) We can find solutions to the issue of meeting our physical needs only by utilising our intellect, and by no other means (including Divine guidance)

Now let us look at the results of this approach in practice. There is no doubt that self-preservation is the demand of every living thing. Wherever life exists, it does everything to survive. This is true of every life form from the tiniest insect to the human being. The survival instinct is innate in the animal kingdom, but in humanity survival instinct is accompanied by intellect. In other words, in humans self-preservation is the demand of the intellect. The intellect protects our own self-interest, and no one else's; thus my intellect will serve to protect my interest, and your intellect will protect yours and yours alone. We can demonstrate this point by means of an example. If a fire breaks out in a cinema, then everyone in the audience will rush to the exit to escape. In their panic, people will be completely unconcerned about each other. Subsequently more will die in the ensuing stampede than directly as a result of the fire, and this is down to the fact that every individual is concerned chiefly with saving his own life. At most some people will also try to save their children (these being an extension of the self). Of course this same urge of self-preservation is innate to the animal kingdom. We can see how much cats, dogs, cows and goats care for their young, but if ever a situation arises in which a mother has to choose between saving herself and her young, she will save herself first, and leave the young behind. Among human beings too we have all heard of cases in which desperately poor parents sell off their own children to survive. Notwithstanding any exceptions to the rule, the fact remains that human intellect will act only to protect one's self-interest, and not the interests of others. At most it might be said that humans protect their progeny as well as themselves. Self-preservation then, is the first principle.

Animals and the future

Moving on, survival instinct may be innate in animals but they are unable to perceive the future. The ability to consider the future is unique to human beings. This means that even after successfully meeting the needs of today, human beings will worry about how they will meet their needs tomorrow. And since people have no idea how long they will live, their anxiety about 'tomorrow' knows no bounds.

To illustrate the limited perception of the animal kingdom, take the cow. As long as she has not eaten her fill, she will not allow another cow near her food. The cow doesn't care how hungry the other cows might be. Her needs are placed above those of all others. But once she has eaten her fill, she will peacefully move aside and chew the cud. She will be completely unconcerned about the food she has left behind. She won't take the remaining food away and store it for later. Of course there are some exceptions such as ants that do store food for a later time, but even this is meant to last only through a harsher short-term period – i.e. the winter, and so even these creatures do not truly store anything for a period beyond the short term. Humans on the other hand are always concerned with hoarding for the long term.

As people grow older and become increasingly aware of how little time they have left on this earth, theoretically they ought to become less concerned with hoarding for the long term. Yet in practice, people actually become worried about what they are leaving behind for their children. From a psychological standpoint, they are attempting to live on through their progeny. Having put aside his savings all his life in order to sustain himself, the individual now focuses on saving for his children. Animals neither worry about tomorrow nor (in the long term) for their offspring. Their lives are entirely focused on self-subsistence, but humans become so obsessed with hoarding to protect their own and their children's interests, that it rarely if ever occurs to them to think in the interests of others; and they take their habit to the grave. Eventually the perceived need to hoard becomes so great that people actually hoard for the sake of hoarding. They are no longer motivated by a need to survive, but by pure greed. Their thirst to forever acquire more and more becomes insatiable. Hence hoarding is the second principle.

In short:

1) Intellect serves to protect self-interest
2) To protect their self-interest, humans become obsessed with acquisition and hoarding
3) It follows that after taking care of themselves, people become consumed in their desire to hoard for their children. At this point therefore, a mere need to survive turns into greed

Let us continue further. Look at any species of animal, such as deer. Every deer has approximately the same level of intelligence;[67] hence there is no question of a hierarchy based on intelligence. They don't attempt to deceive one another, as they don't have the capability. This is due to the fact that in order to deceive, one deer would have to possess more intelligence than another. It is simply not in the nature of any deer to try to earn and save more than the others in its herd.

Differences in intellectual capacity

Unlike nature, the intellectual capacity of human beings varies from individual to individual. Consequently their individual earning capability varies as well. Furthermore, humans are capable of deceiving and swindling one another. Let us consider the root causes of greed and selfishness in human society. It is a battle of wits:

---

[67] In the animal kingdom, abilities are shared by the whole species and not the individuals. For example, all weaver birds are equally capable of weaving and building their nests. Just as one honey bee possesses the ability to build a hive, so do all honey bees possess the same ability. Furthermore, their knowledge doesn't increase with time. Whatever the honey bee knows from birth remains with her all her life. The exact same knowledge has remained in every generation of honey bee for thousands of years. By contrast, every human possesses different capabilities and talents, and his/her knowledge increases over time. Furthermore collective human intelligence varies over the centuries.

Whoever has greater intelligence is usually more successful. A relatively inept personality is no good at deceiving others; in fact he is more often the victim of deception and fraud at the hands of others. The intellect devises all kinds of schemes with the aim of acquiring and saving. This leads to the creation of economic classes. Whoever has a greater intellect therefore has a greater capacity to earn. He is more adept at swindling others and (yet, paradoxically) society deems him to be clever.[68] It follows that once an individual accumulates enough wealth to leave a sizable estate for his children, the next generation automatically attains a privileged status in society on the back of that wealth; and so they join the 'high class'. Conversely, those of a lower intellect (or those deprived people who have not inherited wealth) remain in the working class. In fact their social class is established on this very basis. A powerful argument is put forward to justify this status quo. It is said that he who puts his mind into what he does and works as hard as he can has the right to own what he earns. Indeed, how can we deprive a man of his hard-earned money? On the basis of this argument we cannot justifiably place a limit on how much he keeps. He should be able to earn as much as he likes, and use his wealth to invest in machines, factories, firms, banks, and in fact whatever he likes to buy and build and so further increase his wealth and property. Resources will be placed in private control, and subsequently these resources will become restricted to the rest of the population. This, in short, is capitalism.

Capitalism

It is difficult to counter the basic principles of capitalism because the concept of capitalism and the system itself is the product of the intellect. And since, according to the mechanistic view of life, there is nothing higher than human intellect, we are led to accept that capitalism is morally justified. Karl Marx is generally considered to be the greatest opponent of capitalism, but even he was unable to offer a convincing argument against it. Since he also accepted the mechanistic view of life, he had no suggestions for a higher source of morals than the intellect. So on what basis did he offer a counterargument? He

---

[68] **Translators' note:** In other words, this form of 'intelligence' (cunning) may fall under the category of rational intelligence as it utilises cold logic. Otherwise, cunning is actually identified with *lower* emotional intelligence as it goes hand in hand with a lack of altruism.

argued (in line with Hegelian dialectics) that in view of history no system anywhere in the world can last forever. Every system subsists for a time and then, once its failings become apparent (and oppression ensues), its opponents revolt from within. Eventually a new and opposite system takes the place of the old oppressive model. According to Marx therefore, the capitalism that is established throughout today's world will fall sooner or later, and an opposite model will take its place. The present system is in the hands of tycoons, bankers, and landlords, but the new opposite system will belong to the poor, to the working class and to farmers.

When Marx was asked to explain the cause of this cycle of oppression and revolt, he replied that it is an historical necessity. Here we will not review either communism or this concept of historical necessity in detail. At this time we need only say that even capitalism's greatest opponent, Karl Marx, was unable to effectively counter it, and he blindly accepted the theory of historical necessity.

Conclusion

So far we have seen that according to the mechanistic viewpoint:

1) 'Human sustenance' means meeting the physical needs of humanity

2) Humanity can resolve the issue of meeting its physical needs by utilising the intellect

3) The intellect serves to protect self-interest, and is unconcerned with protecting the interests of others

4) Every individual (or individual's intellect) is chiefly concerned with acquisition and saving, and later in his life he continues the same behaviour both in view of protecting the interests of his progeny, and also out of habit (greed)

5) Different people have various levels of intelligence, and so their capacity to earn also varies.

6) The 'brighter' members of society earn more and are thereby able to acquire more private property. As more and more property and resources become privatised, the availability of these resources becomes restricted to the rest of the population. (This is the outcome of capitalism.)

7) Human intellect alone cannot offer an effective argument against capitalism for the reason that this system is itself the product of intellect

8) Thus human society divides into socioeconomic classes, and with time the rich-poor divide becomes ever more acute

Why we should help the deprived members of society

If we ask a wealthy man to help a poor man, he retorts: 'Why should I help him?' We will be unable to find a satisfactory answer to the question. At best we might appeal to him on humanitarian grounds, to invoke his sympathy. But of course we are appealing only to his feelings. Empathy is not a matter of rational logic, but of emotions. If the wealthy man ignores your plea, then we only say of him that he is cold-hearted and mean. We will not say that he is stupid, i.e. that his refusal to help is down to an intellectual failure, or a logical fallacy. We will say only that he doesn't possess higher emotions (such as compassion). Yet according to the mechanistic view, there is no question of the existence of 'high' and 'low' emotions or mindsets. To the materialist, the 'human' is only a physical being; and insofar as the human (i.e. body) is concerned, there is only a question of 'weak' versus 'strong', and 'pain' versus 'pleasure'. There are no considerations beyond the purely physical.

We might also say to the wealthy man that there may come a day when he is poor and needs charity, and so he should in good conscience be willing to help a needy person today. But he replies: 'No thanks. I have already made a contingency plan to protect myself in case I end up in such a situation. Therefore I have no need to invest in this kind of 'business'. Your proposal has no legs to stand on; but my plan makes good business sense!' And so he will have the final word.

Now let us look at this problem from another angle. We tried to persuade the wealthy man that an act of charity would ultimately be in his best interest. However he concluded that in fact this was not to his advantage at all, and that he preferred to make his own arrangements to secure his future.

To one's own advantage

And what was the underlying point of our argument? We tried to reason with the man, and explain that his act of charity would ultimately be for his own good. From this it is obvious that we cannot persuade anyone to do anything unless we can logically show him how he stands to benefit. For example, we might ask someone: 'Why did you lie?' She will reply: 'What reason would I have to lie?' In fact we all sometimes say this, or we say, 'What have I to gain from lying?' In other words, we seem to acknowledge with every breath that almost everything we say and do is motivated by our self-interest. We will only tell a lie if we think this will profit or protect us. Most of us behave this way throughout our lives but rarely do we stop to consider the underlying reason for it. We are subconsciously acknowledging that we will tell the truth only as long as it doesn't threaten our self-interest. In light of our earlier point that intellect serves to protect our self-interest, it becomes clear that intellect is less concerned about which act is right and wrong, and more about which act will benefit the self. If it is in the interest of the self to tell the truth, then so be it; and if it is more advantageous to lie, then so be it. In short, the intellect is incapable of thinking beyond serving the self.

However, we also observe that there are many materialists who believe in nothing higher than the intellect, and yet they aid the poor, believe that lying is wrong, and conform to a moral code. So what is the reason? In fact there are a multitude of reasons. Western moral philosophers have written much on the subject, but nevertheless they all agree that no moral code can truly appeal to the intellect because any code of ethics necessarily makes self-interest subordinate to the needs of the many, and it is impossible for the intellect to put self-interest aside in this way. Rashdall, the foremost thinker on the subject of ethics, writes:

> Even in the less advanced branches of physical Science, and in the higher reaches even of the most advanced, there is room for wide difference of opinion; and be it observed, this difference is partly due to purely intellectual causes, to the different degrees of intellectual insight, lucidity of mind, logical power, observation and judgement possessed by different men, but only partly. Even here – in a region comparatively remote from the great practical interests which inspire passion and distort judgement – every one knows to what an enormous extent men's opinions are liable to be swayed by such influences as personal loyalty, personal antagonism, fashion, party spirit, caprice, carelessness, laziness, ambition, conceit. Still more obviously do those influences – the influence of the environment on the one hand and the 'personal equation' on

the other — mould men's views upon such matters as speculative Philosophy, History, Social Science, Politics.[69]

Max Planck meanwhile writes:

> The fact is that no person, however clever, can derive the decisive motives of his own conscious actions from the causal law alone; he requires another law — the ethical law, for which the highest intelligence and the most subtle self-analysis are no adequate substitute.[70]

Thus the demand of the intellect is only to serve the self; this is the only law it knows. In this humanity and animals are the same. When a cow is hungry, she goes out into the fields and there she doesn't know or care who the field belongs to (i.e. whether it belongs to her owner or to some other farmer, where she is not supposed to graze). She will eat whatever she sees in front of her. There is no question of 'lawful' versus 'unlawful'. As such, the same is true for humans, with the difference that whilst animals know only one way by which to achieve their aim of feeding themselves, humans can come up with any number of ways and schemes. Note that searching for ways and means of self-preservation isn't a *fault* of the intellect; rather, this is its duty. The intellect is bound to do everything to protect self-interest. Neither can it protect the interests of others, nor can it differentiate between right and wrong. In the end only a fear of the consequences of breaking the law and/or societal pressure act as deterrents against acting 'unlawfully'. In the words of Herbert Spencer, the founder of utilitarianism, the basis of all morality lies in:

> ... mutual dread of vengeance.[71]

However if an individual successfully utilises his intellect to either circumvent the law or to avoid the lynch mob, nothing can stop him from doing exactly as he pleases.

---

[69] Hastings, Rashdall (1907) *The Theory of Good and Evil: A Treatise on Moral Philosophy* Oxford: Clarendon Press Vol. II, p.151-2

[70] Planck, Max (1931) *The Universe in the Light of Modern Physics* (first English edition). London: Allen & Unwin, p.87

[71] Spencer, Herbert (1879) *The Data of Ethics* New York: Cambridge University Press 2012 reprint, p.115

At this stage it should be stressed that all we have discussed on intellect over the last few pages should not lead us to the erroneous conclusion that intellect is the cause of all evil in the world. This is not the case. Intellect is merely a tool which can be used for different tasks, whether good or bad. When we wish to indulge our own individual interests, the intellect will faithfully work on ways and means to this end. But if we submit the intellect to higher values then it will work just as hard in the humanitarian cause. Here we are discussing intellect strictly in light of the materialist view in which 'higher' values are deemed invalid, and so we are presenting intellect as a mere tool for the protection of self-interest. When we discuss higher values later in this book, we will show how this very same intellect can become the benefactor of humanity.[72]

Moving on, if a man is living alone on a deserted island, then the question of unlawful versus lawful, or self-interest versus others' interests does not arise. This question arises only when two or more humans live together. When humans live together sooner or later there is always a clash of interests, and so social and moral laws become necessary. Humans are social creatures, and none can live in isolation. They almost always live in a collective, i.e. a society.

The materialist society

Let us now consider the effect of the mechanistic viewpoint on society.

1) In a materialist society, intellect serves to protect self-interest and so it is constantly working on ways and means of acquiring and saving

2) In a society governed by the dictum 'every man for himself', those with greater intelligence (or cunning) succeed in building ever-increasing wealth

3) The intellect is not concerned with the needs or interests of others, nor is it compelled to do so under the dictates of a moral code. For this reason every individual utilises his intellect solely to acquire and hoard for himself, by means fair or foul

4) To maintain the social order, and to ensure that individuals conduct themselves within certain bounds, society inevitably creates a system of law and punishment. The

---

[72] **Translators' note:** See Chapter 5.

rebellious intellect will conceive of any number of schemes to circumvent the law, and in general those who are less intelligent and come up with poor schemes will be caught

In such a society it is impossible to imagine that anyone would ever stop and consider the question of meeting others' needs and protecting others' interests. Every individual will be concerned only with protecting himself and at most his immediate family.

We have already mentioned that humans are social creatures. This is due in part to the fact that individuals feel more secure when they live as part of a collective. Thus so-called 'herd instinct' is the wider implication of self-interest. The herd instinct originally led primitive human groups to form tribes, and this was the earliest precursor to modern nationalism.

Nationalism

Looking at the larger picture, the way in which individuals treat one another is reflected in the way that a nation treats other nations. The collective wisdom of a nation dictates that it must always act in the 'national interest'. Subsequently it is impossible for one nation to take the needs of another into consideration. Just as the individual intellect does not differentiate between a lawful versus an unlawful means of acquisition, likewise national wisdom does not differentiate when it comes to protecting the national interest. Whatever is in the interests of the nation is right, and whatever goes against the national interest is wrong. An individual who thinks in terms of the national interest is called a patriot, and in nationalist terms, this makes him a great human being. Conversely any individual who acts against the national interest is deemed guilty of high treason, and the punishment for this is death. Hence the saying 'my country, right or wrong' means that acting in the national interest is a mark of greatness, whether or not it is really right or wrong. National wisdom is responsible for this state of affairs, and moreover every nation in the world operates on the same principle.

Modern politics

The best-known proponent of nationalist thought was Machiavelli. His book *The Prince* is considered the bible of modern politics. In this book he has written:

But since a Prince should know how to use the beast's nature wisely, he ought of beasts to choose both the lion and the fox; for the lion cannot guard himself from the toils, nor the fox from wolves. He must therefore be a fox to discern toils, and a lion to drive off wolves.

To rely wholly on the lion is unwise; and for this reason a prudent Prince neither can nor ought to keep his word when to keep it is hurtful to him and the causes which led him to pledge it are removed.[73]

At another point he writes:

And you are to understand that a Prince, and most of all a new Prince, cannot observe all those rules of conduct in respect whereof men are accounted good, being often forced, in order to preserve his Princedom, to act in opposition to good faith, charity, humanity, and religion. He must therefore keep his mind ready to shift as the winds and tides of Fortune turn, and, as I have already said, ought not to quit good courses if he can help it, but should know how to follow evil if he must.[74]

Frederick II (also known as Frederick the Great) was an admirer of Machiavellian thought. He wrote:

The great matter is to conceal one's designs, and to cover up one's character. ... Policy consists rather in profiting by favourable conjunctures than in preparing them in advance. This is why I counsel you not to make treaties depending upon uncertain events, and to keep your hands free. For then you can make your decision, according to time, place, and the condition of your affairs; in a word, according as your interest requires of you. ... Machiavelli says that a disinterested Power, situated among ambitious Powers, could not avoid ultimate destruction. I hate to admit it, but I am obliged to confess that Machiavelli is right. Ambition is necessary to princes, but so is wisdom, measured and enlightened by reason. If the desire for aggrandisement does not procure acquisitions to a pacific prince, at least it sustains his power, because the same means

---

[73] Machiavelli, Niccolo (1532) *The Prince* 1913 reprint, Oxford: Clarendon Press, p.126
[74] Op. cit. p.128-9

which he means to employ in aggressive action will always be ready for defending the State.[75]

Another proponent of Machiavellian thought, Rumelin, wrote that 'the State is autarkic'[76], and that:

> Self regard is its [the State's] appointed duty; the maintenance and development of its own power and well-being, — egoism, if you like to call this egoism, — is the supreme principle of all politics.[77]

The psychological motivation of all the above statements comes from the intellect's demand to serve self-interest over and above all other interests.

The state of the world's nations

This underlying psychology has also manifested itself in today's international relations. And the result? Spalding answers with the following words:

> [M]aterialistic society is a jungle in which nations prey upon nations like wild beasts, all teeth and claws.[78]

If this is the state of the world's nations, what is the state of the people living within each nation? Lewis Mumford writes:

> In America we have created a new race, with healthy physiques, sometimes beautiful bodies, but empty minds: people who have accepted life as an alternation of meaningless routine with insignificant sensation. They deny because of their lack of experience that life has any other meanings or values or possibilities. At their best, these passive barbarians live on an innocent animal level: they sun-tan their bodies, sometimes at

---

[75] Frederick II, *Political Testament* as cited in Murray, Robert H. (1946) *The Individual and the State* London: Hutchinson, p.212-3
[76] Op. cit. p.216
[77] Ibid.
[78] Spalding, H.N. (1939) *Civilization in East and West: An Introduction to the Study of Human Progress* Oxford: Oxford University Press/ Humphrey Milford, p.13

vast public bathing beaches, sometimes under a lamp. They dance, whirl, sway, in mild orgies of vacant sexuality, or they engage in more intimate felicities without a feeling, a sentiment, or an ultimate intention that a copulating cat would not equally share. They dress themselves carefully within the range of uniformity dictated by fashion. Their hair is curled by a machine; and what passes for thought or feeling is also achieved, passively, through the use of a machine – the radio or the moving picture today, or Aldous Huxley's 'feelies' tomorrow.

These people eat, marry, bear children, and go to their grave in a state that is at best hilarious anaesthesia, and at worst is anxiety, fear, and envy, for lack of the necessary means to achieve the fashionable minimum of sensation. Without this minimum, their routine would be unbearable or their vacancy worse. Shopgirls and clerks, millionaires and mechanics, share the same underlying beliefs, engage in the same practices: they have a common contempt for life on any other level than that of animal satisfaction, animal vitality. Deprive them of this, and it is not worth living. Half dead in their work – half alive outside their work. This is their destiny.[79]

This is the state of today's humanity, about which Joad wrote:

While our civilization hangs on the verge of destruction through its inability to control the powers which science has conferred upon it, young men and women wander aimlessly along the road of life without knowing whither they are travelling, or why they travel at all. They are without creed or code, standards or values.[80]

Summary

Over the preceding pages we saw that there are two opposing views of reality. One is the materialist or mechanistic view, which holds that life does not go beyond the physical, and that human beings must necessarily be selfish. By implication every nation must take care of the national interest. Any scheme or act designed to protect self-interest, whether at the individual or collective level, is deemed

---

[79] Mumford, Lewis (1940) *Faith for Living* New York: Harcourt, Brace & Co., p.38-9
[80] Joad, C.E.M. (1940) *Philosophy For Our Times* 1941 reprint, London: Readers' Union, p.12

praiseworthy; and all schemes and acts that are detrimental to self-interest are deemed contemptible. This is the standard of 'good' and 'bad' in the materialist world. Every man must live for himself and his political conduct should accord with this ideal. The other view of life is (Platonian) mysticism, according to which the world is an illusion, and nothing is real. Our aim in life should be to shun the material and hate it. The secret of life is to eliminate all desire and things that bring pleasure. A person is only truly alive if he leads a living death. The more a person destroys his ego, the closer he will get to God. We find spiritual honour only when we disown the physical. To find God, we must leave behind the material world.

The first view outlined above is the creation of those who believe in the mechanistic view of life, and who are 'atheist' in religious terminology. But if we look more closely it becomes clear that this philosophy is not restricted just to atheists but is accepted even by the majority of the world's religious people, who on the one hand believe in God and at the same time lead their lives according to the dictates of materialism. Thus belief or disbelief appears to have no bearing on what is presently happening in practice. Spalding has termed this state of affairs 'this-worldliness'.[81]

The second view outlined above was Platonian philosophy which later influenced religious and mystic movements. But the present form of this view is no longer truly Platonian, nor is it truly identified with spiritualism and mysticism in practice. Rather it is identified with theism, just as materialism is identified solely with atheists and agnostics. Today the followers of all the world's religions are called 'theists', and even Muslims are placed in the same category.[82] Like other theists, Muslims presently believe that the world is corrupt and that those who seek material things are destined for Hell. The world is deemed a prison and no pious man can embrace it. The more a person is humiliated or oppressed on earth, the closer he will be to God. Worldly wealth and respect means nothing. Real success will come

---

[81] Spalding, *Civilization in East and West*, p.87, 164

[82] Muslims are in this state because the religion they practise today is not what was given to them in the Qur'an. Today's religion developed some time later. It has come under the influence of Magian (Zoroastrian) concepts of personality worship and destiny (or fatalism), as well as Jewish customs and historical traditions, and also Christian monastic asceticism. The Qur'an stood firmly against these religious ideas, but Muslims no longer pay heed to it. Instead the Qur'an is merely recited at funerals and Muslims have been practising a mere religion for centuries.

only in the afterlife. Islam (as a religion) was for the poor, it remains for the poor, and God's kingdom will be for the meek and the poor. In fact these beliefs are common to all major religions. Spalding has collectively termed these beliefs 'other-worldliness'.[83]

Everything in the human world is generally placed into one or the other of these two groups. This division is not the product of modern times. It has existed from practically the very beginning, but as we have already stated, *Rabbubiya* (i.e. the development of hidden human potential) cannot happen by adhering to either worldview. The former treats the human as a mere machine and so is concerned only with physical development. But we have observed that the human being is more than the sum of his physical parts. Aside from his physical body he possesses a personality, or self. The materialist denies the existence of the self, so no question arises as to its development; and yet, even as everyone agrees on the right of securing the means of physical development, every man acts solely in self-interest, and the subsequent conflict creates hell on earth. Such is the situation today.

The other view advocates a rejection of the physical world, and so the question of physical development doesn't arise. This leaves only the issue of the soul. The mystic view is that the sooner we abandon our individuality and return to the Real (i.e. Great Spirit, since only the spirit is real), the better. Thus we find that in reality even the mystic does not really speak of developing the self, but rather seeks to merge it with the One.

Attempting to resolve the issue of sustenance under the dictates of materialism has turned the world into a lion's den. Dealing with the same issue under the dictates of mysticism turns human civilisation into a graveyard.

In the next chapter we will see what the Qur'an says on the subject.

---

[83] Spalding, op. cit. p.87, 108

CHAPTER 4
The Qur'anic view

In the last two chapters we discussed the two major worldviews, namely the materialist and the mystic. The Qur'an repudiates them both, and offers its own. We will discuss this shortly, but first we will look at what the Qur'an has to say about the two other worldviews.

The fact that the spiritualist worldview stands on a weak premise is self-evident; so much so that the Qur'an has not given much space to offering a detailed counterargument. It merely states that:

> But as for monasticism, We did not enjoin it upon them: they invented it themselves out of a [mistaken] desire for God's goodly acceptance. 57:27

Monasticism is the escape route for those who cannot face the realities of life. Instead of facing life's challenges, the would-be member of the clergy declares his inability to deal with them, and adopts a defeatist attitude. How can the Creator ordain such a lifestyle when He has clearly decreed:

> And He has made all that is in the heavens and on earth subservient to you, [as a gift] from Himself ... 45:13

Worldly goods as temptation

The Almighty has said that worldly goods and luxuries may be tempting for humans:

> Alluring unto man is the enjoyment of worldly desires through women, and children, and heaped-up treasures of gold

and silver, and horses of high mark, and cattle, and lands. All
this may be enjoyed in the life of this world … 3:14[84]

All things in the natural universe possess both the characteristics
of *jalaal* (power and strength) and *jamaal* (beauty and elegance). For
example, rain clouds bring us both storms and rainbows. The awesome
power of lightning is an essential agent in enabling vegetation to thrive
and create fruits and flowers.[85] Seemingly destructive volcanic activity
leads to the renewal of life via the creation of new islands. The sun is a
burning furnace in which nothing could survive; and yet without it, life
on earth in all its variety would become impossible.

Looking at human history, we find that humans have always either
sought power (*jalaal*), and neglected the aesthetics (*jamaal*) of life; or
conversely they have focused on the aesthetics and neglected power
(along with the progress it might bring). The Qur'an has said this is
humanity's mistake – that our perspective is devoid of balance. *Jalaal*
and *jamaal* are actually from the same source, namely God. He tells us:

All that is in the heavens and all that is on earth extols God's
limitless glory: 64:1

But what does this mean? It means that the activity of the universe
manifests the facets *jamaal* and *jalaal* together, and in so doing reveals
that the source of both power and beauty is one.

To Him belongs all praise (*hamd*) and power 64:1

The full meaning of the word *hamd* means appreciation of beauty –
the kind which spontaneously evokes a feeling of awe. Thus power and
glory and beauty and elegance come from one and the same source.

This second part of the verse also suggests that (as with *jalaal* and
jamaal) 'power' and 'praise' are not contrary to one another but are
actually complimentary. Incidentally the Qur'an also states that all
things are created 'in pairs' (78:6). Thus night and day, darkness and
light, power and beauty, all are complimentary pairs. When we come

---

[84] The second half of this verse tells us that these things are fleeting, and that
the ultimate goal is with God. But we will return to this later.

[85] **Translators' note:** Lightning helps release nitrogen in the
atmosphere, which is then carried to the ground in the rain. This in
turn provides nutrients to the soil.

to recognise them together, we see their true nature, and thus also learn the true nature of Reality. Ignoring the fact of their seeming contradiction, they are actually related to one another by virtue of the fact that one always comes from the other.

> Thus it is, because God makes the night grow longer by shortening the day, and makes the day grow longer by shortening the night 22:61

Hence these supposed conflicting pairs should be seen as a kind of spirit level of God's law. When there is a change in the balance, we see a corresponding change in the observable universe.

Hence we see that *jalaal* and *jamaal* are not opposed to each other, and are not mutually exclusive. (The ancient Persians wrongly treated lightness and darkness as two opposing phenomena, and this dualist thought was behind the creation of Magian religion.) Thus any way of life that advocates the rejection of beauty and elegance cannot be considered Islamic. The true way consists in retaining moderation and balance in everything. Therefore the Qur'an is addressing the mystics when it states:

> O children of Adam! Beautify yourselves for every act of service[86] at the *masjid*,[87] and eat and drink [freely], but do not waste: indeed, He does not love the wasteful! 7:31

In light of the above verse, if a society establishes itself on Qur'anic lines, it will obviously utilise all that is good and beautiful (which will then be reflected in the afterlife as well).

> ... Theirs shall be gardens of perpetual bliss – [gardens] beneath which running waters flow – there they will be adorned with bracelets of gold and will wear green garments of silk and

---

[86] **Translators' note:** Here we have replaced the word 'worship' (as used in the traditional translation) with 'service'. For explanation, see fn 102, 151.

[87] (*Masjid*: another word for mosque.) Obviously in this verse the word '*masjid*' cannot literally mean 'Muslim place of worship', firstly because the verse is addressing humanity ('children of Adam') as a whole, and not just Muslims. Secondly, along with the word *masjid* in the Arabic we see the term 'eat and drink', which shows clearly that the word *masjid* itself is not a reference to a building. It refers to an 'act of service', or 'obey (the Divine law)'.

brocade, [and] they will recline upon couches: how excellent a
recompense, and how goodly a place to rest! 18:31

The Qur'an places much more emphasis on beauty in life than the
average person might realise, as he/she is focusing solely on the
usefulness of such things and overlooking the element of beauty itself.
For example, the Qur'an refers to cattle and sheep from which we use
the skin and wool for our clothes, and we consume the meat. These are
the practical benefits we take from our livestock. The average person
doesn't think beyond this point. But the Qur'an takes it further and
asks us to consider the beauty of the scene when the livestock are
returning to their stables in the evening; or at daybreak, when we take
our livestock out to pasture, and the sun gradually rises over the
horizon. Hence the Qur'an is asking us to consider the aesthetics as
well as the practical usefulness of all things.

And He creates cattle: you derive warmth from them, and
[various other] uses; and from them you obtain food / and you
find beauty in them when you drive them home in the evenings
and when you take them out to pasture in the mornings. 16:5-6

A few verses later the Qur'an adds:

And [it is He who creates] horses and mules and asses for
you to ride, as well as for [their] beauty: and He will yet create
things of which [today] you have no knowledge. 16:8 [88]

Note that the Qur'an sternly rebukes those who would reject the
beautiful and useful things of the world and declare them *haraam*
(prohibited), turning human society into a funeral procession. It has
stated that wealth and power are gifts from God. All messengers have
advised their peoples to strive for these things. Prophet Hud (Eber)
told his people to remember the blessings that God had granted to
Noah's people before them, i.e. the things that helped them to establish
their power and to prosper.

----

[88] **Translators' note:** This verse obviously implies the emergence of
transport such as today's modern cars, trains and planes which are valued
both for their usefulness and for their aesthetic qualities. '*He* will create' in
the above verse implies (as Muhammad Asad has written in his commentary
on the Qur'an) that such transport will come into being via the *God-given*
inventiveness of human beings (as implied in verses 16:8 and 36:42).

> Do but remember how He made you heirs to Noah's people, and endowed you abundantly with power: remember, then, God's blessings, so that you might attain to a happy state! 7:69

Likewise the Prophet Saleh told his people:

> And remember how He made you heirs to [the tribe of] 'Ad, and settled you firmly on earth, so that you [were able to] build for yourselves castles on its plains and hew out mountains [to serve you] as dwellings: 7:74

The Prophet Shoaib (Jethro) told his people:

> And remember [the time] when you were few, and, [how] He made you many [and thus became a strong nation] 7:86

The Qur'an states regarding Abraham's people (tribe) that 'We have given them the Book and the Wisdom'. In addition it states:

> We granted Revelation and wisdom to the House of Abraham, and We bestowed a mighty dominion to them 4:54

The whole story of Moses and the Israelites is a continuation of the history referred to above; and from this we get an idea of how much importance the Qur'an has given to the acquisition of power.[89] It has recorded the outcome of this struggle as follows:

> [And] whereas unto the people who had been deemed utterly low [at one time], We gave them the eastern and western parts of the land that We had blessed as their heritage. 7:137

God's favour (of power and authority for those who struggle in His cause) was promised not just to the children of Israel but in fact to all nations. Hence the early Muslims were also told:

---

[89] **Translators' note:** This should not be taken to mean 'power' in the sense of conquering and securing domination over others. It should be understood in the Qur'anic context of reaching a position of prosperity, progress and success.

And He made you heirs to their lands, and their houses, and
their goods – and [promised you] lands on which you had never
yet set foot: for God has indeed the power (*qadr*) to will
anything (i.e. everything occurs in line with the measures and
scales[90] set by Him) 33:27

When the Prophet Abraham went to what is now present-day
Makkah to lay the foundations of the Ka'bah, he prayed to God with the
following words:

O my Sustainer! Make this a land secure, and grant its
people fruitful sustenance 2:126

God likewise recounted His favour to the Quraish of Makkah:

[He] has given them food against hunger, and made them
safe from danger 106:4

God told the final Messenger:

And found you needy, and enabled you to become self-
sufficient 93:8

We have created all this for the sustenance of human
beings. It is We who bring dead land to life 50:11

Any nation that follows God's law will:

... partake of all the blessings of heaven and earth 5:66

Not only do such people obtain all they need for their sustenance,
but they also gain an honourable status, i.e. dignity and power:

God has promised those of you who have attained to faith
and do righteous deeds that, of a certainty, He will cause them
to accede to power on earth 24:55

---

[90] *Qadr* comes from a root word meaning 'estimate' and 'value', and thus by
extension *Qadr* means both 'power' and 'scale/measure'.

As for anyone – man or woman – who does righteous
deeds, and attains to conviction (*eiman*) – We will certainly
cause him to live a good life 16:97

For them there is the glad tiding [of happiness] in the life of
this world 10:64

Conversely, for those who defy Divine law, the Qur'an states:

What, then, could be the reward of those among you who do
such things but disgrace in the life of this world 2:85

This 'disgrace' takes the form of hunger, fear, and shortage in every
type of sustenance:

[They] taste the all-embracing misery of hunger and fear
16:112 (see also verse 7:130)

Therefore God's rewards for following Divine law are abundance,
economic ease and all the good things in life, and conversely His
punishments are a lack of sustenance and hunger and fear. At another
place the Qur'an states:

But as for him who shall turn away from remembering Me –
his means (of subsistence) will be restricted 20:124

The Qur'an has taken this point further. To the theist, the purpose
of life is to try and strive for a place in Heaven by doing good deeds.
We will leave aside the subject of 'Heaven' here. In the Qur'an, God
tells Adam[91] that *Iblees* (Satan) is his enemy, and warns him not to
allow *Iblees* to lead him out of heaven[92] and into a world of suffering.
At that time, Adam had been living in a heavenly state in which he did
not want for anything:

---

[91] The meanings of the legend of Adam is discussed in my book *Iblees o-Adam*.
[92] **Translators' note:** Here and at other places we have not capitalised the
first letter of the word 'heaven' (and also 'hell'), in order to differentiate
between a 'heavenly' existence on earth and the 'Heaven' of the hereafter,
though at times one can also reflect the other (i.e. the characteristics of
Heaven can have their equivalent on earth's heaven), which is what Parwez
also goes on to explain in the main text. See also Parwez's own comment on
earthly heaven and hell and their afterlife counterparts Chapter 5, fn 110).

At present (with the kind of life you are leading) you do not have to worry about your food or clothing. / You suffer neither from thirst, nor from the heat of sun. 20:118-9

Heavenly existence

In Heaven no one experiences hunger, thirst, or lack of clothing and shelter. In other words, the outstanding feature of Heaven is that no one goes without their basic necessities. Likewise in their 'heaven' Adam and Eve were told:

And We said: 'O Adam, you and your wife reside in this garden, and eat freely[93] from it, both of you, whatever you may wish.' 2:35

In heaven there will be no shortage of food and water and people's needs will be met in full. Neither will anyone have to labour just to survive, nor will anyone become tired (35:35), giving cause for its inhabitants to say:

'All praise is due to God, who has caused all sorrow to leave us.' 35:34

Aside from this, at various places the Qur'an reiterates the point that in heaven neither shall anyone have cause to fear, nor shall they have cause to feel sorrow (2:37, 2:62, 2:112, and others). Everyone will be protected from all harm. Not only will no one worry about unemployment, but all means of sustenance and all aesthetic things and wholesome sources of enjoyment will be provided for as well. Let us now see how the Qur'an describes this heavenly state of affairs:

A garden [of bliss] and with [garments of] silk 76:12

... they will recline on couches 76:13

... clusters of fruit 76:14

---

[93] God addressed the Israelites with these same words after they had been rescued from the Pharaoh and were taking refuge in the valley of Sinai. See verse 2:58.

... vessels of silver and goblets that will [seem to] be crystal 76:15

... garments of green silk and brocade 76:21

... bracelets of gold and pearls 22:23 (also 35:33)

... waited upon with trays and goblets of gold 43:71

... where there are rivers of water that time does not corrupt, and rivers of milk the taste of which never alters, and rivers of wine delightful to those who drink it, and rivers of honey 47:15

... fruit and meat in abundance 52:22

... reclining upon green meadows and carpets rich in beauty 55:76

They will be given a drink of pure wine whereon the seal [of God] will have been set 83:25

... they shall have whatever they may desire 50:35

... and theirs shall be all that they could ask for 36:57

... and there will be found all that the souls might desire, and [all that] the eyes might delight in 43:72

... you will see the brightness of bliss on their faces 83:24

According to the Qur'an this is life in heaven, and it can be achieved by following the Qur'anic program. Note that according to the Qur'an, this life can be acquired not only in the afterlife but on earth as well. Any society that governs itself according to Qur'anic teachings will thus have a heavenly life on earth. All the joyful, abundant and beautiful things (as listed above) of Heaven are obtained on earth, whilst these same things, as applied to the Heaven of the afterlife, are metaphorical. What these metaphors of the afterlife represent cannot be known to us at present, nor are they the subject of our discussion. Suffice it to say again that according to the Qur'an, a 'heavenly life' means ease and happiness here on earth as well as in the hereafter.

From this discussion it becomes clear that according to the Qur'an, the good things of this world are all God's reward. Good conduct is rewarded with the attainment of power and of success in the land.

When there is abundance of sustenance and all needs are met leading to peace and security, then this is heaven on earth. The desire to have attractive and pleasing items is not forbidden by the Almighty. Conversely disgrace, oppression, weakness, fear and hunger are forms of our self-inflicted punishment, coming from our unwillingness to follow His laws. From this it is obvious that the 'spiritualist' worldview according to which all desire is sinful, and life's sufferings such as hunger and destitution are signs of piety, stands in stark contrast to the Qur'anic position.

Let us now review the materialist worldview, according to which there is no life beyond the life of this world, and the only nourishment we require is physical. The entire focus of the materialist is to live well, and meeting all our physical needs is the mark of success. Of course this is also contrary to the Qur'anic position, for the following reasons:

1) According to the Qur'an we don't merely have a physical existence, but we also possess a self or personality that is capable of attaining immortality. Death therefore does not mark the end of human existence

2) According to the materialist, we cannot even meet the needs of all people here on earth, let alone in any future life. In contrast, the Qur'an offers a system that not only meets humanity's physical needs but also makes provisions for unlocking our hidden potential. Thus the human self develops and is fully prepared to enter the next stage (the afterlife)

Note that in our present earthly life, the development of the human self is dependent on the condition of the physical body, and thus it is of the utmost importance that all our physical needs be met. It follows that meeting our physical needs is a means to an end, and not an end in itself. Meeting our physical needs therefore is a step towards the higher goal of unlocking the potential of the human self.

The human self

As we have already noted in Chapter 2, when human beings reached a certain stage of evolution we passed beyond the animal stage and acquired a characteristic that is unique to us, which the Qur'an terms 'Divine Energy' (32:9). Some modern Western thinkers also acknowledge this view of human life. Ouspensky for example has said:

The complicated system of the human soul often appears as dual, and there are serious grounds for such a view. There live in every man, as it were, two beings, one being comprising the mineral, vegetable, animal and human "time and space" world, the other being belonging to some other world. One is the being of "the past", the other the being of "the future". ... And the past and the future find themselves in eternal struggle and eternal conflict in the soul of man. It may be said without the slightest exaggeration that the soul of man is the battle-field [*sic*] of the past and the future.[94]

Nietzsche translated Zoroaster as follows:

I am of today and heretofore, but something is in me that is of the morrow, and the day following, and the hereafter.[95]

In other words, life has passed organically through the mineral, plant and animal stages to finally become human. Once we reached the human stage, we gained a new characteristic, namely the personality, or self. Our future doesn't lie in biological evolution, but in *self* evolution. The human being is of course (biologically) a highly complex animal. It changes from moment to moment, in accordance with the laws of nature. But the human self (*nafs*) is made of Divine Energy and so it is not subject to the laws of nature, i.e. space and time. Biologists tell us that every cell in the body dies and is replaced after a time, and so the body that existed ten years ago is completely different today. However the part of ourselves that we call 'I' or 'me' remains the same and is permanent; it does not change as the body does, and thus it is separate from the body. From this it is clear that every individual is actually a combination of change and permanence. In the words of Berdyeav:

Two diametrically opposed principles struggle in life. One's attitude to the change which takes place in the world must be two-fold. Life is change and without the new there is no life. But change may be betrayal. The realization of human personality presupposes change and newness but it also presupposes the

---

[94] Ouspensky, P.D. (1931) *A New Model of the Universe* 1997 reprint, New York: Dover Publications p.118-9

[95] Nietzsche, Friedrich W. (1891) *Thus Spake Zarathustra* English translation by Thomas Common 2007 reprint, Kansas: Digireads.com, p.81 (slightly edited)

unchanging without which there is no personality. In the development of personality man must be true to himself; he must not betray himself; he must preserve his own features which are foreordained for eternity. It is a necessary thing in life that the process of change which leads to the new shall be combined with fidelity.[96]

This is what makes the human self unique. To quote Bergson again (as we did in Chapter 2):

[The soul is] a thing incapable of decomposition because it is simple, incorruptible because it is indivisible, immortal by virtue of its essence.[97]

Joad writes that even if we admit that the self is subject to change, the fact remains that the self cannot be divided or broken down.

The whole personality is present in everything that we do.[98]

The psychologist and philosopher Erich Fromm has written with regards to the self:

In the same sense we have faith in ourselves. We are aware of the existence of a self, of a core in our personality which is unchangeable and which persists throughout our life in spite of varying circumstances, and regardless of certain changes in opinions and feelings. It is this core which is the reality behind the word 'I', and on which our conviction of our own identity is based. Unless we have faith in the persistence of our self, our feeling of identity is threatened and we become dependent on other people whose approval then becomes the basis for our feeling of identity. Only the person who has faith in himself is able to be faithful to others, because only he can be sure that he will be the same at a future time as he is today and, therefore, to feel and to act as he now expects to. Faith in oneself is a condition of our ability to promise, and since, as

[96] Berdyaev, Nicolas (1949) *The Divine and the Human* (trans. R.M. French) London: Geoffrey Bles, p.50
[97] Bergson, *The Two Sources of Morality and Religion*, p.225
[98] Joad, C.E.M. (1948) *Decadence* London: Faber & Faber, p.208

Nietzsche said, man can be defined by his capacity to promise,
faith is one of the conditions of human existence.[99]

What we have described of the Qur'anic view accords with mystic
thought to a point, since mysticism also advocates the existence of the
soul. Yet from here the two viewpoints diverge. In mysticism the aim is
to discard the ego (the 'I') and merge the soul with the Great Spirit. If
we accept this view, the idea of developing and strengthening the self
becomes void. In light of the Qur'an the self is permanent, and the aim
of life is to strengthen the self to the point that the individual ('I')
becomes indestructible or immortal. To the mystic, the only way to
cleanse the soul is to denounce the world. This concept (as we have
already mentioned) is completely opposed to the Qur'anic worldview.
Hence there is no room for spiritualism or mysticism in the system of
Rabbubiya (total sustenance), which the Qur'an decrees as the ultimate
goal in life. It is clear therefore that the Qur'anic viewpoint is distinct
from both the materialist and the mystic view of life.

In the next chapter we will review the Qur'anic system of
Rabbubiya; and later in this book (Chapter 8) we will also discuss how,
according to the Qur'an, it can be established.

---

[99] Fromm, Eric (1956) *The Art of Loving* (1995 reprint) London:
Thorsons, p.96-7

CHAPTER 5
The Qur'anic system of sustenance

In the last chapter our subject of focus was the human self, and for this reason we had to make use of abstract language. Since abstract concepts are generally difficult to grasp and relate to, we feel it is important that we revisit the subject before we proceed any further.

The fact is that 'human being' is the name of both the body and the personality (self) combined. The purpose of life is to nourish and develop the body in order to keep it in good health, and so pave the way to also develop the human self. However the difficulty lies in the fact that the principle of 'nourishing' the body and that of 'nourishing' the self stand in opposition. The principle of nourishing the body requires that we consume. My body will develop only when I eat. My body will not be nourished if I give my food to someone else instead of eating it myself. To keep up my strength and grow, I must eat. Furthermore, the way my body develops is dependent on what I eat, and not on what I give away to others. Hence the principle of nourishing the body is totally individual-focused, and rests upon what and how much it can get. This is a fixed law and no one can change it.

The principle of nourishing the self meanwhile is exactly the opposite. It is based on how much we give, and how we contribute to the beauty of the universe. What do we give to others to fulfil their needs? In other words, how do we contribute to the sustenance of the human race? The more we give, the more the self will grow. This is what we would call the training and development of the self. To sum up what we have discussed so far:

1) 'Human being' is really a term for both the physical body and the self

2) Both aspects of the human being (physical and self) require nourishment and development

3) The body develops by taking; the self develops by giving
4) These two principles of nourishment are totally opposed to each other. When we receive, our self does not develop, and when we give, our physical body misses out

This is the paradox with which we have to contend and for which we have not been able to find a resolution. Humanity has spent most of its history struggling with striking a balance, and has subsequently swung between deficiency and excess. One group tells us to give away all our worldly goods and to wilfully neglect the body's demands. They tell us that the secret to success lies in the destruction of the body. But this is a fallacy. The human being is both self and body. Another group tells us that we should take for ourselves and thereby attain physical success. They tell us that the purpose of life is to develop our body and our strength, and nothing else. But this too is a fallacy, since again the human being is both body *and* self. If we neglect either one or the other, we fail in our purpose of life.

Human thought has been unable to get past either materialism or spiritualism, and this is because we have not properly understood the root of the problem. As a result the self is faced with a contradiction that is also reflected in society.[100] Psychological conflicts in the society are termed in the Qur'an as *fasaad* (lit. 'chaos', or 'corruption').

The Qur'an tells us that this conflict can be easily resolved. It is possible to establish a system in which the seemingly opposite demands of body and self are simultaneously met, and so both are developed and strengthened. This type of system can be described as a *Nizam-e-Rabbubiya* (Divine system of universal sustenance).

Now let us review the details of this system as it appears in the Qur'an. We should keep both the needs of the body and the self in mind that we have already described. The Qur'an uses the phrase 'life of this world' (*hiyaat-ud-duniyya*) for what we would call 'materialist' or worldly existence, including the notions of self-preservation and protection of kith and kin, and securing the future. Over the coming pages we will use the same phrase. Contrary to this, the Qur'anic view of life affirms that our temporal existence (i.e. of the body) and the afterlife (i.e. the ongoing existence of the self) are both equally valid. This is the Islamic way of life, or system of sustenance. It is a system in which both the needs of the body and of the self are completely met.

---

[100] **Translators' note:** The psychological term for this conflicted mental state is 'cognitive dissonance'.

Hence it becomes possible to attain success and happiness in both the present and future – that is, in this world and in the hereafter.

The effect of self-interest on humanity

The Qur'an tells us that we are concerned solely with indulging our self-interests. We continually hoard until our hunger for more becomes insatiable.

> [They] amass [wealth] and thereupon withhold [it from others] 70:18

> Indeed, man is born with a restless disposition 70:19

('Restless'(halu'an) in Arabic means one whose hunger (for acquisition) is unending.)

> For, indeed, to the love of wealth is he most ardently devoted 100:8

> [He] who amasses wealth and counts it a safeguard / thinking that his wealth will make him live forever! 104:2-3

We are also focused on immediate gain without considering the consequences in the long term:

> But they don't fear the Hereafter 74:53

> You love this fleeting life, / and give no thought to the afterlife [and to Judgment Day]! 75:20-21

> But nay, you prefer the life of this world 87:16

We hoard as much as we can and even become preoccupied with what we will inherit from others:

> And you devour the inheritance [of others] with devouring greed 89:19

We don't hoard merely to satisfy our needs, but merely for the sake of hoarding:

> And you love wealth with boundless love! 89:20

Everyone competes to become richer than everyone else, and this race continues to the grave:

> You are obsessed by greed for more and more / until you go down to your graves 102:1-2

In such a society, certain groups lose touch with the rest of the community and its concerns:

> [You are henceforth] enemies to one another 2:36

Even family members can turn against each other:

> ... Everyone will flee from his brother / and from his mother and father / and from his spouse and his children: / on that day, every one of them will be concerned only with his own state 80:34-7

Instead of working for the benefit of humanity, each nation aims solely to protect its own interests:

> Yea, each one of them wants to be given scrolls spread out! 74:52

(In other words: These nations do not wish to be subject to a law that might hinder their excesses. They want a licence to do as they please, hence 'scroll spread out'.)

In this hellish existence, every nation also schemes to deprive other nations (also distances itself from the rest):

> Every time a new people enters [hell], it curses its sister-people (that went before), until they follow each other, all into the Fire. 7:38

(In Arabic the word 'curse' (*La'a na*) is better understood as 'putting distance between')

> [Do not use] your pledges as a means of deceiving one another in order to supersede them in wealth and power 16:92

Just as every individual feels that he does not need anyone else when he becomes self-sufficient, every self-sufficient nation feels secure in the knowledge that it doesn't need help from other nations. Hence no nation respects the human rights of other nations.[101]

> Indeed man transgresses all bounds / whenever he believes himself to be self-sufficient 96:6-7

Note the profound truth that is summed up succinctly in the two sentences above. Nations of this mentality become arrogant and believe they are beyond reproach:

> Does he, then, think that no one has power over him? 90:5

This mentality eventually reaches the stage whereby those at the top deem themselves to be above the law, and so they will continually take as much from the public as they can, and simultaneously give back as little as possible. If we look around our own societies, we will find the same mentality persisting everywhere. Predators are constantly looking for ways to pounce and transfer money from other people's pockets to their own. They will pay as little as possible to get a job done, whilst overcharging others when they provide any service. In short, they are extremely miserly. This psychology is behind societal breakdown and chaos, and we see it across the world. The Qur'an offers many historical instances as evidence. In particular it discusses the tribe of Madyan and the Prophet Shoaib (Jethro), who did his best to reform his people. He told them:

> 'O my people! Obey[102] God alone: you have no deity (Rabb) other than Him. Clear evidence of the truth has now come to

---

[101] **Translators' note:** It might be argued that in today's climate of increasing global interdependency, nations have become much more conscious of human rights issues and have better learned to respect one another's sovereignty. But in fact all that has happened is that the scope of the problem has enlarged. Instead of nation standing against nation, we have seen the rise of blocs such as East versus West, or first world (West) versus third world (Asia, Africa and Middle East). Western nations respect one another to the extent that they will maintain an entirely different attitude with non-Western states, being far more prepared to impose crippling sanctions and to start wars against them.
[102] **Translators' note:** The traditional text uses the word worship' but we have replaced it with the word 'obey'. In Arabic grammar, although the word

you from your Sustainer. Give, therefore, full measure and weight [in all your dealings], and do not deprive people of what is rightfully theirs; and do not spread corruption on the earth after it has been so well ordered: this is for your own good, if you would but become convinced.' 7:85

'Do not sit in ambush upon the roads leading to truth, thereby hindering those who believe in it, and do not seek to make the path of God crooked.' 7:86[103]

'[So said Shoaib] I see you are happy [with the state of things] at present, but [if you do not desist], I fear the penalty of a Day that will encompass you [in doom]!' 11:84

What else could follow but doom? The Prophet Shoaib warned his people to be fair and equitable in their financial dealings ('give full measure and weight') and not to be the instigators of injustice.

'[Always] give full measure, and be not among those who cause loss [to others].' 26:181

He also warned that they should not be preoccupied with immediate gain, but rather should set their sights on the future:[104]
Keep your vision on the Last Day, and do not act wickedly on earth by spreading corruption (fasaad)! 29:36

---

ibadat means 'worship' as well as 'service' and 'obedience', the use of ibadat specifically as 'worship' is restricted solely to deities and the devil, i.e. supernatural entities. See Lane, E.W. (1968 reprint) An Arabic-English Lexicon in 8 parts Beirut: Librarie du Liban, Book I (Part 5) p.1934: 'the verb is used in these senses [religious service or worship] only when the object is God, or a false god, or the Devil' (Online: http://www.laneslexicon.co.uk Last retrieved 29 June 2012). As such in the above verse, since God is the subject, we could have left it as 'worship'. However, the rest of the verse, as well as the context in which this verse is placed, makes it clear that the discussion is not religion, but socioeconomics. In addition, the word ibadat appears in other verses referring to subjects other than supernatural entities. See for example. verse 3:79 (in which the subject is a prophet, i.e. a human being), and 7:31 (in which the subject is a mosque or masjid, i.e. a building).

[103] **Translators' note:** In other words, they have been warned against designing their socioeconomic system in such a way that it trips up those who wish to live in the path of truth, and makes it impossible for them to survive.

[104] Here we are simply recounting Shoaib's warnings, but later in this book we will also discuss how his people responded. See Chapter 8.

The Qur'an has given us the specific example of the people of Madyan, but as such the problem of seeking immediate gain is common throughout the peoples of the world. They hoard and they restrict resources that are otherwise freely available:

> [The] withholder of good [i.e. resources that are needed by everyone, and] rebellious aggressor, fomenter of distrust [between people] 50:25

Thus they withhold the God-given resources that are meant to be free for all, e.g. by blocking irrigation routes so that water won't reach everybody's fields.

> [And they] deny all assistance [to their fellow people]! 107:7

They are unwilling to spend in the way of the collective good, and even when they are obliged to do so, they give as little as possible, since they are tight-fisted:

> And gives so little [of himself for the collective good], and so grudgingly 53:34

The Qur'an makes a similar statement elsewhere:

> Woe to those who give short measure 83:1

Once this psychology of selfish competition reaches its peak, and every single member of society competes to take everything for himself and to leave as little as possible for all others, the system becomes absolutely corrupted and its doom is inevitable. These are the people about whom the Qur'an has said:

> When they receive their due from [other] people, [they] demand that it be given in full / but when they have to measure or weigh whatever they owe to others, give less than what is due! 83:2-3

These are people who take as much as possible and give as little as possible; but according to the Qur'an there is also a group that does nothing but take and gives nothing away. They live on the blood of others, whilst contributing nothing of value to their society. In Qur'anic phraseology they are termed *mutrafeen* (lit. the 'self-indulgent'). This group comprises religious leaders. Hence the Qur'an states:

> O you who have *eiman* (conviction)! Behold, many of the rabbis and monks do indeed wrongfully devour men's possessions and turn away from the path of God. 9:34

This group also always strongly opposes any moves towards a Qur'anic revolution that would establish the Divine system of sustenance for all. The reason for this is that they can foresee their own destruction as the outcome of this revolution. In the Divine system of sustenance every able member of society is expected to do their part towards its maintenance. There is no place for the lazy and the freeloader; but the religious elite are not in the habit of having to work for a living. Thus wherever and whenever a voice is raised for establishing the Divine system, the religious elite is quick to try and silence it. They provoke the public by declaring that 'this person is inventing new ideas and is attempting to lead us stray from the traditions of our forefathers.' All past attempts to bring about the Divine revolution have always been stifled by manipulative means, and no doubt this will continue in the future.

> And so it is: whenever We sent, before your time, a warner to any community, those of its people who had lost themselves entirely in self-indulgence (*mutrafeen*) would always say, 'Behold, we found our forefathers agreed on what to believe – and indeed, it is but in their footsteps that we follow!' 43:23

In other words, these self-indulgent people do not oppose the Divine revolution out of ignorance; they do so with complete awareness of what they are doing. After all, they are parasites and are used to living off others. They will baulk at the thought of not only having to earn for themselves, but also having to make the fruit of their labour available to others.

Here the Qur'an makes a subtle point when it singles out the 'rabbis and monks' (i.e. religious elite). The capitalists who exploit others still has to invest some of his own capital into their ventures and thus take business risks. But the religious elite never invest a single penny in anything, since they take whatever they want in donations from other people, and so they never need to take a risk. It becomes clear from this that the religious elite are in fact the most extreme type of capitalist. This is why the Qur'an singles out the *mutrafeen* (parasitic people) before even speaking of capitalists in general. To revisit verse 9:34:

> O you who have *eiman* (conviction)! Behold, many of the rabbis and monks do indeed wrongfully devour men's possessions and turn away from the path of God. And there are those who hoard treasures of gold and silver and do not spend them for the sake of God – give them the tiding of grievous suffering [in the life to come]. 9:34

From the Qur'anic viewpoint these *mutrafeen* are the ones who merely seek the 'life of this world' (*hiyaat-ud-duniyya* which we mentioned earlier). They are obsessed solely with immediate gains and self-preservation, and they are blind as far as their own future (in the hereafter) is concerned. Yet ironically, whilst they believe they are highly successful and productive members of society, in reality their entire contribution to humanity weighs less than a grain of sand.

> Say: 'Shall we tell you who are the greatest losers in whatever they may do? / '[It is] they whose labour has gone astray in [the pursuit of nothing but] the life of this world, and who nonetheless think that they are doing good works; / it is they who have chosen to deny their Sustainer's messages and the fact that they are destined to meet Him.' Hence, all their deeds come to nought, and no weight shall We assign to them on Resurrection Day. 18:103-5

It doesn't take much imagination to see why such a society is doomed to self-destruct. As we have already observed, the intellect is only concerned with protecting the self, and since no one knows when he will die, he never places a limit on how much he hoards. His intellect is driven by a fear of insecurity, and so it continues hoarding up to the grave. Of course, whilst his desire to acquire is unlimited, resources are in limited supply. Thus every individual is obsessed with taking as much for himself or herself as possible, and this inevitably leads to conflict. The wider implications of this are that conflicts occur not only at the individual level, but between nations as well. Just as the individual intellect serves self-interest, so national wisdom serves the national interest, and aims to take sole control over available resources, leading to international conflict. As Joad has said:

It follows that a society whose members aim at wealth, power, fame and social position is a society whose values are inconsistent with stability and contentment, since where men value as ends in themselves goods which are limited and dividing, the possessors will be few and the deprived many, with the result that many will be restless and disappointed. Now, restless and disappointed citizens are a source of weakness and instability, as the history of European States immediately prior to the rise of Fascism abundantly testifies.[105]

As far as the *mutrafeen* are concerned, Briffault has said:

[T]he collective organism cannot be healthy when one part seeks to thrive to the detriment of another.[106]

This is the condition of a society that lives by the philosophy of 'immediate gain'. The thinkers of such societies observe the ensuing chaos and inevitably they come together to try and find the reasons for it. However the Qur'an states that the problem is so obvious that we hardly need to set up a commission to investigate the matter. The Qur'an explains this in its own way. It states that people in this situation merely blame God: 'It is God's will – he makes life easy for some, and makes it difficult for some.' (89:15-16). But, says the Qur'an, this claim is completely false. In fact they are deluded and refuse to acknowledge the truth. They console themselves by blaming the outcome of their own wrongdoings on God. In reality they do not suffer without good reason. They bring it upon themselves, when they don't respect the downtrodden who are alone and without support.

But no, no [consider all that you do and fail to do]. You are not generous towards the orphan, / and you do not urge one another to feed the needy, / and you devour the inheritance [of others] with devouring greed, (89:17-19) [107]

What else then can be the fate of such people but for them to face the consequences?

---

[105] Joad, *Decadence*, p.328-9

[106] Briffault, Robert (1919) *The Making of Humanity* London: George Allen & Unwin, p.101

[107] See also verses 69:34, 74:44, 107:3; and for the opposite behaviour of those with *eiman*, see 76:8 and 90:14. Aside from these, verse 93:9 states: 'Do not mistreat the orphan.'

And His grip would be so severe, that it would have no parallel 89:26

... That [hoarded wealth] shall be heated in the fire of hell, and their foreheads and their sides and their backs will be branded with it, and [those people shall be told]: 'These are the treasures which you have laid up for yourselves! Taste, then, [the fruit of] your hoarded treasures!' 9:35

(It should be noted that this hellish outcome is not something that happens only in the afterlife, but manifests itself on earth also).[108]

[Doomed is he] who amasses wealth and counts it as a safeguard, / thinking that his wealth will save him [from calamity] forever! / No, but he shall indeed be left in a crushing torment! / And what will explain to you what that crushing torment will be? / A fire kindled by God, / which will rise over their hearts: / Indeed, it will close in upon them / in endless columns! 104:2-9

(In other words: The rich believe they are immune from all financial crises by virtue of the size of their wealth. But when the system fails, their wealth will offer no security; in fact it will be worthless, leaving them in a state of terror and misery.)

The Qur'an states that such people do not even achieve the status of a 'human being'. They live like animals, which eat, drink, and then die. Leading this kind of meaningless life creates hell on earth.

Indeed, God will admit all those who have conviction and do righteous deeds into gardens through which running waters flow, whereas those who reject the truth may enjoy their [material] life and eat as cattle eat — but shall have the fire for their abode. 47:12

Another viewpoint

---

[108] **Translators' note:** At the time of writing this (August 2011), the UK has just passed through a period of serious rioting in several major cities. Though the reasons are as yet being debated, it is quite clear that in light of the Qur'an, this outcome was inevitable in a climate of the sharpening rich-poor divide, and a deepening recession coming in part from the financial fallout following the bank bailouts.

Aside from this there is another way of life which is termed the 'hereafter' or 'collective interest' or 'pleasant life'. If the subject of our earlier discussion can be summed up in the term 'vested interests', then this alternate viewpoint may be termed 'collective (or open) interest'.

The word *infaaq* appears so frequently in various ways in the Qur'an that its meaning becomes quite obvious. *Nafaq* (from which *infaaq* is derived) refers to a tunnel that is open at both ends. (The antonym of *nafaq* is *sarb*, which is a one-way tunnel closed at the other end.) The derivative word *munafiq* (usually translated as 'hypocrite' in the Qur'an) thus actually refers to someone who enters the house of *deen* through one door and leaves another open for his escape. The meaning of *infaaq* in the Qur'an is to leave resources open to everyone. The word is usually translated as 'to spend (freely)', but this fails to adequately communicate the full meaning of the word. The full meaning of the Qur'anic phrase *infaaq fi sabil-Allah* (usually translated 'spend in the path of God') needs proper explanation. In the Qur'an in fact, *bukhal* is used as the antonym of *infaaq*. *Bukhal* means 'stinginess' or 'meanness', i.e. to 'keep to oneself', or 'to hold onto', or 'hoard'. Contrary to this, the meaning of *infaaq* is to 'keep open' for the benefit of everyone, or 'open up', and to 'remove restrictions'. Therefore any society that bases itself on the principle of *infaaq fi sabil-Allah* is one in which every individual leaves open the fruit of his labour for the benefit of the collective. He/she will not place restrictions on what he/she gives away. Every member of this society will constantly keep the interest of the whole in mind, and thus will place collective interest above self-interest.

> [They] give [others] preference over themselves, even though they themselves are poor 59:9

Let us consider the following analogy. Imagine there is a drought and there is a water shortage. There is only one water pump in the area supplying a limited amount of water. But there are too many people who need to drink. In this situation people start pushing each other out of the way to get to the pump. The Arabic term for this mentality is *shuh-ha-nafs* (lit. 'for oneself'). The Qur'an states that those who place the needs of others above their own are saved from selfishness, and such people will achieve prosperity in the future.

> [They are] saved from their own selfishness; so they shall
> attain to a happy state 59:9

Investing in the self

At another place in the Qur'an *infaaq* does literally refer to 'spending'
on others, but this ultimately means investing in one's own *nafs*. This is
because (as we have mentioned earlier) the nourishment of the self is
dependent on how much we give rather than take.

> And spend for the good of your own selves [pl. s*shuh-ha-
> nafsihee*]. 64:16

The Qur'an has repeatedly and emphatically stated that when we
leave resources open to others, it doesn't mean that others are
benefiting and we are getting nothing in return. In fact such acts serve
to benefit the self.

> And whatever you may spend on others is for your own
> good ... 2:272

> Whoever grows in purity [i.e. provides for others], does so
> for the good of his own self 35:18

Thus the self develops through giving, and reaches a state in which
neither fear nor grief shall touch it.

> ... No fear will they have, and neither shall they grieve 2:274

Everything we give will be compensated in full.

> ... Whatever you may spend will be repaid unto you
> in full 2:272

The Qur'an has at various places also described this giving in terms
of a 'loan' (*qarz*). Usually a loan implies lending in order to get it back
later; but the Qur'anic version has an important implication which we
can best illustrate by means of an analogy. When a cow chews the cud,
it is chewing grass that is not yet digested (it is in 'raw' form). When
the cow subsequently swallows the cud, it is now ready for full
digestion, and this in Arabic is called *qareez*. In the verses relating to

infaaq, on the surface it appears that we are giving to others, but in fact this should be understood in terms of the concept of *qareez*. The system of sustenance is designed such that whatever we give (or loan: *qarz*) in 'raw' form is returned in 'mature' (and thus more clearly beneficial) form:

> If you offer up to God a goodly loan [*qarz hasana*], He will doubly repay you for it and will 'forgive' [*ghafr*] your shortcomings. 64:17

Whatever we contribute towards maintaining the balance of our society is repaid doubly, i.e. it becomes a means of 'security' both for the physical body and for the self. (Usually translated 'forgive your shortcomings' as above, the word *ghafr* really means 'protect' or 'succour', rather than 'forgive'.)

Note that the Divine system of sustenance keeps nothing for itself, but rewards for all contributions in abundance. The meaning of the Arabic word *shakoorun* is 'return in abundance' (from a root word meaning literally, 'to fill'.)

> God is most ready to appreciate [i.e. reward service – *shakoorun*] 64:17

As the self develops via the Divine system, the entire human being is strengthened like a camel that is physically in good shape and so is not easily frightened. (The Arabic word for physical strength and emotional composure or balance is *haleem*).

> ... and [He makes us] patient (*haleem*) 64:17

Aside from any results that would manifest themselves and become obvious, there are also some long-term implications of this system that are not immediately obvious and which we cannot perceive or foresee:

> [He knows] all that is beyond the reach of perception as well as all that can be witnessed. He is the Almighty (*Aziz*), the Wise (*Hakeem*)! 64:18

It should also be kept in mind (with respect to the above verse) that God is Almighty (*Aziz*). Hence it is impossible for any human power to try and hinder the processes of His Law. But we can't get away from God's law of requital (*mukafat*), because He designed it to be perfectly reliable (the Arabic word for this attribute of God is *Hakeem*, lit. 'wisdom'); and so we must necessarily have conviction that whatever we put into the system will inevitably yield results, even though we cannot perceive them in the present.

The Qur'an states that either an abundance or shortage of sustenance (*rizq*) occurs by way of the law of *Rabbubiya*:

> Say: 'Indeed my Lord [*Rabb*] enlarges and restricts the Sustenance to such of his servants as He pleases: and nothing do you spend at all (in His cause) but He replaces [*khilfatun*] it: for He is the Best of those who grant Sustenance.' 34:39[109]

In accordance with this fundamental principle, the more we contribute to the 'collective interest' the more *rizq* will be returned to us. As we have already discussed, when we spend our wealth it appears to us as though we are giving it away with no return. In reality we don't lose it at all, but rather it is returned to us in a 'pleasing' (i.e. different yet beneficial) form. Take the example of trees in autumn, which shed their leaves, and it may seem that they have lost them forever. Yet in the spring, the same trees will produce fresh new foliage (hence, in the above verse, 'He replaces it' – *khilfatun*). This analogy applies to human society as well, insofar as leaving the fruit of our labour open to the collective will benefit us and bring progress in the long term.

> And whatever it be that you spend on others, He [always] replaces (*khilfatun*) it: for He is the best of providers. 34:39

(The Arabic word *khilfatun* also happens to be the word for the aforementioned 'fresh foliage' in our Qur'an-inspired analogy). Another example can be found in a single grain, which, once planted, produces seven ears, with a hundred new grains in each ear:

---

[109] **Translators' note:** 'My Sustainer *grants* ...' On the surface this appears to imply that God bestows wealth or poverty at His own discretion, and humans have no control over their personal circumstances. But in fact the verse means that scarcity and abundance occur due to the processes of Divine (Natural) law, and that all selfish acts will eventually result in scarcity – even in those nations that wrongly believe they are strong and self-sufficient. See the verses preceding 34:39 (in particular 34:34-6).

> The parable of those who spend their possessions for the sake of God is that of a grain out of which grow seven ears, in every ear a hundred grains: for God grants manifold increase to whomever He wills; and God is infinite, all-knowing. 2:261

Hence our contributions to the system are only good for us.

> And whatever good you may spend on others is for your own good, provided that you spend only out of a longing for God's countenance 2:272

The return will be in full, and will not come short.

> For whatever good you may spend will be repaid to you in full, and you shall not be wronged. 2:272

Hence this will also strengthen the self:

> [They spend in order to] strengthen their souls 2:265

In other words, we will broaden our horizons and set the self on the path to immortality.

> Never shall you attain to true piety unless you spend on others out of what you cherish yourselves 3:92

Conversely at another place the Qur'an states that whoever gives (infaaq) out of a feeling of grudging obligation, will not be repaid:

> For only this prevents their spending from being accepted from them ... [they] never spend [on righteous causes – infaaq] without feeling resentment. 9:54 (see also verses 2:264, 3:116 and 4:28)

The true meaning of 'giving openly' (infaaq) therefore means that we should not give either grudgingly, or with any expectation of receiving a reward.

> [They give to the poor and underprivileged members of society with the thought:] 'We feed you for the sake of God alone: we desire no recompense from you, nor thanks.' 76:9

For this reason the *infaaq* which is given in the 'cause of God' (i.e. for the higher purpose of *Rabbubiya*) is for the betterment of the self:

[He] spends his possessions [on others] so that he might grow in purity 92:18

Thus there is no question of seeking thanks or a reward; and so the Qur'an also states:

And do not, through giving, seek to gain for yourself 74:6

By helping to overcome the existing shortfalls in society (i.e. in bringing people to socioeconomic equity), we also absolve the shortcomings in the self:

Could the reward of good (*ehsan*) be anything but good (*ehsan*)? 55:60

(*Ehsan*: lit. 'indemnification'.)

Hence this is the full exposition of the word *infaaq*. The Qur'an requires the establishment of a society in which every citizen makes *infaaq* a principle to live by, and terms such a state *jannat* (lit. 'Paradise' or Heaven).[110] A unique feature of this state is that it provides *rizq* (sustenance) in abundance. We already know that in the legend of Adam and heaven, he could eat whatever and whenever he liked without fear of facing shortage.

Heavenly life

And We said: 'O Adam, you and your wife reside in this garden, and eat freely from it, both of you, whatever you may wish.' 2:35

---

[110] A society that establishes itself according to the law of *Rabbubiya* becomes a heaven on earth, and a society that does not establish itself according to this law will lead a hellish existence. Since, according to the Qur'anic view, life doesn't end with death, heaven and hell likewise begin on earth and continue on the hereafter. In the life after death, the laws of time and space as we know them will be different, and so we cannot comprehend what Heaven and Hell will be like in the hereafter, yet we (as Muslims) have conviction in their existence. In fact, having conviction in the existence of Heaven and Hell is a prerequisite of being a Muslim.

Adam was also warned that if he made the mistake of listening to *Iblees* (Satan, the metaphor for a non-Divine law), then he would be led out of heaven and lose its privileges (i.e. having the necessities of life freely provided):

> It is provided for you that you do not hunger here or feel naked / and that you do not thirst here or suffer from the heat of the sun 20:118-9

He was also warned (as implied in verse 20:117): 'if you leave this heavenly society and choose to follow a law that is not Divinely ordained, then leave aside fulfilling your higher purpose of being, you will have to toil and struggle even to meet your basic needs and so you will lead a life of suffering'. (The key word *fatashqaa* in verse 20:117 means 'suffering' or 'unhappy').

But Adam left his heavenly life and instead brought difficulties upon himself. The events that led up to his leaving heaven and what happened afterwards have been described eloquently in the Qur'an. In heaven Adam was obtaining everything wanted freely and without hardship (2:35), but he was also warned:

> [But] do not approach this one tree (*shajr*), in case you become wrongdoers 2:35

So what was this 'tree' (*shajr*)? A lot of commentators have offered various explanations, but we can find the answer within the meaning of the word *shajr* itself. Aside from 'tree', *shajr* means 'people living in division' or 'discord amongst people'. It also means 'enmity'. From this we can see that *shajr* refers to a lifestyle in which individuals pursue self-interest. 'Adam' was deceived by *Iblees* and thus he lost his paradisiacal life. As a result, Adam and his progeny became:

> ... enemies to one another 2:36

This was the beginning of human life in which self-interest would be placed above collective interest. At another place, the Qur'an states that Satan told Adam:

> 'O Adam! Shall I lead you to the tree of eternal life; and [thus] to a kingdom that will never decay?' 20:120

In short Satan was suggesting to Adam that he could achieve immortality through his children, meaning that he would live forever through them even after his own death. Hence the secret of eternal life would be to reproduce.

> And so the two ate [the fruit of the tree]: and subsequently they became conscious of their nakedness and began to cover themselves with pieced-together leaves from the Garden. And [thus] did Adam disobey his Sustainer, and thus did he fall into grievous error 20:121

The pair thus became 'conscious of their nakedness', i.e. they became sexually aware; and so they were tempted into committing the sexual act out of a belief that they would live on through their children.[111] Adam therefore created a new problem for himself. First, he acted out of his own self-interest, and then he became concerned with safeguarding his progeny as an extension of his self-interest. Consequently his children also became preoccupied with safeguarding their self-interest, and the inevitable conflicts meant that Adam lost his heavenly life.

> [God said:] Down with you all from this [Garden, and be henceforth] enemies to one another! 20:123

Since we have lost our paradisiacal society, we must find a way to re-establish it. This is the purpose of life. It is possible only if the

---

[111] **Translators' note:** It might also be said that Satan instilled in Adam a *belief* in reproduction to the end of achieving physical immortality – a belief which led to the first act of *shirk* in the sense of ideological disobedience, as symbolised by the tree from which Adam and his wife ate. (*Shirk*, lit. polytheism; see also Afterword, fn 224). As a consequence, Adam's people became divided in the pursuit of self-interest, and since they could not hide this from the Almighty they were soon 'exposed' (20:121 figuratively). Subsequently they resorted to adopting certain Divine laws here and there to try and create a facade of good behaviour – hence, they took 'leaves from the Garden' to hide behind – just as today's religions contain some Divine law to have the surface appearance of Truth, when underneath they contain false manmade doctrines. This also explains why the Qur'an subsequently addresses 'Adam' not singularly nor in the dual (in Arabic grammar), but in the *plural* as a people, when they are thrown out of the Garden - 'Down with you *all* ...' (2:36).

children of Adam establish a society in accordance with the Divine law of *Rabbubiya*.

> We shall send you Our Guidance: and those who follow My guidance need have no fear, and neither shall they grieve. 2:38

Similar to the verse above, the Qur'an also states:

> [And anyone] who follows My guidance will not go astray, and neither will he be unhappy 20:123

Thus it follows that falling from the 'Garden' meant that Adam now had to constantly worry about securing his means of sustenance (he was in a state of *fatashqaa* (suffering) – 20:117). However Adam was told that if he led his life under the guidance of *Wahi* (Revelation), then his suffering would cease and he would once again have everything in abundance (20:123). But if after adopting the Qur'anic code he strayed from it, he would once again experience destitution and suffering.

Consequence of abandoning the Qur'an

> But as for him who shall turn away from remembering Me (i.e. abandons Divine Law) – his means [of subsistence] shall be restricted 20:124

The Qur'an also states that whenever humans establish a Divine system they will return to a heavenly state. They will reside in a paradise of abundance:

> There they will have their sustenance by day and by night 19:62

The phrase 'by day and by night' means that there will be constant abundance, and never will there be a time of shortage.

> [This is an enduring life in which] no struggle can assail us, and no weariness can touch us 35:35

Not once will anyone worry about meeting their needs:

They will say: 'All praise is due to God, who has caused all sorrow to leave us ...' 35:34

In other words, these people will be grateful to God for setting them free from the worries of having to sustain themselves and their children. Since there will be no more conflict over the available resources, all feelings of animosity and jealousy will disappear.

...We will have removed whatever unworthy thoughts or feelings may have been [lingering] in their hearts 7:43

Thus all will have peace of mind and will feel secure.

[They will be received with the greeting,] 'Enter here in peace, secure!' 15:46

They will live together in peace and harmony:

[They will be like] brothers, facing one another [in affection] upon thrones of happiness 15:47

This state of abundance will be everlasting:

No weariness shall ever touch them in this [state of abundance], and never shall they have to forgo it 15:48

[They will have] gardens through which running waters flow, where they will live ... gardens of perpetual bliss 9:71[112]

The supreme awesomeness [of that Day] will cause them no grief (i.e. even a major catastrophe on earth will not cause them distress) 21:103

People will see for themselves how God's attribute of *Rabb* (nourishment) manifests itself in their society.

[In that state of happiness] they will call out, 'All praise is due to God, the Sustainer of all the worlds!' 10:10

---

[112] **Translators' note:** We have added this verse to account for Parwez's reference to 'gardens with running streams' – a line that we have otherwise omitted from the original Urdu text in translation.

This is only a brief overview of a society built upon the Divine law of *Rabbubiya*. For more details we can look at any of the Qur'anic verses on the subject of heaven.[113] From these verses we can get a good idea of what kind of life we will lead in a Qur'anic society. The law of *Rabbubiya* ensures that both physical needs and inner needs (i.e. of the self) will be met. However when people abandon the Qur'anic code, they will return to a life of anxiety and want. A manmade society will be unable to meet even an individual's physical needs, let alone the needs of his self. Thus we can see that the Divine system of *Rabbubiya* is designed to address not just either the 'spiritual' or the 'material' aspects of life, but rather both together.

So far in this chapter we have reviewed both material life (individual, focused on immediate gains) and the life of the 'hereafter'(collective, focused on the future), and we have also reviewed the impact that each respective worldview has on human society. Now let us see how the Qur'an compares these two worldviews. The fact is that since the Qur'an's sole aim is to encourage the establishment of a society in accordance with the Divine system of sustenance (*Rabbubiya*), much of the Qur'an is dedicated to providing the details of this system. At times it has plainly stated the principles, and at other times it has used various analogies from nature to illustrate how neatly the Divine system of sustenance operates throughout the universe. It also presents examples from the history of nations that have fallen as a direct result of focusing on self-interest.

Qur'anic claims that appeal to reason

A peculiar feature of the Qur'an is that it does not expect anyone to accept its claims blindly. It provides logical reasoning to support its arguments. It asks us to consider its claims on the basis of the knowledge we acquire, and to accept them only once we are fully satisfied of their veracity. In the same breath it states that we should not reject any of its claims without further investigation. If we reject the Qur'an's claims, then:

---

[113] I (Parwez) have also discussed these characteristics of heaven further in my book, *Jahan e Farda* (*The Life of Tomorrow*) (1969)

Say: 'Produce your evidence - if you truly believe in your
claim [as against the claim of God]!' 27:64

The Qur'an also confidently asserts that try as we might, no one
can actually find a valid argument against its claims on the basis of
human knowledge.

[Humankind] has no evidence [to deny the existence of God
and His laws] 23:117

This is a bold challenge and it is reiterated in the Qur'an many
times. This is because the Qur'an's claims are not based on
presumptions or any speculative concepts but are based on Divine
knowledge and wisdom. Thus the Almighty has no qualms in making
this challenge. He repeatedly admonishes those who fail to use their
God-given faculties of reason and choose to blindly follow their
ancestors' traditions rather than His law.

Now let us return to the main subject of our discussion, namely the
two worldviews of 'self-interest' (which focuses on taking) and
'collective interest' (which, in accordance with the Divine law of
sustenance, focuses on giving). The Qur'an makes a clear comparison
between the two. It states that humanity spends much time and energy
on various aims.

You aim at most divergent ends 92:4

But however divergent these 'aims' may appear to be, in reality all
of them come down to just one of two types: Their underlying
principle is either to give, or it is to take. The individual who learns to
be 'giving' will give whatever surplus he has to others, in line with the
law of *Rabbubiya*:

Thus, as for him who gives [to others] and is
conscious of God, / and thus acts as a testimony of the
ultimate good ... 92:5-6

As a result, the door will open to ease and abundance:

... [For such a person] We make smooth the path
towards ease 92:7

This is one of the two ways of life along with its outcome. Contrary to this, the individual who adopts the other way of life becomes preoccupied with taking and hoarding, and erroneously believes he is completely secure:

> But as for him who is niggardly, and thinks that he is self-sufficient 92:8

Such a person effectively belies the Divine law in practice and brings instability to the system:

> And calls the ultimate good a lie 92:9

Consequently the door to hardship and suffering will soon open:

> For him shall We make easy the path towards hardship 92:10

Of course it follows that such a system cannot last. Revolt will happen sooner or later, and when it does, those who hoarded their wealth will find it is worthless and cannot save them.

> And what will his wealth avail him when he goes down? 92:11

They choose this selfish way of life based on a belief that the only real life is physical. This belief comes either from personal choice, or 'instinct' (i.e. what they are programmed to think from the social environment they grow up in), or it is intellectual (e.g. from education, or an ideology). Either way, this is enough for them. Yet the truth is that manmade systems can never succeed in developing and evolving human life. For this reason the responsibility of evolving human life, says God, rests on Him. For the sustenance (*Rabbubiya*) of the human being (i.e. both the body and the self) God has chosen the code of conduct (or guiding principles) that are best for us.

> Behold, it is indeed for Us to grace [humans] with guidance 92:12

The Almighty has taken on this responsibility because human beings are concerned only with indulging their self-interest. They are caught up in trivial pursuits and are short-sighted. They fail to account for the bigger picture, i.e. collective interest, and to think of the long term (i.e. the hereafter). Contrary to this, God accounts for the immediate and the distant, the present and the future, the individual and the collective.

> And behold, Ours is [the dominion over] the life to come [i.e. the long term] as well as [over] this earlier part [of your life – i.e. the short term] 92:13

God instructs the Messenger to warn people of the consequences of their individualistic living, which we can succinctly explain by means of an analogy: The produce of their fields will burn in the heat. The Qur'an thus states:

> And so I warn you of the raging fire [of hell] 92:14

This is what happens to those who are selfish and seek ways of life that are contrary to the Divine law of sustenance.

> [This is the fire] which none shall have to endure but that most hapless wretch / who gives the lie to the truth and turns away [from it] 92:15-16

Conversely, a society in which every citizen works for the common good (collective interest) and thus maintains balance will be saved from ruin.

> For he who is truly conscious of God (taqwa)[114] shall remain safe from it [the fire] 92:17

In a Qur'anic society each and every individual will endeavour to give for the collective interest, and by extension his self-interest as well:

---

[114] Taqwa (rendered by Asad as 'God-conscious') is most often translated as 'fear of God'. But this simple translation does not adequately explain the full meaning of the term taqwa. The root word from which taqwa is derived (wqe) means 'to look after' and 'custody'. Thus taqwa refers to someone who 'safeguards' the sanctity of the Divine law in every aspect of his life, and thus lives in harmony with the Natural Order. In doing so, such a person becomes protected from all threats and difficulties in life.

He who spends his wealth [on others] so that he might grow
in purity 92:18

In this society no one will give with the expectation of an
immediate reward, because in fact everyone will understand
that they are contributing to a higher purpose – namely the
sustenance (*Rabbubiya*) of humanity.

[They are] not expecting payment for favours received, / but
[give] only out of a longing for the countenance of his Sustainer,
the All-Highest 92:19-20

The positive results of living in a Qur'anic system will quickly
become apparent:

And such, indeed, shall in time be well-pleased. 92:21

Before we proceed further, it is necessary that we elaborate
upon an earlier point. As we have already seen from verse
92:12, God has said that He is the only one Who is able to
provide us with guidance, as human intellect is insufficient for
the task. This statement is the focal point of the Qur'an's
teachings, and from this it is obvious that *Wahi* (Revelation) is a
necessity for humans.

The necessity of Revelation

We have seen that the demand of the intellect is to serve the self, and
likewise national wisdom dictates that we must put national interest
first. In fact the individual feels attached to the group for the simple
reason that belonging to the group makes him feel secure. Neither
does any individual concern himself with looking after the needs of
others, nor does any nation concern itself with the welfare of other
nations. In fact, according to the materialist view, the intellect is
incapable of looking after the interest of others.[115] Just as my eye can

---

[115] When motivated by pure curiosity about the universe, the intellect is
usually perfectly objective in making its discoveries. But when it comes to

only show *me* what it sees, and just as all my senses can serve only me, and not you, my intellect can only protect my self-interest. It follows that neither the individual intellect nor the combined wisdom of a human collective (nation) is capable of producing a system that has the interest of all humanity (i.e. the 'other') at its heart. In order to truly take care of humanity's interests as a whole, we need guidance from a source that is objective and impartial. In Qur'anic terms, this guidance is available in the form of *Wahi* (Revelation). This is why the Qur'an states that human intellect is not sufficient to establish a system of sustenance. True guidance can come only from God.

> Behold, it is indeed for Us to grace [humans] with guidance (*Wahi*) 92:12

Revelation is necessary because we cannot help but try to look after our own interests, whilst God takes into account the needs of everyone as a whole.

Now we return to our main subject of discussion. The Qur'an at another place states that people focus only on immediate gains, and fail to consider the long term.

> They know only the outer surface of this world's life, whereas they are utterly unaware of the ultimate things [i.e. the long term]. 30:7

But if, instead of speculating, they did their research, they would find that the ultimate (or long-term) secret of life is to be found in taking care of the collective interest, and not in the program of indulging self-interest. There are hundreds of departments of research in the human world, but if we consider them together we find that they all fall into one of three fundamental types: 1) human sciences, e.g. medicine, philosophy, psychology, etc. 2) natural sciences, e.g. physics, chemistry, biology, etc. 3) human history. The Qur'an states that we

---

making discoveries in the realm of human sciences (i.e. society, economics etc.), the intellect is incapable of retaining objectivity. This is because of clashes of interests between individuals and societies, and we know that the individual intellect focuses on self-interest. When the intellect is left to its own devices it can only create a satanic system, one in which every human becomes an enemy to others (20:123). However, when intellect is subordinated to Divine law, then – and only then – it becomes capable of bringing a heavenly system into being.

must investigate all three of these subject types and ask ourselves: Is the universe operating on a principle of self-interest (taking, or *bukhl* i.e. hoarding), or is it operating on the principle of collective interest (giving, or *infaaq*)? First let us take an individual human being (as a subject of human sciences).

Have they never learned to look within themselves? 30:8

In the human body, all organs and their parts are constantly working to pass on whatever they receive to nourish other parts. The stomach, liver, lungs, heart, brain, veins, arteries, and every cell in fact – are all working hard day and night to process whatever nutrient or stimulus they receive and pass it on rapidly to the rest of the body. The system of the human body is thus operating on the principle of giving. But if the stomach (for example) begins operating on the principle of taking (*bukhl*), and thereby stores all incoming food and fails to pass it onto the digestive system, then soon the whole body machinery stops. If the heart abandons the principle of giving (*aatta*) for even a second, death will soon follow. If the veins and arteries cease transporting blood through the body, then the whole system will shut down. Thus we can see that life itself depends on the principle of giving.

Moving on from the human sciences to the natural sciences, we can observe the same principle in action here as well. All life on earth relies on heat and light. The sun continually supplies both in abundance, and does so without holding back. This same principle applies to other natural phenomena as well, as they are all participants in the natural law of *Rabbubiya*. The process leads to positive results throughout the universe. If just one part was to adopt the principle of taking, there would be chaos throughout the universe.

God has not created the heavens and the earth and all that is between them without truth (*haqq*), for an appointed term 30:8

Moving on again, let us consider the third department. Looking at the history of humanity, we find that any nation operating a 'selfish' socioeconomic system (i.e. based upon the principle of self-interest) has always met its destruction. Meanwhile, the nations that have founded their systems on the basis of collective interest have prospered; and as soon as they have abandoned this principle, leading to inequity via selfish individuals, then these systems have fallen apart.

Historical testimony

> Have they [i.e. the unbelieving nations of today], then, never journeyed about the earth and beheld what happened in the end to those [civilisations] who lived before their time? 30:9

Note that in the above verse, the Qur'an is asking if the 'unbelieving nations' (i.e. the nations of today that reject Divine law) have considered what happened to the nations of old that came before them. The verse continues by emphasising that much greater civilisations have fallen before:

> Greater were they in power than they [the present unbelieving nations] are 30:9

These civilisations had also amassed more wealth, and had made a greater impact on the earth (i.e. political, cultural and economic).

> And they left a stronger impact on the earth, and built it up even better than these [are doing] 30:9

But ultimately their way of life proved to be futile. Messengers were sent to bring the truth to them, but they refused to change their habits and lifestyles. As a result, these civilisations fell apart.

> And to them [too] came their Messengers with all evidence of the truth: and so, [when they rejected the truth and perished] it was not God who wronged them, but it was they who had wronged themselves. 30:9

Any nation that produces socioeconomic inequity in its society and thus creates imbalance in every department of its life, becomes chaotic and disorderly. Thus these civilisations were destroyed because of the unchanging Divine principle that life requires balance and stability:

> In the long run evil in the extreme will be the End of those who do evil; for they rejected God's messages and held them up to ridicule. 30:10

When the situation has not yet deteriorated to the point of causing a revolt, it may appear to any outsider that the ruling class in these selfish societies are friends working together and taking care of each other. But in fact once the situation reaches a crisis point, and the social structure begins to falter, only then does the reality become manifest: These people were not really friends at all; they were just using one another. It is at this point that we see them going their separate ways to safeguard their own self-interests:

> They will have no intercessor from among their 'Partners';[116] and they themselves will reject their 'Partners' 30:13

(In other words, all the people with whom they had collaborated for selfish ends will not be able to intercede on their behalf. In fact they will deny having had any association with them.)

This type of nation and a way of life can be thus distinguished from the other (30:14), which, by contrast, makes the Divine system of *Rabbubiya* its ideal, and establishes and develops itself according to Qur'anic dictates. Such a nation creates a heaven on earth:

> Those who attained *eiman* (conviction) and did righteous deeds shall be made happy in a garden of delight 30:15

We have already seen that the Qur'an places much importance on the need to make our worldly life comfortable and free of hardship. However it also states that such a life is only truly possible when the system of *Rabbubiya* is both universal (i.e. it accounts for *all* of humanity, and not just a section of it), and is forward-looking (i.e. it accounts for the long-term goal of also developing the human self). Conversely, if a system focuses solely on physical development for material benefits, its socioeconomic prosperity will have no value. Instead it will lead itself to its own destruction. In such a society the value of worldly life is no more than *la'u* and *la'ab*. The Arabic word *la'u* means all alluring temptations that distract people from their higher purpose, and the word *la'ab* refers to a directionless programme in which there is movement, but we get nowhere, much like a boat that is stuck in a whirlpool.

---

[116] **Translators' note:** ('Partners' taken from Abdullah Yusuf Ali's translation). This phrase is usually rendered as 'partners they associate with God' – implying, of course, false gods. But insofar as the object of 'obedience' here is selfish desire, 'partner' in the sense of 'human powers' (i.e. a ruling class) alone applies.

Worldly life as *la'u* and *la'ab*

Thus the materialist way of life is incapable of taking humanity to its higher goal, i.e. it provides no means of sustenance for the self (and by extension for its immortality).

> Know this [O humanity], that the life of this world is but a play and a passing delight, (*la'ab*) and a beautiful show (*la'u*) 57:20

In other words, leading a selfish (materialist) life brings socioeconomic progress for the sake of progress, and it focuses on superficial aesthetics that are nothing but a distraction in the way of our true destination. The only goal that remains in such a setup is the creation and maintenance of a privileged class or group; it acquires ever-increasing wealth, it is the most advantaged in every sphere of life, and has no qualms in leaving all others trailing behind:

> [It is the cause of] your empty (*fakhr*) competitiveness with one another, and [of your] greed for more and more riches and children ... the life of this world is nothing but the enjoyment of delusion (*ghuroor*) 57:20

(In Arabic, *fakhr* refers to an udder that appears large but is empty in reality; and *ghuroor* refers again to an udder that appears large, but actually contains only a small amount of milk.)

However, this kind of existence whereby social and economic prosperity are symbols of pride and status can be likened to a farmer who, upon seeing a few fragile shoots following light rain, becomes overly confident about his crop's potential:

> Its parable is that of rain: the herbage which it causes to grow delights the tillers of the soil 57:20

However the farmer is celebrating too soon. It only takes a bit of heat for the shoots to wither and die:

> But then it withers, and you can see it turn yellow; and in the end it crumbles into dust. 57:20

We can easily foresee the outcome for those who pin their hopes on a weak crop. Their future is bleak, and their example serves as an ample warning to others.

> But [the abiding truth of man's condition will become fully apparent] in the life to come: severe suffering 57:20

There is only one way to avoid this bleak future, and that is to direct our efforts to accord with Divine law:

> [Severe suffering] or God's forgiveness and His goodly acceptance: 57:20

But if we merely set our sights on selfish and trivial ends, then, as we have already shown, our accumulated wealth will be worthless no matter how valuable we perceive it to be.

> For the life of this world is nothing but an enjoyment of self-delusion (ghuroor). 57:20

The Qur'an also acknowledges that competitiveness is deep-rooted in the human psyche. God tells us that he does not wish to crush our competitive spirit, because it represents a hidden strength of the self. However He exhorts us to redirect our competitiveness so that we utilise it for the good, and not for selfish ends. In other words we should compete[117] to establish a system of sustenance, which provides for the security and development of all humanity.

> [Hence], vie with one another in seeking to attain to your Sustainer's forgiveness 57:21

Thus the Qur'an tells us to strive for a 'heavenly' system that is (at present) beyond the reach of our perception:

---

[117] With reference to 'competition (for the good)' (manaafasat, lit. 'aspire'), the Qur'an states elsewhere – after describing the benefits of a heavenly existence – 'let those who have (high) aspirations, aspire' – i.e. to advance towards a 'heavenly life' (83:26). In another surah (as well as others) it states: 'Vie, therefore, with one another in doing good works.' (2:148). The Qur'an is thus teaching us to direct our competitiveness in the way of good rather than for selfish aims; hence in 23:60-61 the Qur'an tells us to try and outdo one another in giving (not taking).

And [thus bring humanity] to a paradise as vast as the
heavens and the earth 57:21

It is only by adhering to the Divine programme that such a 'heaven'
can come into being:

[It] has been readied for those who have conviction in God
and His Apostle 57:21

This law is not exclusively for any particular nation or society. Any
nation that chooses to adopt the Divine system will gain its benefits:

Such is the bounty of God which He grants to
whomever He wills 57:21

Therefore true socioeconomic prosperity comes only when a
society builds its foundations upon God's law:

For God is limitless in His great bounty 57:21

We should also compare the trivial pursuits of this earthly life and
the meaningful existence of the hereafter from another angle. We have
already seen that humanity's physical or material development
depends on physical nourishment; but the development of the self
comes only when we uphold the permanent values which are provided
in Revelation. As long there is no conflict between our means of
acquisition and the Divine law of *Rabbubiya*, we will have no barriers
in the way of our success. However the question is: When the two
come into conflict, what do we do? The Qur'an states that in such an
event we should prioritise the permanent values over our worldly
interests and make sacrifices. This is because the permanent values
are ultimately more valuable than our material interests, since the
latter have only a short-term value. However, when the Qur'an
declares the material to be ultimately 'trivial' or worthless, we
shouldn't take this to mean that we ought to reject the material world
(as would the mystics). If we take this statement in its proper context,
then its true meaning becomes clear.

A universal law

Moving on, the Qur'an states (as previously mentioned) that any system based on materialist principles is bound to self-destruct. Conversely, any system that safeguards humanity's collective interest and provides its sustenance (including that of the human self) must necessarily be founded upon a great truth. And this great truth is that the entire universe is operating upon one and the same law. For this reason it is impossible for humanity to succeed until it conducts itself in harmony with this same law. A society that conducts its worldly affairs according to manmade laws that are not harmonious with (universal) moral principles will bring about nothing but destruction. This fundamental point is repeated in the Qur'an in various ways. It states that the Divine law of *Rabbubiya* which governs the natural universe should also govern human society. It follows that anyone who wishes to introduce his/her own law or code of conduct in defiance of God's law is in fact guilty of attempting to place another authority on par with that of Him (the Qur'anic word for which is *shirk*):

> And yet, some people choose to serve certain earthly things or beings as deities [i.e. they believe that there should be two different 'gods' or laws; one to rule the physical world (the Divine or nature)[118] and the other (human) to rule our earthly lives] 21:21

If this is their chosen way of life, then they should remember that if they introduce human laws into society that are opposed to Divine law, the result can only be chaos (*fasaad*):

> Had there been in those two realms (heaven and earth) any deities other than God, both those realms would surely have fallen into ruin (*fasaad*)! 21:22

The crux of the law of *Rabbubiya* is that God is the Almighty and sole Sovereign of the whole universe, including the human realm. Thus His law is universally applicable; it is above all others:

> [His Almightiness is] above anything that men may devise by way of definition! 21:22

---

[118] **Translators' note:** Here we have used both 'Divine' and 'nature' to account both for secularists who separate their religious and worldly lives, and atheists who do not acknowledge the existence of the Divine.

The law of *Wahdat* (Unity)

That there is only one law in effect throughout the universe is an established fact in modern science. Hans Driesch thus contemplates:[119]

> The doctrine that the universe is *one ordered whole* may be called the *monism of order.* ... There can be no doubt that this monism, were it true, would supersede all other theories of natural order. Everything would prove to have been pro-visionary and would merge into the concept of monism. There would be no limited systems, for there would be only *the one* system; and, strange to say, there would be no "laws of Nature" with regard to independent repeatable kinds of becoming, for there would be but *one* law, and no kind of independence. ... There would be one organism, so to say; or, in other terms, the universe would be *the one* organism.[120]

Another prominent scientist writes:

> We see plan both in the organic and the lifeless world. The more we know of the laws and arrangement of the elements and of their combinations, as well as of the stars and planets, just so much the more clearly is law apparent.[121]

Therefore the notion that we should adopt our own code of conduct that conflicts with the universal law is patently false. The

---

[119] **Translators' note:** We have altered this sentence to read 'Driesch *contemplates*' it' (instead of 'Driesch writes') because we find that in he did not in fact subscribe to a 'monism of order'. In the above passage that Parwez has cited, Driesch is merely reviewing monism and a few pages later he concludes (albeit reluctantly): 'Personally, I confess that, while a monism of order for the reasons explained is not altogether impossible – though even then it is not quite satisfactory, – *I myself feel forced to accept the dualistic doctrine*, in spite of all logical postulates.' (Driesch, Hans (1914) *The Problem of Individuality* London: Macmillan, p.74. Emphasis added.). We might add that Parwez is at least partly correct in stating that monism is an established fact in modern science: Quantum physicists in recent years have been searching for a 'theory of everything' to explain the totality of the universe with one fundamental law (notwithstanding that they are seeking a purely physical theory). In this respect modern science is at least motivated by *physical* monism.
[120] Ibid. p.63-4. Emphasis in original.
[121] Dwight, Thomas (1911) *Thoughts of a Catholic Anatomist* New York: Longman, Green & Co., p.241

Qur'an states that those who adopt such a mentality are not comprised solely of atheists, but includes those who believe in a Higher law, and yet choose to follow manmade systems (secularists). Hence, says the Qur'an, if we ask such people: 'Who created the universe and set the sun and the moon on their appointed courses?' they will acknowledge: 'God'. (29:60) Thereafter the Qur'an asks: If they accept this truth, why are they looking elsewhere for laws by which to govern themselves? Why don't they adopt Divine law in human society?

> How perverted, then, are their minds! 29:60

Furthermore, when asked who sends down the rain and gives life to crops, they will again answer that it is God (29:63). Given that they also accept this fact, the Qur'an asks why they wish to establish their own manmade (selfish) systems, instead of adopting the universal law which would safeguard the collective interest of humanity and take it to its higher destination. If we really claim to believe in God, then the only real way to prove it is to wholeheartedly adopt, in toto, the permanent values that reflect God's Divine attributes. This is the only way that society will retain *husn* (just proportion) and *nazm* (order/balance). It is a fallacy to pick and choose some of these values and set aside others just to suit ourselves.[122] The Arabic term for this is *alhaad*, meaning 'to move aside', or 'deviate'. The Arabic word for 'grave' (*l'had*) also literally means 'to set aside', based on a certain type of grave in Muslim tradition.

> [O people of conviction!] Stand aloof from all who deviate (*alhaad*) concerning His attributes 7:180

In other words, these people may accept that the laws of nature apply to the whole universe, but as far as the human equation is concerned they prefer to rely upon their own concepts of law, or they split human life into two departments (religion and state) and give Divine principles the priority in one, whilst setting them aside in the other. Those who prefer to devise their own laws for economy instead of adopting Divine principles should note that the dictates of self-interest make life and all material things a mere distraction (*la'u*) and

---

[122] **Translators' note:** This 'pick and choose' behaviour is what is described in metaphor in the story of Adam, when he and his wife cover themselves with fig leaves (as described in our earlier footnote in Chapter 5, fn 110).

ultimately meaningless (la'ab) (57:20). Life is real and meaningful only when our vision is forward-looking and takes the interests of the whole of humanity into account.

> [For those who live by the selfish principle] the life of this world is nothing but a passing delight and a play – whereas, behold, the life in the hereafter is indeed the only [true] life: if they but knew this! 29:64

> For it is He [alone] who is God in heaven and God on earth, and He alone is truly wise, all knowing. 43:84

Human beings believe that the natural universe is like an unthinking machine, and that therefore it is fine for God's law to take care of it, but human beings have free will so they should decide their own affairs by rights. This however is based on a logical fallacy.

Fitrat-Allah (Divine pattern)

The Qur'an tells us that the existence of the entire universe is down to the law of creation (fitrat-Allah), and the very same law is responsible for the creation of Adam (30:30). In the words of Ouspensky:

> It is impossible to study a system of the universe without studying man. At the same time it is impossible to study man without studying the universe. Man is an image of the world. He was created by the same laws which created the whole of the world. By knowing and understanding himself he will know and understand the whole world, all the laws that create and govern the world. And at the same time by studying the world and the laws that govern the world he will learn and understand the laws that govern him. In this connection some laws are understood and assimilated more easily by studying the objective world, while man can only understand other laws by studying himself. The study of the world and the study of man must therefore run parallel, one helping the other.[123]

Thus the same laws and processes that brought the universe into being also brought human beings into existence. These laws have

---

[123] Ouspensky, P.D. (1949) In Search of the Miraculous (2001 reprint) New York: Harcourt p.75

never changed. They are fundamentally firm and finely balanced. However this fact can only really be appreciated through study and the acquisition of knowledge.

> And so, set your face steadfastly towards the faith (deen), turning away from all that is false, in accordance with the natural pattern (fitra) on which God has created man: [there is] no change in what God has thus created – this is the ever-true [point of] conviction; but most people know it not. 30:30

If we study the universe it will soon become abundantly clear that the human being is insignificant compared to the universe:

> Greater indeed than the creation of man is the creation of the heavens and the earth: yet most men do not understand [what this implies]. 40:57

Hence it is a fallacy that on the one hand human beings accept that the mind-boggling working of the universe is in control of a Higher law, whilst on the other they insist on implementing their own limited ideas in their own realm and expect a fruitful result of the type they observe in the natural universe. This is the major failure of human thought. The Qur'an clearly states that there are two types of people: 1) those who bring equity to humanity via the Divine law of sustenance, and 2) those who bring inequity into humanity via manmade laws. These two groups can be likened to a seeing man versus a blind man.

> But [then] the blind and the seeing are not equal; and neither [are] those who have conviction and do good works and the doers of evil. 40:58

We need only to look to human history for proof of this fact; but we don't even do this much.

> How seldom do you keep this in mind! 40:58

From the example of human history we can easily see that all nations that rejected Divine law and followed their own programmes eventually created inequity in their societies, and thus proved the futility of their own ideas.

[The Messengers came to try and put a stop to] their arrogant behaviour on earth, and their devising of evil [programmes against God's messages]. Yet [in the end] such evil scheming will engulf none but its authors 35:43

This is a universal law of God. In the Qur'an it is termed *sunnat-Allah* (lit. 'habit of God') or law of God. There is neither any change in these laws, nor do they alter their course.

No change will you ever find in God's way (*sunnat-Allah*); no deviation will you ever find in God's way! 35:43

Thus no manmade system can ever succeed. The secret to true success is to adopt His law, since it takes both the present and the future into consideration, and it ensures the prosperity of both the individual and the collective.

Does man imagine that it is his due to have all that he might wish for / despite the fact that [both] the life to come and this present [one] belong to God [alone]? 53:24-25

So how can these short-sighted people, who think only of short-term gains, and who have no thought for the future, ever succeed? (75:20-1, 76:27, 87:16, 92:13, 93:4). Of course those who work hard for their worldly gains will (in accordance with the natural law of requital) see the fruit of their efforts repaid in full:

As for those who care for [no more than] the life of this world and its bounties – We shall repay them in full for all that they did in this [life], and they shall not be deprived of their just due therein: 11:15

However their success is short-lived (6:44). Long-term endurance comes only to those who submit to the Divine law of Sustenance (6:45). There cannot be any blessings for those whose focus is on immediate and short-term gains:

For there are people who [merely] pray, 'O our Sustainer! Give us in this world' – and such shall not partake in the blessings of the life to come. 2:200

However those who make the Divine law of *Rabbubiya* their ideal will find that the effort of every individual will bring positive results.

Hence they will achieve prosperity for all in both the present and in the long term, and they will be saved from destruction.

> But there are those among them who pray, 'O our Sustainer! Grant us good in this world and good in the life to come, and keep us safe from suffering through the fire': / it is these [people] who shall have their portion [of happiness] in return for what they have earned. And God is swift in reckoning. 2:201-2

The Divine system of sustenance thus offers us success in both the present and the future:

> To him who cares for [just the material gains of] this fleeting life We readily grant as much as We please, [giving] to whomever it is Our will [to give]; but in the end We consign him to [the suffering of] Hell; which he will have to endure disgraced and disowned! / But as for those who care for the [good of the] life to come, and strive for it as it ought to be striven for, and are [true] people of conviction (*eiman*) – they are the ones whose striving finds favour [with God]! 17:18-9

Elsewhere the Qur'an states that we can differentiate between the followers of the two respective viewpoints (Divine versus materialist) from the analogy of the 'vineyards'. The first man owns two vineyards, and follows his own conception of law with a view to keeping whatever he grows for himself. The other man (who does not have his own land) has a vision in keeping with Divine law. The former man believes he is doing better than his friend, because he keeps the crops for himself and attains wealth and status. This man arrogantly believes that his wealth brings him complete security, and that his vineyard will last forever; but eventually calamity strikes as a natural outcome of his defective manmade law, and he is ruined (see 18:34-42).

The Qur'an similarly uses the following analogy: Those who on the one hand accept that crops grow thanks to God's natural law and yet on the other prefer to manage the distribution of the produce as they see fit, with the claim that no Higher law applies to them, will find that their crops will vanish as though they had never even sprouted:

> The parable of the life of this world is that of rain which We send down from the sky, and which is absorbed by the plants of the earth whereof men and animals draw nourishment ... and [when] they who dwell on it believe that they have gained

mastery over it – there comes down upon it Our judgment, by
night or by day, and We cause it to become [like] a field mowed
down, as if there had been none there yesterday. 10:24

After this analogy the Qur'an states that in the end we can only
obtain peace and security when we live by the universal law of
Rabbubiya (sustenance):

And [know that] God invites [humanity] to the abode
of peace 10:25

This is why the Qur'an repeatedly emphasises that proper
development can only be achieved by having a consistent vision for
both the present and the future:

Beware of [God's insight into] all that lies open before
you [at present] and all that is hidden from you [in the
distant future], so that you might be graced with His
'mercy' (*Rahmat*). 36:45

(The root word *rhm* – from which *Rahmat* is derived – refers to a
womb, containing the ideal atmosphere which provides protection
from the external environment during pregnancy, whilst at the same
time allowing for the complete development of an unborn child. This
word thus provides an obvious analogy for what is meant by having a
consistent vision for the present (material development) and the
future (self development).[124])

Elsewhere the Qur'an states clearly:

And they will ask you as to what they should spend [in
God's cause]. Say: 'Whatever is surplus to your needs.' 2:219

The Qur'an further tells us that this point has been made clear so
that we might learn to keep both the present and the future in mind:

In this way God makes clear unto you His messages,
so that you might reflect / on this world and on the life to
come. 2:219-20

---

[124] **Translators' note:** From the above analysis of the word *Rahmat* we can also
see that the word 'mercy' is not an accurate translation for this Qur'anic concept.

The Qur'an likens such a society to:

> [It is like] a 'goodly tree' (*shajar-e-tayyab*) firmly rooted,
> [reaching out] with its branches towards the sky, / yielding its
> fruit at all times by its Sustainer's leave. 14:24-5

Thus the Divine law of sustenance guarantees stability for human society both in the present and the future. Continuing with the analogy of the 'good tree':

> God grants firmness to those who have attained to faith
> through the word that is unshakably true in the life of this world
> as well as in the life to come. 14:28

Therefore the only valid way of life is one in which we have a clear vision for the future:

> O you who have conviction! Remain conscious of God, and
> let every human being look to what he sends ahead for
> tomorrow! 59:18

In doing so, we will ensure that our present and future will be bright (4:134). Meanwhile, says the Qur'an, those who merely focus on securing their self-interest and immediate gains should know that there is only one way of life that guarantees enduring prosperity, and it is one that is forward-looking:

> But no, you prefer the life of this world, / although the
> life to come is better and more enduring. 87:16-17 (see
> also 92:13 and 93:4)

It is only in following the Divine law of sustenance that the present and the future ('beginning and end') both become 'praiseworthy' (worthy of *hamd*):

> To Him all praise (*hamd*) is due, at the beginning and
> at the end 28:70

(**Note:** When we observe something of beauty and of exquisite quality, with perfect proportions and balance, the spontaneous feeling of appreciation it invokes is termed *hamd*. It means literally 'praise', or 'thanks' because the feeling is directed not at the object, but at its maker. Such a feeling will be invoked spontaneously only within someone who has full knowledge of the subject they are observing. Note therefore that this Arabic word is used exclusively with reference to the Divine Maker (God) and no other entity. Hence this makes sense of the context in which this word is used in the phrase 'the beginning and end are praiseworthy'.)

In other words, there is only one Divine law and it God's alone. There can be no other law in operation. When it is made subject to Divine law, the beginning and end of the life of humanity are 'praiseworthy' – i.e. the whole of human society reaches an ideal or perfect and beautiful state both in the present and the future. God's law already prevails throughout the universe, and even human beings are not exempt from it. We should bear this in mind in every decision we take and in every action:

> And with Him rests all judgment; and to Him shall you all be brought back. 28:70

We cannot escape the grip of His authority. We will reap what we sow. Our destiny lies in our own hands, but this means that we cannot lead a meaningless life and expect a positive result. Indeed, a positive result can come only when we lead our lives in accordance with the Qur'anic system of sustenance.

CHAPTER 6
The right of ownership

In the last chapter we saw that there is one 'way of life' according to which every individual aspires to protect his or her self-interest, and is unconcerned with the interests of others. The other way of life is one in which every individual is concerned with taking care of the whole of society, and makes the fruit of his or her labour freely available for the benefit of others. Since self-interest is innate to the animal kingdom, it appears to justify the selfish way of life for humanity. Logic thus dictates that everyone should be self-focused. The Qur'anic phrase for this selfish and rebellious mentality is *Iblees* or Satan. In other words, it is a mentality that rebels against the law of God. It bases all its decisions in light of selfish desires. It constantly pushes us to save and hoard, and convinces us that sharing our wealth will only lead to hardship and regret:

> Satan threatens you with the prospect of poverty and bids you to be miserly (*fahsha*)[125] 2:268

A self-serving mentality (Satan) influences the individual's attitude towards his/her wealth and children:

> Then (O Satan) entice whomsoever you can with your voice … and be their partner in [what they do with their] worldly goods and children 17:64

---

[125] The word *fahsha* (miserly) is also synonymous with the Arabic term *bukhl* (hoarding), because miserliness leads to a mean personality, and the development of bad character. Hence the Arabs (who culturally identified generosity with nobility) even used the word *fahsha* as a derogatory term for anyone with a bad character.

Satan's influence is so utterly powerful that it can easily lead us wherever it likes:

> [Satan said]: I shall most certainly cause his [Adam's] descendants – all but a few – to obey me blindly (*ihtanaka*)! 17:62

Let us look at the word *ihtanaka* more closely. It means literally to 'put a rope around the lower jaw (*hanak*) [of a horse]'.[126] To lead the animal in such a manner is thus termed *ihtanaka*. The Qur'an thus tells us that our desire to protect the interests of ourselves and our children is so strong that it can be likened to a rope which leads us about, and we cannot resist it. It goes without saying that persuading an individual to change this mentality – i.e. to put the collective interest above his self-interest – is a very difficult task. It is so difficult in fact, that the Qur'an has likened it to taking a path up a steep and treacherous mountain:

> But he would not try to ascend the steep uphill road ... 90:11

Human intellect justifies its refusal to abandon the selfish mentality with the argument that every person has a different capacity to earn, and so whoever earns more should have the right to own what he earns. In fact it is considered an injustice to take the earnings of one person and give them to others. Making someone hand over £16 out of the £20 that he has earned in a day, leaving him with only £4 is surely unfair. Of course, if he does so voluntarily, that is another matter. At any rate it is his money and he has the right to dispose of it as he wishes.

Capital worship – reasoning

If we look closely we will see that the structure of self-interest and capitalism is based on this understanding of ownership. The Qur'an has referred to Qaroon (Korah, the Jewish major magnate who lived during Moses' time) as the symbol of capitalism. When he was asked

---

[126] **Translators' note:** See also M. Asad's note on this same verse (17:62)

how on earth he justified keeping and hoarding so much wealth when the people around him were starving to death, his response was:

> 'This [wealth] has been given to me only by virtue of the knowledge [i.e. business acumen] I possess!' 28:78

He meant of course that no one had the right to tell him to give up what he had rightfully made for himself utilising his own talents. The Qur'an tells us that all self-serving people and wealthy classes have operated on the same reasoning throughout the ages, and that it is the root of all chaos and conflict.

> When We grant him affluence by Our grace, he says [to himself], 'I have been given this by virtue of [my own] wisdom!' 39:49 (see also 40:83 and 41:50)

The Qur'an provides an analysis of their argument and also reveals its fallacy. Let us review it here. There are, broadly speaking, two types of earning capacity, which we will call skilled and unskilled. Both groups work from 9 to 5 every day. The skilled worker earns £20 in one day, while the unskilled worker earns £2.[127] Note that two factors will determine the level of income: 1) effort, and 2) qualification. Arguably we can say that when it comes to effort – that is, how much time and energy is given to a job – there is no difference between skilled and unskilled workers. Both workers may be colleagues at the same plant, working the same number of hours. Qualification however, is what sets them apart. Since the skilled worker is deemed more highly qualified than the other, this is said to justify his higher pay rate, and furthermore it is his right to keep what he has earned due to the more sophisticated part he plays at the plant. Subsequently he is able to acquire more capital, and invest it in real estate, business, etc., which in turn leads to even more capital. When the skilled worker dies, his capital is inherited by his children. The next generation has no need to acquire skills or indeed to work, as they already have all the money they need (and more), as well as having the means to increase it even more via investments.

The Qur'an tells us that we should consider the following:

---

[127] At this point we will not raise the moral issue of why one earns far more than the other based on his skill. The fact is that this is the present status quo in all manmade society.

1) Intelligence (qualifications or business acumen)
2) Property and business acquired from existing (earned and saved) capital

Next we should ask ourselves how much of these we rightfully own.

Intelligence

We know that the individual's level of intelligence is determined by a number of factors:

- Nature (i.e. any intelligence or God-given talents that might be genetically determined)
- Social environment
- Education
- Opportunities to hone our existing skills and talents

All of the above factors can be summed up by saying that where we are born ultimately has a bearing on our individual intelligence. Which of these is in our control? Which of these directly involves our own effort or contribution? If someone has an innate talent, in fact it is granted to him by the Almighty.[128] If we happen to be brought up in a good social environment, we cannot say that this is in our control any more than we could if our social environment was detrimental to our intellectual development. Likewise we cannot control the kind of schooling we get. The schools in our area might be poor, or indeed there might be no schools at all.

Property and business acquired from existing capital

Now we turn our attention to investments (oil, land, property, industry) that we make with existing capital, which then enable us to acquire even more. Every one of these investments ultimately has a connection to the land, i.e. the resources of the earth. This is why the Qur'an has used the term *arz* (lit. earth) for economic life, since every

---

[128] Hence the Qur'an states: '[God] taught man what he did not know! / No, indeed, man becomes grossly arrogant / whenever he believes himself to be self-sufficient' (96:5-7)

resource comes from the earth. The Qur'an asks: do humans contribute in any way to the creation of the earth and the natural processes that produce its resources, such as, water, heat, light, air, minerals, etc.? (Do humans truly do anything to justify a claim to owning these resources?) The Qur'an makes this fundamental point in the following words:

> Have you ever considered the seed which you cast upon the soil? 56:63

The fact is that all we really do is prepare the field and plant the seed. Do we have the power literally to germinate the seed and make it grow? The Qur'an asks whether we have that power, or whether it is down to His laws over which we have no control:

> Is it you who cause it to grow – or are We the cause of its growth? 56:64

If God decided not to give the crop a chance to develop, and instead chose to destroy it before it ripened, could we prevent this from happening? Not only our harvest, but the time and effort we had spent on cultivating the crop would go to waste:

> [For,] were it Our will, We could indeed turn it into chaff, and you would be left bewildered 56:65

The part we play

Moving on, the Qur'an asks us to consider the water upon which we depend for our crops and indeed for our very lives.

> Have you ever considered the water which you drink? / Is it you who cause it to come down from the clouds – or are We the cause of its coming down? 56:68-9

The Qur'an also alludes to the water cycle, and the fact that seawater evaporates and comes down again as fresh water, free of salt. If the salt remained in the water, could we do anything about it?

> [The rain comes down sweet – but] were it Our will, We could make it salty and bitter [i.e. unpalatable]: why, then, do you not give thanks [to Us]? 56:70

Finally the Qur'an also asks us whether the fuels that we derive from the earth are created by us:

> Have you ever considered the fire which you kindle? / Is it you who have brought into being the tree that serves as its fuel – or are We the cause of its coming into being? 56:71-2

The Qur'an challenges us by asking how much of a part we really play in creating these resources, compared with the part that the universal process of *Rabbubiya* plays. Everything owes its existence to Divine law. The only part that humans play is their effort in procuring natural resources. The rest is down to God. We can liken this to a business partnership in which humans are the workers, and God is the provider of capital and resources. Therefore it is only natural that humans should keep a share of what they earn, and God should also have His share. However God tells us that His share is being put aside as a trust fund which will benefit humanity, and so it is our duty to contribute to it.

> All this is a means to remind you [that none of these resources are created by you], and a comfort for all who are lost and hungry in the wilderness [of their lives]. 56:73

To reiterate, God tells us in the above verse that He has set aside this 'trust' for those who are 'hungry and lost', i.e. the deprived sections of society. Thus we must constantly contribute towards it:

> Extol, then [through your work and deeds], the limitless glory[129] of your Sustainer's mighty name! 56:74

---

[129] The phrases *Rabb-e-kal azeem* and *Rabb-e-kal aalaah* need closer inspection. The Qur'an states that every one of us is concerned only with providing for ourselves and our children. As such this is an issue of *Rabbubiya* (sustenance), but at this level it is the same as the animal kingdom, since even animals provide for themselves and their offspring. Thus this is only a basic issue of sustenance and is limited in scope. Conversely the Divine law of *Rabbubiya* encompasses every facet of life (hence the phrase, *Rabb-il-aalameen* (Sustainer of the whole universe)). Likewise the two phrases

Similarly the Qur'an asks us to consider the food we eat in terms of the part we play in producing it, versus the part that Divine law plays. It explains that in accordance with the universal law of sustenance, rain comes down and the earth opens up, allowing a shoot to come up and develop into a fully grown plant. We get a variety of fruit and vegetables, lush vegetation for other uses, and of course a source of nutrition for every living creature including our livestock. (80:24-32)

> And fruits and herbage, / for you and for your animals to enjoy. 80:31-2 (see also 36:35, 23:18-21, 14:25)

Elsewhere the Qur'an tells us that God has 'spread the earth' (i.e. the land is broken up into continents with the movement of tectonic plates) and has placed mountains throughout it (mountains being the result of land masses gradually coming together). This set up, says the Qur'an, has allowed for farming and water systems (including natural and manmade forms of irrigation: Streams and rivers that always have their source on mountains and other highland, dams, and canals). This in turn creates an abundance of foliage and greenery. The Qur'an tells us that if we ponder over all of this we will find that it provides an insight into the process of *Rabbubiya* and also serves as an ample reminder of this (50:7-9). From water we thus obtain all our food and a means of sustenance:

> And We send down water from the skies, rich in blessings, and with it cause gardens to grow, and fields of grain, / and tall palm-trees with their thickly-clustered dates, / as sustenance apportioned to humanity (50:10-11)

After this the Qur'an again asks us: Who is behind all these means of sustenance and provision of livelihood? If He were to withhold the means of sustenance would we have either the power or the means to obtain our sustenance another way?

> Or is there any that could provide you with sustenance if He should withhold His provision [from you]? 67:21

Rabb-e-kal azeem and *Rabb-e-kal aalaah* refer to God's supremacy and greatness (i.e. highness/loftiness). Thus we are expected to prove the veracity of these two phrases (and by extension, the truth) by putting them into practice on earth.

For example, if the earth's water were to disappear underground and fresh water failed to evaporate from the sea, thus cutting off our entire supply, what could we do about it?

> Say [to those who deny the truth]: 'What do you think? If all of a sudden all your water were to vanish underground, who [but God] could provide you with water from fresh springs?' 67:30

It is clear therefore that He 'spreads the earth', and 'gathers the clouds', bringing us fresh water, the element of life. In so doing, He provides us with all that we need for our subsistence.

> [God is the One] Who has made the earth a resting-place for you and the sky a canopy, and has sent down water from the sky and thereby brought forth fruits for your sustenance 2:22

God is responsible for all of this, but instead of utilising the resources He provides in harmony with His law of sustenance, we invent our own concepts of law and mismanage our resources accordingly.

> Do not, then, claim that there is any power that could rival God, when you know [that He is the One] 2:22

Our allotted share

Clearly then we are only entitled to our share based on the effort that we put in. The rest belongs to God:

> [He has provided you with various fruit-bearing trees as well as other trees and plants, so] eat of their fruit when it comes to fruition, and give [the poor, in accordance with His decree] their due on harvest day. 6:141

Another verse in the Qur'an reminds us (by way of an environmental message) that the earthly resources we take for granted are not provided solely for our own benefit, but exist to sustain all life on earth as well:

> [And He has] provided a means of livelihood for you [O humanity] as well as for all [other living creatures] whose sustenance does not depend on you 15:20

> And the earth has He spread out for all living beings 55:10

In addition the Qur'an tells us that God has created a law of 'balance' (*meezan*, lit. scale). Thus we are told to keep this balance in mind by striving to retain justice and to not wrongfully deprive anyone (or indeed anything) of their due right:

> Weigh, therefore, [every decision and act] with equity, and cut not the measure short! 55:9

From this it should now be clear that all natural resources are God-given, and their purpose is to sustain the whole of humanity. For this reason no one has the right to create artificial barriers and divisions and declare ownership of these resources:

> [To all human beings, regardless of whether they have conviction in God's law or not] We freely endow with some of your Sustainer's gifts, since your Sustainer's giving is never confined [to one kind of man]. 17:20

Private ownership prohibited

Let us note the principle once again that all the natural resources freely given to us by God are ultimately from the earth. For this reason the Qur'an states with respect to 'earth' that it should be left open for the benefit of humanity. Bearing this in mind, along with all the verses we have reviewed above, makes it clear that there should be no question of private ownership:

> Say [O Messenger]: 'Would you indeed deny Him who has created the earth in two aeons? And do you claim that there is any power that could rival Him, the Sustainer of the worlds (*Rabb-il-aalameen*)?' 41:9

In addition the Qur'an states:

> For He [after creating the earth,] placed firm mountains on it, [towering] above its surface, and bestowed [so many]

blessings on it, and equitably apportioned its means of subsistence to all who would seek it: [and all this He created] in four aeons 41:10 (see also 15:19-20 76:30-31)

The earth is thus the medium for the production of all means of subsistence, which are provided freely for the benefit of humanity. It is human beings that have created artificial borders and divisions by way of declaring their ownership of various resources. This is obviously a rebellion against the Almighty and His Divine law of sustenance. In light of the fact that all natural resources are made freely available by God with no expectation of anything in return, the concept of private ownership is a complete falsehood. Wind, water, light, heat and the earth, all of which exist for our sustenance and are freely given by God, should actually be left equally open for all human beings.

Earning capacity

To return to our earlier discussion, there are three factors that affect earning capacity. (We will omit pre-existing or saved capital from our discussion, as this counts as a surplus of earnings that have either been hoarded or inherited, and thus cannot be considered a direct factor.)

1) Effort
2) Intelligence (talent or skill)
3) Means of production (raw natural resources)

Now let us review each of these in turn.

Effort

'Effort' refers to our sense of determination or resoluteness. In practice it means the amount of time and energy we give to our job, and it is based entirely on our willpower. Under this category we might broadly identify three types of people:

i) Those who always do their utmost to complete a task and work hard
ii) Those who (despite having the capability) are simply too lazy to work

iii)   Those who, either due to disability or by virtue of illness or
        an accident, are incapable of working

Obviously all those in the first group will be equal as far as effort is
concerned; that is, the same rule applies to them all: The harder they
work, the more they will earn. (They may differ only in terms of skills
and qualifications, but we will return to this later.) Thus if one
labourer works outside for 6 hours, and an engineer at his desk works
the same number of hours, and both as hard as they can in their tasks,
then they will be considered equal (in terms of effort) and so should
earn the same amount of pay.

The second group, being lazy, are not entitled to any pay (or, if
they do happen to do a little work, albeit not to their full capacity, they
will be entitled to an appropriate amount of pay):

Man can have nothing [more] than what he strives for 53:39

This is an unalterable truth (a permanent value). It is unacceptable
for someone to make no effort to work, leaving others to take on the
weight of his responsibilities.

No bearer of burdens shall be made to bear another's
burden 53:38

This of course is only just and fair. In the Qur'anic law of
sustenance there is no place for those who benefit from the fruit of
others' labour, and who fail to work for themselves despite having the
capacity to do so. They are termed *mutrafeen*, and include both lazy
people and those who are rich and do not feel compelled to work and
yet live lavish lifestyles.

Now we come to the third group, comprising of those who are
incapable of working through no fault of their own. To put it bluntly,
they do not qualify for 'wages'. However the Qur'anic system of
sustenance includes *ehsan* (indemnification) as well as *adl* (justice). In
short the word *ehsan* refers to making up for any deficiency or
shortfall that may appear in society. By compensating those who
cannot work, society will retain proportion (*husn*) and balance.
Therefore those in our third group will receive everything they need
by virtue of the principle of *ehsan* and not *adl* (which would apply to
wages based on effort).

So far we have limited our discussion to effort. Now we will move onto skills (including qualification, talent and experience) that affect earning capacity, and basic necessities.

Skill

Here too we can broadly split people into one of three types of skill set:

1) Those who have exceptional skills and so are able to build wealth beyond their needs
2) Those who, due to a lack of skills, are unable even to meet their basic needs
3) Those who (due to severe disability or illness) cannot earn anything at all

(Here we will omit a fourth group of people who possess the skill to work, but are not willing to make use of those skills)

The Qur'an states that exceptional skills or talents are God-given gifts and not of our own making, or in our control.

> For, whatever good thing comes to you, comes from God 16:53

It logically follows that whatever fortune we might make as a result of our God-given talent is not really ours by right.

> And on some of you God has bestowed more abundant means of sustenance than on others 16:71

According to the above verse therefore, whatever we might earn by virtue of our skills actually belongs to God. This excess wealth therefore will be spent on others in accordance with His Divine law of sustenance. It will be spent on those belonging in the second skill set group above, who are 'needy' (*saa'il*) in Qur'anic terms, and the third group above (which the Qur'an terms *mehroom*, or deprived).

> And in their wealth and possessions [was assigned] the right of he who asked (*saa'il*), and he who [for whatever reason] was unable [to ask] (*mehroom*). 51:19

Notice the use of the word 'right' (*haqq*, truth) in the above verse. These deprived and needy people have a *right* to have a share from out of others' wealth, i.e. they are entitled to it, and therefore this is not charity. As we have already mentioned, generated wealth actually belongs to God, and He has allocated it specifically to those who are *saa'il* and *mehroom*.

Means of production

We have already noted that every resource on earth is given freely to us by God. There is no question therefore of any human claiming a sole right to these resources. This is why the Qur'an asks us why we are not leaving all resources open for the benefit of everybody, when these all belong to God:

> And why should you not spend freely in the cause of God, seeing that God's [alone] is the heritage of the heavens and the earth? 57:10

Now let us return to the issue raised at the beginning of this chapter: Those with a greater capacity to earn tend to claim sole ownership of their accumulated wealth because, according to their logic, they have made this wealth using their own skills and talents. Since they then use this same wealth to purchase real estate and business, they claim ownership of the wealth generated from these investments as well. As we have already mentioned, this argument forms the very basis of capitalism. If we review this argument in light of the Qur'an, the reality of the situation quickly becomes clear.

Why the difference in earning capacity?

Here a question arises: If an individual with a high earning capacity is not the master of his own surplus wealth by right, then why does earning capacity vary so much in human beings? Why has God not granted every individual the same skills and capabilities, thereby avoiding the problem of economic inequity in human society? The Qur'an of course answers this question as well.

We have already noted that in the animal kingdom there is generally no variance in skill within the members of any given species. For example, all deer have the same skills, because they have no concept of competing by hoarding and thus never face issues such as socioeconomic inequity. However we should also note that aside from living and dying, they have no 'purpose' in life (at most they live long enough to breed). Intellectually speaking, they are born and die in the same state (that is, they do not improve their level of intellect). They are incapable of innovation; they cannot change the world. However God has given human beings creative faculties. An individual comes into the world and by utilising his creative faculties he or she can literally change the world. This being made of mere clay is able to produce art, culture, architecture and music. Humanity takes the raw materials of nature and creates a new world for himself. Note however that this creative process continuously presents us with challenges. When we undertake a task, the first stage involves planning, which requires intellectual effort. The next stage is to execute that plan, which requires physical effort. If the world's people had exactly the same skill set, then a division of labour would become impossible. It is for this reason that we find a variation in skills amongst human beings.

> It is We who distribute their means of livelihood among them in the life of this world, and raise some of them by degrees above others, to the end that they might benefit from one another's help 43:32

In short, God has granted all people different abilities so that a variety of skills can be utilised as and when they are needed. The Qur'an thus tells us that differences in skill and talent exist solely for the division of labour and to provide different creative opportunities. This fact is accepted amongst our thinkers as well. Mumford writes:

> The human community, as Aristotle observed, is an association of people who need each other. And they need each other for two reasons: spiritually in order to find themselves in the full dimensions of the group: practically to take advantage of their differences.[130]

Similarly Mason writes:

> Indeed, inequality [i.e. differences in skill and talent] leads to versatility among humanity at large, whereby

---

[130] Mumford, Lewis (1951) *The Conduct of Life* 1970 reprint, New York: Harcourt Brace Jovanovich, p.36

creative activity is stimulated and creative freedom is extended to wider fields of attainment.[131]

But this should not be taken to mean that the Qur'an agrees with either the Platonian idea that human beings should be permanently divided into classes, or the Hindu idea that every person is divided into different castes by birth. The Qur'an is in fact totally opposed to such ideas. It actually states that every human being is equal at birth, and so they should receive equal opportunities in their education and upbringing. This in fact is the very essence of *Rabbubiya*. Thereafter every individual should be entitled to be employed in lines of work that are best suited to his abilities and interests. If we must use the word 'class' or 'hierarchy', then it must only ever be understood in terms of the division of labour, and nothing more. Our birth and background therefore is irrelevant. No man will become a labourer just because his father was a labourer; and no man will be an engineer just because his father was an engineer. Both are treated as the children of Adam. The Qur'an affords them equal opportunities in training and education. If a labourer's son has the right skills and intellectual capacity, he can become an engineer, and if an engineer's son proves to have better physical capability than intellectual capability, he will find employment better suited to his talents.

A society will self-destruct when there is inequity, not due to differences in physical or mental abilities, but because of a lack of equal opportunities. According to Mason:

> Mankind subconsciously understands liberty is not endangered by inequalities when different fields exist for creative development, commensurate with varying degrees of competence or desire. It is not inequality of ability, but inequality of opportunity to express one's ability in the form of creative activity at a stimulating exchange value that causes economic discontent.[132]

The Qur'an does not accept the concept of division into classes. It treats everyone as a child of Adam and gives them equal opportunities, in order to unlock and develop the hidden potential of every

---

[131] Mason, J.W.T. (1926) *Creative Freedom* New York: Harper & Brothers, p.169 (Text in brackets is added by us)
[132] Ibid. p.170

individual. But this is only possible in a society that has established a system of sustenance.

Why the difference in individual talent?

There is no doubt that when every individual is equally receiving the best in education and training, then his intellectual capability will increase. Nevertheless individual differences in intellectual capability, talent, and temperament will remain, regardless of how advanced the overall society becomes. As this fact is self-evident, we need not discuss why these individual differences remain and what the implications of these differences are. Suffice it to say that the modern academic world has done much research on this topic (and continues to do so today). Neurological researchers say that individual intellectual difference is dependent on the structure of the brain. They carry out analyses of brain cells (neurons) and sections and try to explain intellectual differences in terms of problems or deficiencies in certain areas of the brain. But such research is still relatively new and much work has yet to be done.[133] Ouspensky meanwhile has said that neurons are not ultimately composed of the material. At any rate, with the lack of knowledge yielded by research to date, we can safely say that the causes of intellectual difference have not so far been adequately identified. In fact it doesn't even matter how intellectually advanced humanity becomes as a whole, for individual differences will always remain. The Qur'an states that our fundamental error is connecting intellectual difference to economic division, even though the actual purpose of intellectual difference is solely to allow for the division of labour which is essential for the creative process. This colossal error in human thought is responsible for all the evil that has turned our earth into a veritable hell. Our folly is in holding fast to this idea regardless of the consequences. We have adopted the attitude that if those with a greater intellectual capability give their hard-earned wealth to those with a lower capability, then it will be like treating the donkey and the horse as equal. But this is a misconception. Greater intellectual capability is not of our own making. It is granted to us by God. Therefore no one can claim ownership of anything that we earn by utilising these God-given talents. God has given us all these various talents as a means of providing sustenance to those who either

---

[133] **Translators' note:** Today much research in this area also focuses on genetic causes of intellectual differences.

have fewer skills or who for whatever reason are entirely incapable of working. In holding onto surplus wealth and failing to give others their rightful share, we are effectively refusing to acknowledge that our gifts have been granted to us by the Almighty. The Qur'an succinctly highlights this most important issue as follows:

> And on some of you God has bestowed more abundant means of sustenance than on others: and yet, they who are more abundantly favoured are unwilling to share their sustenance with those whom their right hands possess, so that they [all] might be equal in this respect. [In so doing] will they deny God's blessings? 16:71

The Qur'an further states that in continuing this behaviour, these same people are defying the law of *Rabbubiya* itself:

> Have you ever considered [the kind of man] who belies all moral law? / Behold, it is this [kind of man] that thrusts the orphan away, / and feels no urge to feed the needy. 107:1-3

The Qur'an states that natural resources are produced from the earth at a given and proportionate rate in order to retain balance, but if people with their ingenuity were able to get hold of the entire supply of these resources, then goodness knows what damage they might do.

> If God were to enlarge the provision for His Servants, they would indeed transgress beyond all bounds through the earth; but He sends (it) down in due measure as He pleases. For He is with His Servants well-acquainted, watchful. 42:27

It is clear from this that according to the Qur'an an individual can only rightfully keep a share of what he earns from his labour, or effort. He cannot claim ownership of either his skills or any means of production. These belong to God and He entrusts them to the whole of humanity. Therefore the capitalist argument that those with greater capabilities have the right to earn more, and have the right to keep it all, is a fallacy. It is a falsehood. As we have already mentioned, no secular system or ideology (i.e. that which denies the existence of God, denies the existence of the self, the hereafter and the permanent values) has so far been able to counter the capitalist viewpoint. Hence Marx was unable to effectively answer the question of why a more capable person should be prepared to give his hard-earned money to those with lesser earning capability (and we will expand on this later[134]). An effective reply can only come from someone who acknowledges the existence of the self and the need of its development, and this in turn necessitates a conviction in God and the 'Last Day'. Yet ironically the capitalists obtain support for their argument from the religious class; in fact the religious class is itself a product of capitalism (note that by 'religious class' we are not referring to *deen*, a word which in any case cannot be equated with religion, but to manmade religious concepts).[135] The religious class teach that whatever we earn, we have a right to keep, and furthermore, we have the right to keep all our inheritance as well. They tell us that according to *shari'ah* (Muslim law) no one can lawfully be deprived of his or her property. When they speak of *shari'ah* they mean a law taken from the time of kings (monarchy) which was designed to serve those with vested interests (this *shari'ah* has no sanction in the Book of God).

Mentality of a Jewish tribe

They also present the argument that if the needs of all people were met, then there would be no poor and needy left, and so charity would become obsolete. They imply that it is necessary for the poor and the needy classes to exist so that those who give charity can earn the 'points' they need to get into Heaven. They also tell us that if the concept of ownership was abolished, the inheritance laws of the Qur'an would become obsolete. We will return later to the question of the actual function of 'charity' and inheritance in light of the Qur'an.[136] For now let us review the weakness of this argument. It implies that we shouldn't care at all for the wellbeing of the poorest in society – i.e. we should avoid all true efforts to improve their condition. The reason for this is that if all were to become better off, then all social and healthcare services would shut down. There would be no more need for medicine, and doctors would become redundant. To explain this fraud by the religious class, the Qur'an has referred to the example of a

---

[134] **Translators' note:** – For Marx's failed socialist principle, 'historical necessity', see Chapter 7; see also brief discussion on 'incentive' in Chapter 10; and the Qur'anic 'incentive' in Chapter 8.

[135] For a detailed explanation of the differences between *deen* and *mazhab* (religion), see my book *Asbaab-e-Zawal-e-Ummat* (*Causes of the Decline of the Ummah*).

[136] **Translators' note:** See Chapter 8.

certain Jewish tribe. They used to evict weak and vulnerable people from their homes, and when rival tribes eventually captured these people, this particular Jewish tribe would collect donations in order to pay the ransom for their release (2:83-5). Since their religion taught them that freeing captured people is a 'good deed', they were actually trying to earn 'points' for their salvation. They had gone to the extent of creating a perpetual poor class as a means to this end. A similar psychology persists today amongst those with vested interests; they allow the continued existence of under-privileged and impoverished classes, and use charity as a means of earning the reward of good deeds.[137] The Qur'an tells us that people of this ilk not only live in disgrace on this earth, but are also guaranteed nothing but self-destruction in their future.

> What then could be the reward of those among you who do such things, except disgrace in the life of this world and, on the Day of Resurrection, consignment to most grievous suffering? 2:85

Today's Muslims are in much the same state.

Aside from all that we have discussed in this chapter, we must also bear the following in mind. A *momin* in the Qur'an is someone with full conviction (*eiman*) in the purpose of life: Every individual is to work as hard as he can within his or her capacity, to keep only what he needs out of his wages, and to leave the rest open for the benefit of society. In short, the individual places collective interest above self interest. Therefore the question of whether or not an individual can claim ownership of wealth and estate is irrelevant in the eyes of a 'group of believers'[138] (*jamaat-e-momineen*). As far as this group is concerned, all resources and surplus produce belongs to God (and thus is to be distributed to the underprivileged and impoverished sections of society as a matter of human right). Hence we find that with Qur'anic guidance, this most difficult issue of ownership is easily resolved.

---

[137] **Translators' note:** And in the case of those who don't believe in the Divine or the hereafter, they exploit it for publicity and popularity in society.

[138] **Translators' note:** 'Believer', insofar as it implies 'faith' rather than conviction based on logic and knowledge, is not the best word for translating the Qur'anic word *momin* (singular of *momineen*), but we have used it in this translation for lack of an alternative single word. Similarly, we have in places utilised 'unbeliever' for the Qur'anic *kafir* (plural: *kafireen*), though the better word in this case is 'rejecter'.

CHAPTER 7
The fundamental principle

The Qur'anic position on the two worldviews (materialist and spiritualist) has been covered in the previous chapters. In short, it states that the purpose of life is to bring prosperity in human existence both in the present and the future, and that the way to achieve this is for every individual to be concerned with securing the means of sustenance for the whole of humanity. Such a lifestyle obviously would mean the end of capitalism and all vested interests that have turned the world into a living hell. Marx[139] also desired to see the end of capitalism, but he couldn't find a firm ethical foundation upon which to base his arguments, for the reason that he himself was a materialist. Neither could he accept the Divine law of *Rabbubiya*, nor the permanent values, nor the life after death, nor the law of requital. His desire to see the end of capitalism was a noble one, but noble desires can only be realised if they are based on the firm foundations of truth. Marx had no such support, and so he derived his support from the idea of 'historical necessity'.

Lucien Laurat has written:

> In founding socialist aspirations on a rational economic law of social development, instead of justifying them on moral grounds valid at any time and in any place, Marx and Engels proclaimed socialism a historical necessity.[140]

---

[139] In this book I have not discussed either Marxism or communism in any detail as it is not my intent to make a comparative study. Nevertheless we will examine some pertinent points of this ideology in brief towards the end of this book (Chapter 11).

[140] Laurat, Lucien (1940) *Marxism and Democracy* (trans. Edward Fitzgerald) London: Gollancz, p.16

However this argument was insufficient and subsequently it fell at the first hurdle. Lenin, the disciple of Marx, soon abandoned it and followed a path of his own. Stalin came after Lenin, and he changed the fundamental ideals of socialism. The movement initiated by Lenin and Stalin was based on hatred and vengeance, and these have also come to form the basis of communist propaganda. They preach: 'Capitalism is a curse. The rich suck the blood of the poor and the working class. Rise up and take your revenge against them.' But this is an emotional appeal and not a rational or objective one. It is not based on truth. The Qur'an makes its invitation on the basis of truth, appealing to logic and not to emotions.

Philosophy of historical necessity

As we have already noted, Marx's 'historical necessity' means that no system can remain the same forever. According to Marxist theory, every system exists and is stable for a time, until eventually an internal rebellion gives birth to a new opposing system of ideas. With time, this new system takes the place of the old outdated model that preceded it. The blind force of history has always been this way, and so it will continue. History has no concern as to whether a system is good or bad. History simply witnesses that for every system that is in vogue, good or bad, its opposite will certainly come into being. The system in vogue today is capitalism. Historical necessity, according to Marx, will bring an end to this system and replace it with a system of the labourer and the farmer (the 'dictatorship of the proletariat'). Eventually this system too will come to pass, and it too will be replaced by something that is opposite to it.

The Qur'anic concept

In light of the Qur'an, this concept is emotional and irrational. The Qur'an states that the universe is not running upon blind forces, but that there is one God who is all-knowing and all-wise, and that the universe is operating in accordance with His Divine programme. Every change and every movement of the universe comes to pass in accordance with His law and thus has a purpose. These changes and movements are always constructive and evolutionary; they never lead to decline. In fact we observe that the universe is the stage of the continuous interplay of both constructive and destructive forces (*haqq* – truth and *baatil* – falsehood). In this conflict the constructive force always defeats the destructive force and thus the overall movement of the universe is constructive (or positive). Hence this interplay of the two forces is the driving force of evolution.

> Nay, but [by the very act of creation] We hurl the truth [*haqq*] against falsehood [*baatil*], and it crushes the latter: and ah! it withers away. 21:18 (see also 17:81 and 34:49)

That *haqq* always proves true and *baatil* always 'withers away' is not a random or accidental process, but rather, as we have already observed, it all happens in accordance with the Divine plan.

> But then, had God so willed, He could have sealed your heart: for God blots out all falsehood, and by His words proves the truth to be true. 42:24

Having explained this fundamental principle, the Qur'an tells us to apply it to the human equation. It states that there two types of system (or nation). The first is one in which every individual is concerned only with protecting his self-interest. It is *baatil* and thus destructive (i.e. it is not in harmony with the Divine law of sustenance or *Rabbubiya*). Hence it cannot prevail. Contrary to this is the other system in which every individual endeavours in the cause of benefiting humanity. This system is *haqq*, and thus constructive (i.e. it is in harmony with the Divine law of *Rabbubiya*). It is everlasting. Now we will see how the Qur'an provides clear concrete examples to illustrate an abstract truth. Every day we see that after rainfall, twigs, scum, and other impurities rise to the surface of rivers and streams and all are carried away, leaving clear water behind, which will be absorbed into the earth.

> [Whenever] He sends down water from the sky, and [once-dry] river-beds are running high according to their measure, the stream carries scum on its surface 13:17

In the same verse the Qur'an provides an additional example, this time of mineral processing, in which we treat rocks in order to obtain useful metal:

> And, likewise, from that [metal] which they smelt in the fire in order to make ornaments or utensils, scum [rises]. 13:17

Thus these analogies both serve to explain *haqq* and *baatil*:

> In this way God presents the parable of truth (*haqq*) and falsehood (*baatil*): for, as far as the scum is concerned, it passes away as dross; but that which is of benefit to man abides on earth. 13:17

The fundamental principle of immortality

The Qur'an teaches that only a system that benefits the whole of humanity can prevail. Thus all human economic and social systems are subject to the mortality vs. immortality principle:

1) A system or ideal which is based on the 'selfish' principle (whether at the individual or societal level) is bound to be destroyed
2) A system that aims to benefit humanity as a whole can prevail forever

Thus only a system in which self-interest is made subordinate to the collective interest will be everlasting. This is an unchanging truth, even as everything else is constantly in motion and is dynamic. In other words, the principle of *Rabbubiya* is the sole guarantee of long-term abundance and prosperity and this fact can never be altered; otherwise everything else in the universe is subject to change.

> All that lives on earth or in the heavens is bound to pass away: / but your Sustainer's Self will live forever, full of majesty, glory and honour 55:26-7 (see also 28:88)

(In other words: Everything in the universe undergoes changes all the time, but these have no effect on Divine laws. These laws have been given by the Sustainer Who is beyond change and is full of majesty, glory and honour.)

Issue of good and evil

The most difficult question on the minds of thinkers has always been that of morality, i.e. what acts are good and what are evil, and to date there has never been a consensus, even though the question has haunted humanity from its very beginning. It is not the style of the

Qur'an to directly address philosophical questions in detail. Instead it focuses on important principles, and only touches on the aspects of human life that are directly affected by them. It avoids getting into minor details and trivial concerns, but simultaneously offers easy solutions to major and pragmatic human problems. It tells us that when we utilise our God-given gifts (skills and means of production) to develop and nurture humanity, it is *khair* – 'good'; and if, to the contrary, we hoard to protect our self-interest, then it is *shar* – 'evil'.

> And they should not think – the misers who cling to all that God has granted them out of His bounty – that this is good (*khair*) for them: no, it is bad (*shar*) for them 3:180

This therefore is the Qur'anic standard by which we can differentiate between good and evil, and by which we can test the veracity of all human endeavours. Huxley has also defined good and evil in the same terms, when he says:

> Good is that which makes for unity; Evil is that which makes for separateness.[141]

The Qur'anic one-word answer

Today everyone asks: 'What are the teachings of Islam? And what are the implications of putting these teachings into practice?' But generally the answers that people give only add to pre-existing misconceptions and confusion, and thus fail to satisfy anyone. This question is not new; in fact it was first raised when the Qur'an was revealed. It was asked of all the early Muslims whenever they went round inviting others to Islam. The Qur'an has recorded the question as follows:

> But [when] those who are conscious of God are asked, 'What is it that your Sustainer has bestowed from on high?'16:30

It has also supplied a one word answer:

---

[141] Huxley, Aldous (1937) *Ends and Means: An Enquiry into the Nature of Ideals and into the Methods employed for their Realization* 1965 reprint, London: Chatto & Windus, p.303

> They answer, 'Goodness!' (*khair*) 16:30

Hence the answer is that God has revealed something that is 'good' – everything that will bring prosperity and happiness both on earth and in the hereafter. The rest of the verse above thus reads:

> Good fortune awaits, in this world, all who persevere in doing good; but their ultimate state will be far better still: for, how excellent indeed will be the state of the God-conscious [in the life to come]! 16:30

The next verse summarises the point in just a few words:

> [They will have] all that they might desire 16:31

This therefore is what is meant by 'good' (*khair*). The *ummah* (Muslim nation) was established solely for the purpose of making this invitation to the good:

> [God guides you so that] there might grow out of you a community [of people] who invite towards all that is good 3:104

Those who stand in the way of this invitation have been termed *jahannami* (Hell bound):

> (God will sentence them): 'Throw, throw into Hell every contumacious rejecter (of truth)! / Who forbade what was good, transgressed all bounds, cast doubts and suspicions ...' 50:25

This is the implication of the Qur'an's teachings – good fortune both on earth and in the hereafter (16:30). Thus anyone who puts these teachings into practice is a true person of conviction (*momin*).

> It is they, they who are truly believers (*momineen*)! 8:4

In the eyes of God they have greater honour and live in dignity, and so are protected from chaos and destruction:

> Theirs shall be great dignity in their Sustainer's sight, and forgiveness of sins (i.e. their shortcomings are made up for)[142] and a most excellent sustenance 8:4

In fact every messenger in history was sent to preach the same teaching. Hence in the Qur'an Noah's people were told that if they followed the Divine programme, all means of subsistence would be available to them in abundance; their crops would be well-watered, and they would have plenty in terms of possessions and children:

> He will let loose the sky over you with abundance / and will aid you with worldly goods and children, and will bestow upon you gardens, and bestow upon you running waters. 71:11-12

The same promise was given to the followers of Moses and Jesus:

> And if they would but truly observe the Torah and the Gospel and all [Revelation] that has been bestowed from above upon them by their Sustainer, they would indeed partake of all the blessings of heaven and earth. 5:66

If the earlier People of the Book had observed the teachings of the Revelation, they would have brought peace and prosperity to the whole of humanity. Unfortunately the religious elite introduced their own ideas for selfish reasons and so changed the Divine *deen* into something else, and profited greatly from their exploitation of the people. Their people in turn were influenced by these false teachings, and they too became preoccupied with hoarding. Subsequently instead of a heaven on earth, they created hell for themselves.

> O you who have conviction! Behold, many of the rabbis and monks do indeed wrongfully devour people's possessions and turn away from the path of God. But as for all who hoard up treasures of gold and silver and do not spend them for the sake of God – give them the news of grievous suffering [in the life to come]: / on the Day when that [hoarded wealth] shall be heated in the fire of hell and their foreheads and their sides and their backs will be branded with it [those sinners shall be told:] 'These are the treasures which you have laid up

---

[142] See explanation of verse 64:17 (*ghafr*) in Chapter 5.

for yourselves! Taste, then, [the fruit of] your hoarded treasures!' 9:34-5

Concluding the debate

From the above we can clearly see that the Qur'an provides a firm and fundamental principle on the difference between truth and falsehood:

> In this way God presents the parable of truth (*haqq*) and falsehood (*baatil*): for, as far as the scum is concerned, it passes away as [does] dross; *but that which is of benefit to man abides on earth.*13:17

This is the pivotal principle about which the entire teachings of the Qur'an revolve. The Qur'an teaches us that the whole of humanity is one: One *ummah*, one nation, and one party (*jamaat*).[143] However individual selfishness and vested interests have divided humanity into factions of every kind. The teachings of the Qur'an aim to abolish these differences and unite humanity as one family again. Had restoring oneness not been the aim of the Divine programme, then capitalism would have been laid down as a permanent principle, thereby permitting the rich-poor divide, and allowing the wealthy classes to become infinitely richer without any ill consequences. Hence the Qur'an clearly states:

> And were it not [the aim of the Qur'an] that all people would become one community, We might indeed have provided the Rejecters with roofs of silver for their houses, and [silver] stairways to ascend on, / and [silver] doors for their houses, and [silver] couches on which to recline, / and gold [beyond count] 43:33-5

But as we already know, capitalism is focused only on immediate gains; and this makes the *Rabbubiya* of humanity impossible:

> Yet all this would have been nothing but a [fleeting] enjoyment in the life of this world 43:35

It follows that under capitalism and its perpetual rich-poor divide humanity can never become one and united. Thus God has decreed

---

[143] **Translators' note:** The *jamaat* is discussed in Chapters 8-10.

that immortality can only be gained under a system that aims to provide universal sustenance for humanity. This is an absolute truth.

But the life to come, in the eyes of your Sustainer, is for the righteous. 43:35

CHAPTER 8
Establishment

In the previous chapter we saw that when people are left to their own devices and so have no particular direction in life, they inevitably choose the path of selfishness. They hoard only for themselves and are entirely uninterested in how others are faring. The intellect of the individual tells him that he must rely only on what he can get for himself. This is a world of 'every man for himself'. If tomorrow brings hard times, no one will be willing to help him. He and his family will be ruined. Of course from the intellect's viewpoint this belief is hardly without foundation. The individual needs only to look at the ways of the world for proof; and as such, the intellect is telling the truth. In the world we live in (by and large a capitalistic society) it is certainly true that when an individual gets into financial hardship, there is usually no one there to support him. He must rely entirely on what he has in his wallet.

Obviously with this being the accepted norm it is very difficult to explain to those who have never known any differently that this way of life is a falsehood, and that the true path to success is to keep only what we need and to give the rest of what we earn to society. It goes without saying that if it is so difficult to get an individual to understand the truth, then getting him to put it into practice is even harder. The Qur'an is not oblivious to this problem, but it is direct in its approach and doesn't shirk from getting people to face reality. In fact the Qur'an has stated that even when both alternatives are presented to people, and they clearly can see which is falsehood and which is truth, the vast majority of them will still be unwilling to adopt the latter (i.e. that which takes care of the collective interest).

The path of least resistance

They will find this alternative too daunting and too difficult even to contemplate. The Qur'an tells us that it has shown us both paths.

> [Have We not] shown him the two highways [of good and evil]? 90:10

The problem is that human beings tend to pick the path that seems easier. The other path, whilst noble, is like climbing a mountain, and they are not willing to make the effort.

> But he would not try to ascend the steep uphill road ... 90:11

And what, asks the Qur'an, is entailed in climbing this 'steep uphill road'? It answers as follows:

> And what could make you conceive what it is, that steep uphill road? / [It is] the freeing of one's neck [from oppression] / or the giving of food on a day of shortage / of an orphan near of kin, / or of a needy [stranger] lying in the dust 90:12-16

(In other words, the uphill road involves building a system that frees everyone from hardship, ensures that all are provided with what they need for their sustenance, ensures that the isolated and vulnerable members of society are taken care of, and raises the living standard of those who have always been downtrodden and impoverished.)

Obviously then, the Qur'an urges humanity to abolish their present way of life and replace it with a way of life based on truth. How then, can humanity be mobilised to make this uphill climb? How can we get from the present state of society to one in which everyone is a willing benefactor of others? This is the vital question. The Qur'an answers this question in much detail, and in fact it draws up a full programme to the achievement of this end.

Eiman – The first prerequisite

The first step in this programme is to instil some fundamental truths in human hearts, in order to help them develop a sense of *eiman* (conviction)[144] in Islamic idealism. The first truth is that apart from the intellect there is another source of knowledge called *Wahi* (Revelation), which was transmitted to humanity via the messengers. Bergson writes on this subject:

> That reason is the distinguishing mark of man none will deny. That it is a thing of superior value, in the sense in which a fine work of art is indeed valuable, will also be granted. But we must explain how it is that its orders are absolute and why they are obeyed. Reason can only put forth reasons, which we are apparently always at liberty to counter with other reasons. Let us not then merely assert that reason, present in each of us, compels our respect and commands our obedience by virtue of its paramount value. We must add that there are, behind reason, the men who have made mankind divine, and who have thus stamped a divine character on reason, which is the essential attribute of man. It is these men who draw us towards an ideal society, while we yield to the pressure of the real one.[145]

It is universally accepted there is only one set of laws in operation throughout the universe. Therefore it naturally follows that the same law of *Rabbubiya* which is in operation in the natural universe is applicable to the human equation as well, and so this is the only one we should adopt. Humanity can never prosper with the adoption of any other law. This *oneness* of law ultimately means that there is but *one* Creator.

It follows that one Creator will bring out one creation, and this in turn means that humanity is also one single family. The Qur'an has placed enormous emphasis on this fact, which forms the very foundation of the law of *Rabbubiya*. It tells us that the whole of humanity originates from a single cell.

> It is He who has created you [all] out of one living entity 7:189

---

[144] These fundamental assumptions are more often termed the 'permanent values' or eternal truths, which are immutable. Whoever learns and accepts these values in totality is said to enter a state of *eiman*. Thus the word is better translated not as 'faith', but as 'conviction'.

[145] Bergson, *The Two Sources of Morality and Religion*, p.54

The various nations of humanity are mere branches of the same tree; they belong to one brotherhood; and indeed are one organism. Therefore humanity should learn to advance and progress as one, leaving none behind.

> The creation of you all and the raising up of you all is but like [the creation and raising up of] a single soul 31:28[146]

It is only selfish desires that have resulted in the division of humanity. The mission statement of *Wahi* is to eliminate these differences and restore the oneness of humanity.

> All humanity was once one single community 2:213

The way to unite humanity is to adopt the Divine (universal) law of *Rabbubiya* as our ideal. The ultimate mission of each messenger was to unite humanity with this ideal (beginning by bringing together his own people as one united *Ummah*).

The oneness of humanity is a self-evident truth, and the whole world was bound to accept it eventually. We could provide hundreds of references from Western scholars on this matter, but we will look instead at the most recent official proclamation of this fact. In 1950, UNESCO resolved to initiate a programme for disseminating information 'designed to remove what is generally known as racial prejudice'.[147] Its Department of Social Sciences formed a committee comprising a number of international experts from various fields of the human sciences, and tasked them with writing a report detailing their combined research on humanity as a race.[148] In their report, dated 1952, they stated:

---

[146] **Translators' note:** In other words, the individual should be concerned for the fate of humanity as a whole in the same way he/she is concerned for his/her own fate.

[147] Department of Social Sciences, 1952. *The Race Concept: Results of an Inquiry*   Paris: UNESCO,   p.6.   Online: http://unesdoc.unesco.org/images/0007/000733/073351eo.pdf   Last retrieved 15 June 2012

[148] **Translators' note:** We have added details of the research committee and the report that are not mentioned explicitly in Parwez's original text. (Details obtained from the Introduction of the report, referenced in previous footnote).

> Scientists are generally agreed that all men belong to
> a single species, Homo sapiens, and are derived from a
> common stock ...[149]

The aim of the Qur'an is to make humans realise this fundamental fact and universally accept it. Furthermore, human life is not solely connected with the physical body and this world. It continues after physical death. Hence it is imperative that we develop the human self as well as the human body, because immortality can only be achieved with the development of a balanced personality.

In order to develop a balanced personality, we must accept that there is no action without reaction (in accordance with the law of requital). Everything we do has a consequence, and this will manifest itself whether sooner or later (of course the law of 'cause and effect' is already accepted in science). Thus a 'good' act (being constructive) will develop the human self, whilst an 'evil' act (being destructive) will harm the self.

The secret to developing the self therefore is unity of purpose; human beings must collectively work to the best of their individual capabilities and everything they earn or achieve must be left open for the sustenance and development of everyone. In so doing, God's Divine attribute of *Rabb-il-aalameen* (Sustainer of the universe)[150] will be realised in practice. Hence the more an individual gives to others for their overall development, the more his self will develop; and since the purpose of life is to develop the self, he will do his utmost to contribute towards the betterment of humanity.

These then are the fundamental truths which the Qur'an instils in human hearts. This leads to *eiman* – the first prerequisite for climbing that 'steep uphill road' towards the Divine system of sustenance.

Education – The second prerequisite

Once these basic truths are accepted by a group of people – that is, they have attained 'conviction' or *eiman* – the next step is to build upon this *eiman* by taking them through a more intensive education programme to give them comprehensive knowledge of Qur'anic teachings. Subsequently their increasing knowledge of the law of *Rabbubiya* inspires them to try and form a Qur'anic community

---

[149] Ibid. p.11
[150] For explanation of *Rabb-il-aalameen*, see Chapter 6, fn 129.

(*jamaat*[151]). Those responsible for providing this education fully impress on their students that there is no room in the Divine system for the concept of rulers and the ruled, and that whoever decides to adopt this way of life must do so absolutely willingly, and must completely dedicate him/herself to the higher purpose of life, i.e. the *Rabbubiya* of humanity. The students understand that in so doing they are developing their selves and thus gradually evolving in line with the attributes of God.

> It is not conceivable that a human being to whom God had granted the Book, and sound judgment, and prophethood, should thereafter have said to people, 'Obey[152] me beside God'; but rather [he urged them], 'Become men of God by spreading the knowledge of the Divine writ, and by your own deep study [of it]. 3:79

The students are then instructed to share what they have learned with others. This is the way to disseminate knowledge and educate all of society. Eventually those who are fortunate enough to fully realise the significance of what they have learned become determined to put these teachings into practice, and become united in their purpose. Since their hearts and minds are fundamentally altered, it follows that they gradually distance themselves from the existing (manmade) system. This marks the beginning of a new system that will eventually replace the old. The members of this germinating society remain in close contact and support each other, united by a common conviction in the principles that they uphold and abide by at all times and in whatever they do. They also convene regularly and encourage public participation in their discussions. This creates an environment in which new people are introduced to Qur'anic knowledge, thus facilitating its dissemination in the wider community. The process of creating this learning environment is termed *qiaam-e-salaat*.

---

[151] **Translators' note:** *Jamaat* is a word usually used by Muslims to denote the Muslim community, but its meaning simply is 'party' or 'group'.
[152] Here we have replaced the word 'worship' used in the traditional translation with the word 'obey'. Whilst the Arabic word *ibadat* means both 'worship' and 'service', the word 'worship' does not apply to a human being (in this case, a prophet), for linguistic reasons given in fn 102.

Establishing *salaat*

Since at present we have reduced the scope of *salaat* to mere ritualistic prayer, it is difficult for most people to fully comprehend its true meaning. As a result we tend to find the Qur'anic phrase *qiaam-e-salaat* inaccurately translated as 'establish prayers', and in practice this is taken to mean 'commitment to prayer', i.e. to ritually *worshipping* God. Most people today cannot see what 'worship' has to with socioeconomic affairs, and justly so. Yet the misconception regarding the true meaning of *salaat* is hardly new. Revelation (*Wahi*) was always the source of *deen* as a 'way of life', but over time people always altered it so that it was just a religion (*mazhab*) indistinguishable from any other. In other words, the practical elements of *deen* were gradually changed into meaningless rituals and the original practical principles were completely removed from people's lives. Every previous nation has done this, and Muslims are no exception. The Qur'an explains this religious tampering of the past and present. Shoaib (Jethro in the Bible) was sent to the people of Madyan with the Divine message. At first, this nation understood this message in strictly religious terms. They thought he was merely trying to form a community of worship, and so they let him preach, thinking that this new 'religion' would not really affect their way of life at all. But they soon began to comprehend the real implications of Shoaib's invitation – that his 'prayer' was not confined to the walls of a temple but reached far beyond it. This came to them as a great surprise. Hence, records the Qur'an, they asked him:

> They said: 'O Shoaib! does your 'prayer' (*salaat*) teach that we should stop the worship which our fathers practised, or that we should stop doing what we like with our property?' 11:87

Let us consider what the people of Madyan were objecting to and thereby determine the real meaning of *salaat*. They were saying: 'We thought you were teaching a form of worship, but your *salaat* is very strange! It tells us that we are not allowed to do what we like with our property and wealth. But what has worship got to do with economy?'

Here we can see the similarity between the thinking of these people with that of today's Muslims. Both are treating *salaat* as worship. At any rate, to establish a Divine system of *Rabbubiya* the second prerequisite after *eiman* is to create a mindset in people who will then become dedicated to their purpose at all times, whether 'standing, sitting, [or] lying down on their sides' (3:191, 4:103). In Qur'anic terms this is *qiaam-e-salaat*. The Arabic word *sala* means to (closely) follow the law of God. *Masallee* refers to a horse which runs almost alongside the first horse in a race, but never overtakes it. Therefore the full meaning of *qiaam-e-salaat* is to establish a society in which every individual closely follows the laws of God, i.e. a society in which everyone complies with the Divine system of sustenance. Note that congregations of 'prayer' are also a part of the *qiaam-e-salaat*. However the system of *salaat* is not merely about forming prayer congregations. It encompasses everything in the life of a *momin* (person of conviction).

Establishing *salaat* and *zakaat*

Salaat and *Rabbubiya* have a close interconnected relationship. For this reason the Qur'an frequently refers to establishing *salaat* and *zakaat* together. The phrase 'constant in prayer, and give in charity' (traditional translation) appears numerous times in the Qur'an. The difficulty however is that just as we have reduced the meaning of *salaat* to mere ritual worship we have reduced the meaning of *zakaat* to 'charity'. Thus a given individual can hoard as much wealth as he pleases, as long as he gives 2.5% of his annual earnings to charity. Yet *zakaat* actually means 'growth', and so 'giving *zakaat*' really means 'provide the means of sustenance'. Now we can see the real meaning of the phrases 'establishing *salaat*' and 'giving *zakaat*'. Together they mean the creation of a society in which every individual 1) has the permanent values (fundamental truths outlined above) instilled in his mind, 2) is completely dedicated to living in accordance with God's laws, and 3) freely chooses to make the provision of sustenance to others his highest priority. The Qur'an reveals the inevitable outcome of establishing such a society, when it states:

> *Salaat* restrains [humans] from self-deceiving [*munkar*] and unjust [*fahsha*] [153] deeds 29:45

The Qur'an is thus telling us that following the programme of *salaat* will help us avoid miserliness [*fahsha*] and to restrain the self-deluding tendency of the intellect which encourages us to hoard in the

---

[153] **Translators' note:** *Fahsha* (meaning miserly and injustice) as another word for *bukhal*, is mentioned at the beginning of Chapter 6.

first place [*munkar*]. Once these behaviours have been eliminated the people will endeavour instead to 'give *zakaat*' (Arabic: *eeta-e-zakaat* – i.e. provide all means of sustenance to society, and not just a certain fixed rate). Hence *qiaam-e-salaat* (establishing *salaat*) changes the mindset of a society, bringing about an 'intellectual revolution'. This means that the individual subordinates his self-interest in light of permanent values. We have already seen (as the Qur'an tells us) that when people are left to their own devices, they will try to usurp all means of resources, and their hunger for more is insatiable. As a result they hoard their wealth and lock it away.

> And amass [wealth] and thereupon withhold [it from their fellow-men] / Indeed, man is born with a restless disposition [i.e. his hunger is insatiable]. 70:18-19

When times are difficult and they lose their wealth for whatever reason, people complain and feel sorry for themselves; and when they have plenty, they tend to hoard and tie up their wealth in investments that benefit no one but themselves:

> [As a rule,] whenever misfortune touches him, he is filled with self-pity; / and whenever good fortune comes to him, he selfishly withholds it [from others]. 70:19-21

The Qur'an offers a single remedy for this mentality, and that is to establish *salaat*. It states that miserliness is a common trait in human beings, but when they establish a system of *salaat*, then this mentality is soon eradicated.

> [Those] who are steadfast in their *salaat* 70:23

In other words, with this change in mindset they accept the fact that they are not the sole beneficiaries of whatever they earn. Every needy and underprivileged member of society has a right to that wealth as well:

> And those in whose wealth is a recognised right [i.e. those who know that their wealth is not only for their own use, but for others as well] / For the [needy] who asks and him who is prevented [for whatever reason from asking] 70:24-5

So what is the nature of the psychological change that is brought about through *salaat*? And in light of the Qur'an, who are the *musalleen* ('praying ones')?

The praying ones

At another place in the Qur'an it is stated that the 'Hell-bound' will be asked: 'What crime did you commit to bring you here?' They will reply: 'We were not *praying ones*, and we failed to provide for those who could not meet their needs':

> 'What led you into Hell-Fire?' / They will say, 'We were not of *those who prayed (musalleen)*; / 'Nor were we of those who fed the indigent.' 74:42-4 (see also 75:31)

The Qur'an also states that after giving human beings the faculties of intellect, sight and hearing, God also showed them the true way of life and then left it to them to decide whether to adopt it or reject it.

> We made him a being endowed with hearing and sight. / Indeed, We have shown him the way: [and it rests with him to prove himself] either grateful or ungrateful [i.e. whether or not humans will adopt God's law, the only way by which to attain a state of abundance – *shakoorun*[154]]. 76:2-3

The Qur'an also tells that if we stray from the true path, then we will lose our liberties and our opportunities to grow in life will dry up like a stream. Our horizons will be greatly limited, and the self will cease to develop. Thus the price for rejecting the truth and choosing to oppress the weak is hellfire:

> [Now,] behold, for those who deny the truth We have readied chains and shackles, and a blazing flame 76:4

Conversely those who choose to adopt the truth will broaden their horizons. They will lead rich fulfilled lives, and there will be no limits as to what they can achieve. Such people are termed *abrar* in the

---

[154] **Translators' note:** As mentioned in Chapter 5, the meaning of *shukoorun* is 'return in abundance', from a root word meaning literally, 'to fill'.

Qur'an. The word *abrar* means literally 'vast', or 'open'[155] in the sense implying freedom, (though it is usually rendered in Qur'an translations as 'righteous' or 'pious').

Borne of the heart

These 'pious' people will take a drink that will give them peace and bliss (i.e. they will be rewarded for having adopted the law of God). The Qur'an describes this state in metaphor:

> The truly virtuous shall drink from a cup flavoured with the calyx of sweet-smelling flowers 76:5

So what is the source of this 'drink'? It is the human heart itself – the place where the permanent values were instilled – and from which flowed the good deeds that benefited humanity:

> A Fountain where the devotees of God do drink, making it flow in everlasting abundance. 76:6

This system will not have been forced on anyone. It will have been established by dedicated and willing individuals.

> [They are ones who willingly] fulfil their vows 76:7

They will realise that if they fail to establish a Divine system, another society will be established in its place, one in which evil will become the norm, to the point that even good people who can see it for what it is will be unable to escape from it:

> ... And they fear a Day whose evil flies far and wide. 76:7

In order to try and prevent this outcome, the 'believers' will voluntarily provide to the needy, the underprivileged and the vulnerable:

---

[155] The Qur'an has said that this state of 'vastness' in horizons (*abrar*) will only be achieved when we willingly leave our most valued possessions open to society. (3:92)

> [They will] give food – however great be their own want of it
> – to the needy, and the orphan, and the captive. 76:8

They will do all of this with no desire for thanks or reward, and with no thought of serving their self-interest.

> [They will do this with the mindset:] 'We feed you for the sake of God alone: we desire no recompense from you, nor thanks' 76:9

These then are the founding principles of the system of sustenance: The system must be borne of the heart, and it must be designed to benefit humanity. The people who undergo this dramatic psychological change are termed *musalleen* ('devotees' or 'followers').

Moving on, the Qur'an tells us that *deen* ultimately means the establishment of the Divine system of *Rabbubiya*, and that the route to this establishment is *salaat*. Therefore he who does not establish the Divine system is effectively a rejecter of *deen* (traditionally known as an 'unbeliever'). And whoever treats *salaat* merely as a ritual prayer and yet fails to provide the means of sustenance to society will find that his prayer actually destroys him. The Qur'an states:

> Have you ever considered [the kind of man] who belies the *deen*? / Behold, it is this [kind of man] who pushes the orphan away / and feels no urge to feed the needy / Woe, then, upon those devotees [*musallee*] / who are [knowingly] neglectful of their *salaat* 107:1-5

These prayers become the cause of their destruction for psychological reasons. If they abandon *salaat* altogether (in whatever form), then at least they might feel that their failures as a society are due to the fact that they have abandoned their religious duty and forgotten God. But if they believe that *salaat* is a ritual prayer, and they themselves pray regularly, then they are deluded. Evidently they believe that the ills in their society are down to something other than a neglect of *salaat*. These are the type of devotees who fail to see that their understanding of *salaat* is not really *salaat* at all. What type of *salaat* actually reduces the sustenance of humanity?

> Those who want only to be seen [as good people in the community] / But refuse [to meet] others' needs [of sustenance]! 107:6-7

According to the Qur'an one peculiar feature of the *momin* is their dedication to actively meeting the needs of others.

> [They are] active in deeds of *zakaat* [i.e. fulfilling the needs of all] 23:4

We can see here how the Qur'an has clarified the meaning of 'giving *zakaat'*. It has placed the word in context of a programme of action. It is the duty of the believers to set it up. This is the very *raison d'être* of the *momineen*.

> Those [are the ones] who, if We firmly establish them on earth, will establish *salaat*, and give *zakaat* 22:41 (see also 20:55)

There are a couple of points here that we should also consider. First, the duty of 'giving *zakaat'* can only be fulfilled when there is a governing body set up expressly for the purpose. Obviously if the meaning of 'giving *zakaat'* is merely charity, then there is no need for such a government. After all, it is possible to give charity under any manmade system. From this it should be clear that 'giving *zakaat'* is not a simple case of giving to charity. It actually means the establishment of a system, the purpose of which is to provide the means of sustenance to the whole of humanity.

Secondly, it has been made clear in this verse that the Islamic system will 'give *zakaat'* (*eeta-e-zakaat*), i.e. 'giving' will be the responsibility of the administration. Therefore the general notion that the Islamic government collects *zakaat* from the people is at odds with the Qur'anic concept of *zakaat*. In fact the Qur'an tells us that the system is designed to *give* to the people, not to *take* from the people. The fact is that the contemporary meaning we have given to *zakaat* is the cause of this misconception. We treat *zakaat* as charity at the individual level. But in *deen*, 'giving *zakaat'* really means 'to provide the means of sustenance to humanity', and thus the very reason for establishing this system is to make this provision possible.

We have seen that the fundamental principle in the system of *Rabbubiya* is a conviction in the 'Last Day' (i.e. setting our sights on the future) rather than a focus on short-term gains. It follows that those who have set their sights on the future will endeavour to establish a system of *Rabbubiya* or sustenance (i.e. the establishment of a system which will give *zakaat* to the whole of humanity). But those whose focus is on short-term gains are incapable of setting up a system revolving around *zakaat*. For this reason the Qur'an has declared:

> [As for] those who do not spend in *zakaat*: it is they, they who deny the truth of the life to come! 41:7

Conversely it goes without saying that those who establish *salaat* and give *zakaat* are the ones with a vision for the future.

> [Those] who establish *salaat* and spend in *zakaat*: it is they, they who in their innermost are certain of the life to come! 31:4

This is a *deen-e-qayyam*.[156]

> This is a *deen* right and straight (*deen-e-qayyam*). 98:5

The Qur'anic concepts of *salaat* and *zakaat* are entirely interdependent, to the extent that if a group of people give *zakaat* but do so reluctantly, then their *salaat* is wasted and is worthless.

> The only reasons why their contributions are not accepted are … that they establish *salaat* reluctantly; and they never give *zakaat* without resentment. 9:54

Hopefully we can now see the meaning of *qiaam-e-salaat* (establishing *salaat*). It means the creation of an environment in which people will not only instil the permanent values in their own minds and hearts, but will also instil them in others. Therefore setting up a system of sustenance requires the following:

1) The ideals which we have discussed above must become embedded in the individual's psyche
2) A group of such likeminded individuals must offer mutual support to one another and collectively decide to set up the Divine system

---

[156] **Translators' note:** As mentioned in Chapter 1, the Qur'anic term *deen-e-qayyam* refers to a system that is founded on the principles of proportion and balance, and which brings out similar qualities of proportion and balance in society.

This is how people can be equipped to take the first steps along the Qur'anic 'steep uphill road'. The Qur'an has stated that the way up this road is for each individual to possess the following attributes:

[He will be] of those who believe, and who enjoin patience, and who enjoin compassion [upon one another]. 90:17

In other words, those who have conviction in the Divine system of universal sustenance will encourage one another to remain steadfast. They also enjoin others to share all resources bestowed on them by the Almighty.

Incentive

Generally speaking, society only functions when people have an incentive to work. As long as society doesn't lose sight of its ideals (and thus lose its incentive to work), and as long as no other (false) incentives are introduced, people as a whole will retain their character and society will remain stable. Incentive therefore is the lifeblood of society. Freud, the father of modern psychology, thus writes:

Civilised society, which exacts good conduct and does not trouble itself about the impulses underlying it, has thus won over to obedience a great many people who are not thereby following the dictates of their own natures. Encouraged by this success, society has suffered itself to be led into straining the normal standard to the highest possible point, and thus it has forced its members into a yet greater estrangement from their instinctual dispositions. They are consequently subjected to an unceasing suppression of instinct, the resulting strain of which betrays itself in the most remarkable phenomena of reaction and compensation formations. ... [T]he pressure of civilization brings in its train no pathological results, but is shown in malformations of character, and in the perpetual readiness of the inhibited instincts to break through to gratification at any suitable opportunity. Anyone thus compelled to act continually in the sense of precepts which are not the expression of instinctual inclinations, is living, psychologically speaking, beyond his means, and might objectively be designated a hypocrite, whether this difference be clearly known to

him or not. It is undeniable that our contemporary
civilization is extraordinarily favourable to the production
of this form of hypocrisy.[157]

It is not within the scope of this book for us to explain the Qur'anic
concept of 'hypocrisy' and the peculiar features of a hypocritical
personality. Suffice it to say that the findings of Freud and other
modern psychologists corroborate the Qur'anic statements on the
subject. Here we will see how the Qur'an provides the incentives that
become the foundation of the system of *Rabbubiya*. This entire
programme is summed up with the phrase 'establishing *salaat*'.
Professor Hawtrey has written:

> What differentiates economic systems from one
> another is the character of the motives they invoke to
> induce people to work.[158]

Next we will examine the Qur'anic incentives that underpin its
system, how strong they are, how logical, and how much they appeal to
the intellect.

Along with instigating the Qur'anic incentives in the populace, i.e.
establishing *salaat*, the people must become accustomed to sharing
their wealth with others in practice. They must continually be given
opportunities to this end, so that they learn to give the greater part of
their personal wealth for the sake of the collective interest. The Qur'an
uses the term *fi sabil-Allah* for this type of expenditure.

Instructions for the transitional period

The Qur'an does use a word that might be translated as 'charity' or
'alms', and this is *sadaqaat*. All the instructions that the Qur'an
provides on how and why to give *sadaqaat* relate to a transitional
period. We will return to *sadaqaat* later. We should note for now that
this 'transitional period' refers to the stage in which the system of
Rabbubiya is actively being set up, but the process is not yet complete.
In other words this refers to the early stages of its establishment,

---

[157] Freud, Sigmund (1925) *On Creativity and the Unconscious: Papers on the
Psychology of Art, Literature, Love, and Religion* New York: Harper, p.217-8
[158] Hawtrey, Ralph G. (1944) *Economic Destiny* London: Longman,
Green & Co., p.345

when only a small number of people (*jamaat*, group) have reached a state of conviction. The transitional stage prepares these people in such a way as to gradually take the whole of society to the last stage. They are taught that whilst they can keep what they need for themselves, they must share the rest of their earnings with society for the collective interest as well. By putting these principles into practice, they develop the habit of thinking in terms of the collective interest until such a time that the system itself will become responsible for taking the means of sustenance and wealth and redistributing it to everybody. (This of course would be the final stage in establishing the system of *Rabbubiya*.)

> Those who, when they spend on others, are neither extravagant nor miserly, but hold a just (balance) between those (two extremes) 25:67

Elsewhere the Qur'an states:

> And give the near of kin what is his by right, as well as to the needy and the wayfarer, but do not squander [your wealth] senselessly. 17:26

The Qur'an states that *sadaqaat* can be given openly or in secret (2:271). It also teaches that wealth should always circulate, and that it should not remain just in the hands of the wealthy:

> [The wealth is to be given to God] so that it may not be [a benefit] circulating among those of you who are [already] rich 59:7

At another place in the Qur'an we are told the consequences of allowing the hoarding of wealth:

> Say: If it be that your fathers, your sons, your brothers, your mates, or your kindred; the wealth that you have gained; the commerce in which you fear a decline; or the properties in which you delight – are dearer to you than God, Or His Messenger, or the striving in His cause – then wait until God brings about His decision: and God guides not the rebellious. 9:24

We are also warned of the dangers of interest (*riba*) as follows:

> Those who devour interest [*riba*] behave like someone whom the Evil One has driven mad with his touch, for they say: "Trade is like interest," but God has permitted trade and forbidden interest. Those who become aware of their Sustainer's warning and thereafter desist, shall be pardoned for the past, and it will be for God to judge; but those who repeat (the offence) are destined for the Fire; they will abide therein (forever). 2:275

Looking more closely at the implications of these instructions, we can see that this *jamaat* (group) will reach a state in which they no longer have a desire to acquire private property.

No more private property

1) There is no longer any question of the private ownership of land, because it has been said that all resources must be left open to everyone (41:10)
2) When there is no private ownership of land, then all real estate business, whether for selling or letting, becomes obsolete. This includes renting residential properties. Of course people still *need* somewhere to live, but the state will provide accommodation to fulfil this need
3) No one can hoard money since this is forbidden, and wealth cannot be allowed to circulate just amongst a particular (wealthy) class
4) People should not deliberately spend their surplus wealth on things that they don't really need, nor should they be miserly in order to try and save money (see verse 25:67 cited earlier)
5) No one can charge interest, no matter how small the rate, on a loan

Under such circumstances, even if someone has surplus wealth, what can he use it for? It will actually become a burden to him, because the Qur'anic system will give him no opportunities to either keep or privately spend this surplus. It might be suggested that this money be invested in factories and commercial enterprise. This is all well and good, but what of the produce and the profit that comes from these businesses? We will return again to our problem of surplus wealth.

Thus we can see that the Qur'an's instructions leave no room for the acquisition of surplus wealth. When it comes to fulfilling needs, the system assumes responsibility. We will return to this in detail later.

In short, this practical education programme will bring about the kind of psychological change in society that will gradually teach people the habit of working for the collective interest and for the benefit of humanity, rather than for immediate gains.

> Pious is he who ... spends his substance – however much he himself may cherish it – upon his near of kin, and the orphans, and the needy, and the wayfarer, and the beggars, and for the freeing of human beings from bondage; 2:117 (see also 76:8)

It will also nurture the following character traits:

> [They] love all that come to them in search of refuge, and who harbour no grudge in their hearts for whatever they [the refugees] may have been given, but rather give them preference over themselves, even though poverty be their own lot 59:9

Formation of the *jamaat*

Once the psychological state of the *jamaat* reaches its peak, the higher purpose (i.e. the creation of an ideal society) for which they were trained finally becomes manifest. In today's terms this means the emergence of a distinct party; and it emerges for the simple reason that we cannot bring about a revolution in any society until a party or movement comes into being for the purpose. On this subject Ouspensky quotes his mentor Gurdjieff as follows:

> Everything I have said till now I have said about the whole of humanity. But as I pointed out before, the evolution of humanity can proceed only through the evolution of a certain group, which, in its turn, will influence and lead the rest of humanity.[159]

But this *jamaat* will not impose itself by force or coercion, nor can it do so through any nepotistic influence, or with bribery. As we have already seen, this party will comprise a group of people who have

---

[159] Ouspensky , *In Search of the Miraculous*, p.309

made the law of Divine universal sustenance their ideal, who have willingly dedicated themselves to establishing a system based upon it, and who are absolutely convinced that this system is the only guaranteed means to success both in the short term and in the future. In short, the people in this *jamaat* will come to rely on one another and will support and strengthen one another by virtue of their common idealism. Their hearts are united, and they are single-minded in their purpose. It follows that this is the foundation of a 'pious' society. Ouspensky thus writes (citing Gurdjieff):

> Men understand one another so imperfectly because they live always by different emotions. And when they feel similar emotions simultaneously, then and then only do they understand one another.[160]

Thus when such a group of people come together and are united in their purpose, they are said to be leading a collective life. So how does this *jamaat* come into being? Ouspensky again cites Gurdjieff:

> The rule of common responsibility must be borne well in mind. It has another side also. Members of a group are responsible not only for the mistakes of others, but also for their failures. The success of one is the success of all. The failure of one is the failure of all. A grave mistake on the part of one, such as for instance the breaking of a fundamental rule, inevitably leads to the dissolution of the whole group.[161]

This is the purpose about which the final Messenger was told:

> Hence, proclaim openly all that you have been commanded [to say], and turn away from those who join false deities with God 15:94

He was instructed to ensure that those who were ready to take part in the Divine programme received full support and protection:

> ... Lower your wing [in gentleness] to the believers 15:88

---

[160] Ouspensky P.D. (1922) *Tertium Organum* (trans. Claude Bragdon) 1970 reprint, New York: Vintage Books, p.198
[161] Ouspensky, *In Search of the Miraculous* p.231

The Messenger was also told that when opposition inevitably came from vested interests, God's law and those who joined him would be sufficient to help him thwart these opponents:

> O Prophet! God is enough for you and those of the believers who follow you! 8:64

Hence this society emulates the attributes of God in its chosen mission, which is to ultimately provide universal sustenance to all of humanity. This is achieved by means of a social contract between the state (God's central authority) and the people. The people agree to willingly and absolutely entrust their possessions and their lives to the central authority that administers the system of *Rabbubiya*; and in return, the central authority guarantees a heaven on earth.

> Behold, God has bought of the believers their lives and their possessions, promising them paradise in return 9:111

Social contract with God

We have already noted that an ideal state (or 'heaven on earth') is one in which all basic necessities (food, clothing, shelter and security) are made available universally. Thus in practice the social contract with God is an agreement whereby the administration provides basic necessities universally to society; and in return, the surplus wealth that people generate using their God-given talents and abilities is also freely returned to society. This societal setup saves humanity from the doom shared by manmade systems – i.e. those that focus on self-interest rather than the collective interest.

> O you who have attained to conviction! Shall I point out to you a bargain that will save you from grievous suffering [in this world and in the life to come]? 61:10

To reiterate, every capable individual keeps only what he needs, and gives all his surplus back to the treasury:

> And they ask you as to what they should spend [for the needy, in God's cause]. Say: 'Whatever is surplus to your needs.' 2:219

After all, what is the use of hoarding in a society that already has all of its needs met?

Meaning of 'God' in context

Let us now consider the following verse:

> And there is no living creature on earth [including humanity and by extension human society] but depends for its sustenance on God 11:6 (see also 17:31, 29:60). [162]

Before going any further, we must understand an important point about the above verse. In this verse, as well as in verse 9:111 cited a little earlier, the key word is 'God'. Both verses refer to a society which is established to implement the law of God. So 'God' is synonymous with 'law of God'. The question is: How did we reach this conclusion? I have written much on this subject elsewhere, and so it is not necessary to explain it in detail here. Nevertheless, for those who are not familiar with my writings, it should suffice to say that when it comes to humanity, God's work must be done through human hands. For example, God has said that the *kalima* (the Word) will overcome or be proved true (10:33, 40:6), and He will establish *deen al-haqq* (*deen* of truth – 48:28, 61:9). This means that the Divine system is bound to succeed all others. But this cannot happen automatically. In history, truth overcame through the actions of the final Messenger and his party of supporters, on the battlefields of Badr Hunayn. Truth did not prevail until this party (*jamaat al-momineen*) came into existence. Hence the Qur'an states:

> He it is who has sent forth His Apostle with the [task of spreading] guidance and the *deen* of truth, to the end that He makes it prevail over every [false] *deen* ... / Muhammad is the Messenger of God; and those who are with him are firm and unyielding towards all rejecters of the truth [*kafireen*], [but] compassionate amongst one another 48:28-9

It was their tough stance against the opponents of truth that enabled the *deen al-haqq* to overcome and establish itself over all

---

162 **Translators' note:** The point of this verse is that just as nothing in nature can survive without the Sustainer, no human society can thrive without the Sustainer either.

manmade systems. When, at Hudaibiyah near Makkah, the soldiers of the *jamaat* swore their allegiance to the Messenger and pledged their lives, the Qur'an states that they were in fact swearing their allegiance to the Almighty:

> Behold, all who pledge their allegiance to thee pledge their allegiance to God: the hand of God is [placed] over their hands 48:10

Of course God did not *literally* place a hand over theirs, but this was done *in effect* through human agency – that is, through the central authority set up in His name. Similarly, when the Messenger's supporters threw their arrows against their opponents during the battle of Badr, the Qur'an says that it was God who threw the arrows:

> And it was not you who threw [the arrow], when you threw it, but it was God who threw it 8:17 [163]

Therefore God fulfils His responsibilities through human agency, that is, the Divine system of sustenance, which in turn is built upon His law. The Qur'an has emphasised the point in the following verse:

> Thus, when they are told, 'Spend on others out of what God has provided for your sustenance,' the rejecters of the truth say to those who believe, 'Shall we feed anyone whom, if [your] God had so intended, He could have fed [Himself]? Clearly, you are but lost in error!' 36:47

The Qur'an is thus exposing the flaw in their logic. Of course God will not personally provide sustenance to the people Himself, but this will be done through His Divine system. To fully understand why their logic is flawed, we should consider the following. The Qur'an tells us that God is the Sustainer of the nations of the world (*Rabb-il-*

---

[163] **Translators' note:** Other translations of the Qur'an render the wording in the above verse as 'you threw (dust)' or, in the case of Asad, 'cast terror' (which we have replaced with 'threw the arrow' to comply with Parwez's choice of words). But Asad adds the following commentary on this verse: 'Since the verb *rams* (lit., "he cast" or "flung") applies also to the act of "shooting an arrow" or "flinging a spear", it might be explained here as a reference to the Prophet's active participation in the battle.' This explains Parwez's translation of 'threw the arrow'.

aalameen). It tells us that 'there is no living creature on earth but depends for its sustenance on God' (11:6) and that we should not commit infanticide out of a fear of poverty since God 'shall provide sustenance for them as well as for you' (17:31). Obviously if the Almighty has taken the responsibility of fulfilling the needs of society, then it means that no one can remain without. But we observe that countless people die of hunger every day. Famine claims millions of lives. There are many children who die simply because of malnutrition. Naturally (God forbid) we might wonder how, if He is responsible for fulfilling our needs, there is so much suffering based on shortage in the world. However in light of our discussion on the subject, this verse does not mean that God will *personally* intervene and take care of humanity. These responsibilities must be fulfilled through human hands – i.e. by a system. If a system is established in accordance with Divine law, then God's responsibility is automatically fulfilled, and it becomes a testament to the world of how God takes care of humanity.

> Say: 'Am I, then, to seek a sustainer other than God, when He is the Sustainer of all things?' And whatever [injustice] any human being commits [by not adopting His law] rests upon Him alone 6:164

However if a society is established on manmade laws, then the means of sustenance will be unequally distributed – i.e. we will see injustice and some will inevitably go without.

In the natural universe the law of *Rabbubiya* operates by itself – i.e. it is a natural law. However in the human domain this *Rabbubiya* operates *only* when humans themselves choose to adopt it. When a society establishes itself in the name of God, this means that the administration will take on the responsibilities that God has promised to fulfil in the Qur'an; and in return, every member of society will likewise fulfil their duties and obligations (9:111). However the people will fulfil their duties and comply with the system only as long as the system fulfils its responsibilities to them.

In light of all that we have discussed, let us now reconsider the verse in which it is written:

> And there is no living creature on earth [including humanity and by extension human society] but depends for its sustenance on God 11:6

The verse is clearly saying that the responsibility of sustenance will fall upon the society that has established itself in accordance with God's law. The Qur'an states that if God freely provides us with our means of sustenance, then what need is there for us to hoard?

What need to hoard?

The fact is that we collect and save only to protect ourselves and our children from unforeseen circumstances in the future. But when God assumes the responsibility of providing the means of sustenance for ourselves and our children (via the system), then there is no more need to hoard.

> It is We who shall provide sustenance for them (your children) as well as for you. 17:31

In fact we tend to hoard only because we fear that when we grow old and can no longer earn, we may not be able to provide for ourselves and our children (2:266). However such a thought should not even enter the mind if we are living in a system of *Rabbubiya*, since this system provides for everyone at every stage of life. But perhaps we also think we are saving for a rainy day, for a time of unforeseen disaster. Again the Qur'an provides a response:

> No calamity can ever befall the earth, and neither your own selves, unless it be [laid down] in Our decree before We bring it into being: indeed, all this is easy for God 57:22

In other words, this system makes provisions for a potential disaster, since having a contingency plan for external or internal calamities is 'easy for God'. Hence if someone partially or completely loses their capacity to earn after illness or an accident, the system will ensure that he never goes without. At any rate, those with a greater earning capacity do not treat their wealth as their private property, but something that is created to benefit humanity. It is only in 'selfish' societies (in which we are encouraged to compete for self-interest) that people not only equate wealth with status, but are even willing to exploit others in their quest to get it. In a society that secures sustenance for everyone, hoarding becomes an obsolete concept. It is only a fear of future *insecurity* that compels people to hoard.

> Satan threatens you with the prospect of poverty and bids
> you to be miserly (*fahsha*) 2:268

Conversely the system of *Rabbubiya* eliminates all fear of insecurity since it guarantees sustenance to all of humanity:

> ... Whereas God promises you His forgiveness (*ghafr*)[164]
> and bounty 2:268

The Qur'an has thus explained the difference between a manmade and a Divine system in just a few words. In the former, every individual is responsible for meeting his own needs, and so is unconcerned with the needs of others. In this type of society, the individual is worried only about his own future. He lives in constant fear of a day in which he is unable (for whatever reason) to provide for himself and for his children. This powerful feeling of insecurity is the underlying root of the need to hoard to the grave (102:1-2). The obsession with hoarding in turn leads people to use deceptive and exploitative means to meet their needs.

In the latter of our two systems, the responsibility of taking care of every individual rests with the administration. In this society no one feels insecure about his future. He is happy in his work, and sleeps soundly at night. He never feels he has to lie or deceive or steal. This type of society is established by the group of people (*jamaat*) that we described earlier in this chapter. They neither fear for what lies in their future, nor are they anxious about the potential misuse of their earnings by the administration, since such things are impossible in the system of *Rabbubiya*. There is no fundamental difference between the administrators and the rest of the public. There are no rulers and the ruled. Hence the people are told in no uncertain terms:

> No sustenance do I ever demand of them, nor do I demand
> that they feed Me 51:57 (see also 6:41 and 23:87)

In other words, just as all the citizens have their rights and obligations, so does the administration. The process works both ways and there is no difference between them. Those who run the

---

[164] **Translators' note:** As already mentioned in Chapter 5, though the word *ghafr* is usually translated as 'forgive', the word *ghafr* actually means 'protect' or 'succour'.

administration do not expect to receive a higher rate of pay simply because of their position:

> I have asked no reward whatever of you: my reward rests with none but God 10:72

After all, the administrators are members of the same society:

> For I have been bidden to be among those who have submitted to Him [i.e. a member of the society that has submitted]. 10:72

Of course, aside from needs, there is another emotional motive behind the acquisition of wealth, and that is the desire to climb the social ladder and achieve power and status. The Qur'an refers to this desire using two words: *Tafaakhur* ('arrogance') and *takaasur* ('obsession with greed'). But in a society established on the law of *Rabbubiya*, the people have a different idea about what constitutes 'status' and what is 'valuable'.

At present, society equates wealth with respect and status. The more wealth that any given individual has, the greater his status and his perceived respectability. In a Divine system however, individual status is determined by *taqwa* – lit. the 'God-fearing', or piety.[165] This means that those who do their duties to the best of their abilities (and thereby contribute the most to society) are deemed to have greater social status or respect (3:14-15). Hence in such a society there is no desire to hoard as a means to this end.

Business not for profit

To summarise, when the system of *Rabbubiya* is fully established and the administration takes on the responsibility of providing the means of sustenance for all, then neither do individuals feel the need to hoard their surplus wealth, nor do they feel the need to acquire private property. At this stage we might also justly predict the end of businesses that exist to make profit. In fact, the very concept of business itself will have changed. At such a time those who produce goods and services will continue to do so, and consumers will simply

---

[165] **Translators' note:** Asad translates *taqwa* as 'God-consciousness'. See also fn 114 for further explanation of this phrase.

take and utilise these goods and services as and when they need them. This will be possible because the system will provide for the needs of both producers and consumers. As things stand at present, whenever a society is overwhelmed by the consequences of its self-created problems (i.e. it enters recession and there is a shortage of circulating money), the best it can do is introduce some sort of bartering system to exchange tangible goods instead of money. With regards to bartering it has been said that:

> It is axiomatic that exchange is just if, and only if, the exchanged values are equal[166]

Of course this raises the question of how to assign value to a given item (or service). For example, a cobbler makes a pair of shoes and he wants to offer them in exchange for some wheat. How much wheat would be the equivalent value of the shoes? This is the issue at present, but if the system is meeting the needs of the cobbler and the farmer, then perceived 'value' does not come into question. Instead it will be a question solely of need. This is why, in the Qur'anic system of sustenance, this 'business' issue will no longer need a solution, since the issue will no longer exist. In the Qur'anic way of life, 'business' will simply come to mean the facilities which distribute goods and services. As we have already noted, the administrative authority will meet the needs of all people, that is, employees and employers alike. For argument's sake, we might call this their 'return'.

To clarify, since their needs are already being met, the question will never arise as to how much they should be paid for the work they do. Instead, they will all work to the best of their capability for the collective interest, secure in the knowledge that the administration will cater for their needs – and that ultimately this is the 'return' for their efforts.

---

[166] Simons, Yves Rene (1951) *Philosophy of Democratic Government* 1993 reprint, London: University of Notre Dame Press, 'IV. Democratic Equality' (subsection: Equality Versus Exploitation). Online (University of Notre Dame website): http://maritain.nd.edu/jmc/etext/pdg.htm Last retrieved 03 August 2012.

Unlimited powers

Note that the biggest hindrance to the establishment of a system of sustenance is the individual's fear of 'giving away' the surplus which, so his intellect tells him, he ought to be saving for the future. But once the Divine system is established, the intellect becomes satisfied that the administration will provide for both the individual and his children. If the individual is faced with a crisis, he knows that the system will fully support him and he will not be left alone to deal with it himself. He is saved from worrying about anything. When he is no longer anxious about his livelihood and the upkeep of his children, and is free to put his mind to other things, then we can only imagine what he might achieve. It is only his material insecurities and his fears for the future that continually divert his creative energies and prevent him from fulfilling his potential. Otherwise humanity has almost no limit in its power and creative potential. It takes all manner of raw materials and hidden forces in nature, and puts them to good use. Every human being thus reaches the height of his abilities. All live well and in dignity. All are equal and none are downtrodden. Humanity can face any adversity and overcome it.

We can see that not only does the system of *Rabbubiya* free the human mind from the fear of destitution, but in addition it instils a sense of conviction that whatever we 'give' to society will ultimately nourish the individual 'self'. The more we give, the more the self will develop; this is how we will achieve immortality and God's attributes will become manifest within us. The individual will happily work as hard as he can, knowing that the more he produces and gives away, the better it is for his self. If need be, he will gladly give away his most prized possession, since he will know that 1) If he dies, his children will be looked after 2) If he pledges his life to protect the Divine system, he knows that he will be entitled to immortality. If he becomes a martyr, he will be deemed victorious.

A society of this type is an unstoppable force. The world remains in awe of how the final Messenger took a small group of individuals and, in a relatively short period, turned them into the most advanced people on earth. Research institutes have even been set up to find out how they achieved so much in so little time. However the world doesn't seem to realise that the Messenger achieved this only because he formed a society that was built upon the Divine system of sustenance, and the marvellous achievements of this new civilisation are really just the fruits of this system. The Messenger had educated his people with Qur'anic principles, convinced them of the veracity of these teachings, and then established the system in practice:

> [Muhammad] shall convey Your messages to them, and impart Revelation to them as well as wisdom, and cause them to grow in purity 2:129

(In other words: The Messenger would educate and establish a society which would unlock the potential of its people in accordance with God's guidance.)

A new civilisation was thus born, and it spread from East to West. When this civilisation conformed with God's law, then He was their friend and helper (9:100).

Relationship between individual and society

The most important issue at the present time is that of the 'individual' versus the 'collective'. Western materialism is a reaction to the Christian spiritualist doctrine that rejects the physical world, and similarly, modern European ideas regarding the individual and the collective have come about as a result of an adverse reaction to Christian monasticism. The fundamental teaching of monasticism is that collective or societal life has no meaning, and that the true meaning of life is to seek individual salvation – that is, for the 'soul'; and in order to achieve salvation, individuals should cut themselves off from society and lead an isolated life. Modern thinkers and scientists have reacted against this Christian spiritualist position and have totally rejected the existence of the 'soul'[167], choosing materialism instead. Likewise they have rejected the monastic concept of solitary life, redirecting their focus towards collective life; and they have declared that the only real existence is to be found in society. In different parts of the world, this society or collective is either called a 'nation', or it is called a 'state'. Thus from the nineteenth century onward, the idea that the individual should live and die for his nation (or state) gained widespread acceptance in Europe. Outside of his social existence, the concept of individual existence became not only irrelevant, but a falsehood. Hence the modern purpose of life is to submerge individual identity in society, much like the parts of a

---

[167] By 'soul' we mean the human self, which continues to exist after physical death.

machine that have no individuality and exist only for the machine. The parts do not question why they work for the machine; they blindly go on working in its interests. Hence in this particular relationship between the individual and the state, the position of the individual is reduced to that of an automaton. In fact this European belief itself has become a kind of religion, one in which the state is practically a deity and the individual is its devotee. The state demands the supreme sacrifice from its people in the same way that a pagan god supposedly demanded sacrifices to appease it. Hence Huxley writes on the subject of 'nationalism':

> A principal cause of war is nationalism, and nationalism is immensely popular because it is psychologically satisfying to individual nationalists. Every nationalism is an idolatrous religion, in which the god is the personified state, represented in many instances by a more or less deified king or dictator.[168]

Murray meanwhile writes:

> [It] is because direct experience of God has largely ceased that the devil of Nationalism has entered the empty house.[169]

The reality is that the ruling class, in their hunger for power, has simply changed the subject of 'reverence' from 'kings' to the more ambiguous concept of 'state'. A state is an abstract concept, and to this day no political thinker has been able to put forward a clear and unequivocal definition of what the 'state' is. However, looking more closely we find that the underlying motivation of the concept is really about power and control. Hence we are constantly told to strengthen the nation, which in practice really means that we should help strengthen the hand of the ruling elite. When we are also told not to act against the interests of the state, i.e. to rebel against it, we are really being warned not to take any action which could potentially weaken the hold of the elite over the masses. The communists claim that they advocate a 'people's government', but here too 'people' doesn't mean the public as a whole, but rather just the ruling class. Jack Belden writes on the subject of the Chinese Cultural Revolution:

---

[168] Huxley, *Ends and Means*, p.97
[169] Murray, J.M. (1944) *Adam and Eve: An Essay towards a New and Better Society* London: Andrew Dakers, p.67

The Communists' use of the word "people" sounds somewhat mystical to a Western ear. The Chinese emperor used to call himself the Son of Heaven. Now the Chinese Communists call themselves Sons of the People. In other words, the people have replaced God and the Communists have replaced the emperor. The emperor used to rule because he had the command of Heaven; the Communists rule because they have the command of the people. In old China, the people lived under the despotism of the dead and had to pay obeisance to their ancestors. Now, the Communists say the people are the ancestors and obeisance should be paid to them. To put this in Western terms, the sovereign emperor has been replaced by the sovereign people; and the divine will has been replaced by the general will. If all wills must submit to the supreme will, then it follows that the individual must also bow down to the people. ...

In proclaiming the power of the common people, many of the followers of Mao Tze-tung put forth doctrines more characteristic of the Middle Ages than of Marxism. "Follow the masses," they say, proclaiming that the people are always good, that the people can do no wrong. Thus they pave the way to absolutism, for obviously if the people can do no wrong, then the power that represents the people can also do no wrong.[170]

At any rate in Europe it has become accepted that 'true existence' is the state, or nation, or society; and the individual is merely the means by which to establish it. Individual identity is irrelevant. If it is in the state's interest to keep its people alive, then it will certainly keep them alive; and if it requires that they must die, then it will ensure that their lives are sacrificed for it. This principle is at work in all corners of the modern world. The only difference is that in some countries, the government cares not how the people are meeting their needs, or how they are passing their days, whilst in others (the 'welfare states') it is said that the government is responsible for meeting their physical needs to varying degrees. However this type of welfare can be likened to keeping animals at a farm. The people's needs are being met only because of their usefulness to the state. Free education and healthcare is provided only to ensure that people can remain productive and can keep working like machines.[171]

---

[170] Belden, Jack (1940) *China Shakes the World* New York: Harper & Brothers, p.504-5

[171] I (Parwez) read the well-known communist M.D. Kammari's book *Socialism and the Individual* (1949, Foreign Languages Publishing

The Qur'anic position

The Qur'an places much emphasis on the importance of the individual, so much so in fact that it deems the killing of one human being to be the same as killing the whole of humanity, and deems the saving of one human being as the equivalent of saving the whole of humanity:

> We taught the children of Israel that if anyone slays a human being unless it be [in punishment] for murder or for spreading corruption on earth – it shall be as though he had slain all humankind; whereas, if anyone saves a life, it shall be as though he had saved the lives of all humankind 5:32

The purpose of the Qur'an's teachings is to develop and strengthen the individual self. Its claim that every individual is responsible for his deeds and the results of those deeds ultimately determine the fate of his self will prove to be a self-evident fact:

> Whoever, therefore, chooses to see, does so for his own good; and whoever chooses to remain blind, does so to his own hurt. 6:104

The crux of the Qur'anic teaching therefore is to perfect the self. It follows that any other philosophy, or ideology, or religion that is detrimental to individuality in any way is to be rejected. However it also says that the perfection of the self cannot happen without the *jamaat* (community). Hence it is vital for the individual that he be a part of the *jamaat*:

> O you who have attained to conviction! Remain conscious of God, and *be among those* who are true to their word! 9:119

House, Moscow) with interest to see what socialism offers the individual, and the purpose of taking care of his needs. On the one hand she writes that socialist society ensures the 'universal development of the individual, of all physical and spiritual faculties' (1950 reprint, p.48). However I was disappointed to find that all this really amounts to is that individual capabilities and talents should be developed solely to vastly improve his productivity. She has not supplied any real details as to what in her mind constitutes 'spiritual' development.

The Qur'an further states that the human self can only be saved from destruction if the individual lives among people who encourage positive and constructive deeds from one another, and so become a support to one another (103:3). This is a fundamental teaching of the Qur'an. Hence according to the Qur'an, the *jamaat* is the only means of perfecting the individual self. Whilst in Western thought, the self is the means and the state is the end, the Qur'an teaches that the opposite is true. According to Iqbal, the relationship between the individual and the state is like that of a traveller and the caravan with which he travels.[172] Hence a society formed in accordance with the Qur'anic system of sustenance is like a caravan, formed for the purpose of taking each and every individual to his destination. If however the people of the caravan do not take the individual to his destination, then they are not in a caravan at all, but are a bunch of thieves and bandits. The Qur'an has explained the point in the following verse:

> O you who have attained to conviction! Be patient in adversity, and vie in perseverance, and strengthen each other, and remain conscious of God, so that you might prosper. 3:200

The ultimate objective of this society becomes apparent in the last few words of the above verse: 'that you might prosper', i.e. so that the self may unlock its full potential, like the seed that produces a field of crops. A state that fails to unlock the potential of the individual and thus fails to take him to his higher destination is based upon falsehood – i.e. *baatil*; and when subsequently such a state forces people to work in its interests and meet its demands, this is nothing short of tyranny. Conversely a state that is founded upon truth (*haqq*) will itself become the means for the individual to develop his self. Most importantly, it will do so freely, meaning that it will demand nothing in return.

In a state founded upon falsehood (i.e. one in which the individual surrenders his identity in the state) it is easy to form a ruling party in what is generally called a 'one-party' system. In order to maintain power and party discipline, force becomes a necessity. It soon becomes clear that this 'people's party' is really nothing more than a military dictatorship in which individual members are mere soldiers and the leading members are their commanders. The soldier's duty is to obey orders without question and that is all. He has no opinions of

---

[172] In verse 73:1 the Qur'an also calls the Messenger *muzzamil*, 'leader of the caravan' (although traditional translations often erroneously use another meaning, 'the enwrapped one').

his own, and he never thinks for himself – indeed, nor is he required to
do so. No one asks for his input or to contribute an idea. The ideal
soldier is one whose sense of self is utterly annihilated. Any soldier
who shows signs of retaining his sense of individuality is always
crushed (and in fact this is true even of democratic states). China of
course is one example of a state governed by a one-party system. Jack
Belden, who was so awed by the revolution in China that he called it a
'cataclysmic change',[173] has made the following observation:

> In general, it may be said that the Communists are trying to
> unify China by the enthronement of the social right over the
> individual right. If you want to express your individuality, you do
> not belong. You must indulge in self-examination. You must
> come to the group and be criticized. You must acknowledge
> your errors. You must work for society, not yourself.[174]

Therefore, whilst a communist society does indeed take care of the
individual, it does so at the cost of individuality. The Qur'an has
described a similar situation in history, namely that of the ancient
Egyptians. Their Pharaoh claimed:

> [Pharaoh] said: 'I am your sustainer (Rabb) All-
> Highest!' 79:24

(In other words, other than claming divinity, he claimed he was
meeting the needs of his people, hence 'sustainer' – Rabb)

Pharaoh further said that since the land and the rivers of Egypt
were in his control and his system administered them, this justified his
claim that he was the people's sustainer (43:51). He also presented a
similar claim before Moses (and made a point of reminding Moses that
the royal household had raised him as one of their own), but the
Messenger's response revealed the fundamental difference between
the Pharaoh's system of rule and God's Rabbubiya:

> [Moses replied] And as for that favour of which you
> tauntingly remind me – [was it not] due to your having enslaved
> the children of Israel? 26:22

---

173 Belden, op. cit. p.3
174 Op. cit. p.489

The Pharaoh of course maintained his power by exploiting the Israelites and moulding them to suit his purpose. He had effectively emasculated their nation by slaughtering any men who might have rebelled against him, whilst nurturing the gentler and more feminine qualities of their nation (hence, 'killed their sons and spared their women' – 2:49). Generations of Israelites were also raised in Egyptian ways and norms, turning them into intellectual slaves, and thereby destroying their individual identity (2:49, 14:6).

This therefore was the reality of the 'sustenance' provided by the Pharaoh and the Egyptian elite; the means of production was entirely in their control, and they exploited the ordinary people. It was a powerful ancient dictatorship. The fact remains that in a false system – whether we call it a society, a nation, a state, or a people's government – the individual has no real existence. Conversely, *jamaat* of the Divine system of sustenance (*Rabbubiya*) is formed expressly for the purpose of developing every individual to his full potential. Of course this creates a problem: On the one hand, complete law and order is absolutely essential to retain stability in a system; and on the other, the concept of nurturing individuality demands that there must be ample room for freedom of thought and speech. In short, there has to be a balance between authority and freedom, which is not an easy task. This was the crucial point in fact, about which the Messenger was told:

> Behold, We shall bestow upon you a weighty message (i.e. We will entrust you with a great and heavy responsibility) 73:5

> [Have we not helped you with the responsibility] that had weighed so heavily on your back? 94:3

There is insufficient room in this book to discuss the subject of the final Messenger's weighty responsibility and how he succeeded in establishing a society that allowed authority and individual freedom to coexist instead of clashing. The balance of discipline and civil liberties as exhibited in this system is perhaps unmatched in history, and which few of the children of Adam may have witnessed. If we are ever to see it again, then we can only do so by adopting the Qur'anic system of sustenance. This is the system in which the concept of 'ruler and the ruled' is completely eliminated, and every individual is a friend of society. The law that holds this society together is not of their making, but has been given to them by the Almighty. Subsequently there is complete law and order and the state remains stable, and at the same time each individual is free to develop his self.

As we have already stated, the demands of the present age are compelling the world to gradually move towards the principles of the Qur'an. As a result, the very same Europeans who at one time said that true existence could be found only in the collective, and the individual had no value, are now stating the opposite; they are saying that the perfection of the self is the true and only purpose of society. In 1941 Columbia University held the 'Conference on Science, Philosophy, and Religion in Their Relation to the Democratic Way of Life', with the aim of ascertaining whether modern democratic systems had any justification in science, philosophy or religion. Howard Selsam comments that the Conference:

> ... expressed as the *common factor in its viewpoints* insistence on "the dignity and worth of the human personality." "World reconstruction," the Conference report said, "must take this principle as its basic postulate. Any theoretical derogation from the respect due to the human personality, like any political or economic use of one person as a tool in the hands of others, tends to break down the whole structure of civilized life, and is in itself a negation of one of the most significant aspects of human culture and civilization."[175]

Economist Alexander Lovedey, who at one time worked at the League of Nations Secretariat, writes:

> Individuals are equal not in their faculties or in their utility as means by which some end may be achieved, but as an end in themselves. Society is concerned with the life and functioning of all its members and for that life and functioning the individual must enjoy adequate freedom. ... The test of right must be life; the life of the individual; of the individual as an end in himself.[176]

Martin Buber meanwhile writes:

> Not before a man can say "*I*" in perfect reality – that is, finding himself – can he in perfect reality say "*Thou*" –

---

[175] As cited in Selsam, Howard (1943) *Socialism and Ethics* New York: International Publishers, p.203. Emphasis in original.

[176] Lovedey, Alexander (1950) *The Only Way: A Study of Democracy in Danger* London: William Hodge & Co., p.4

that is, to God. ... He who ceases to make a response ceases to hear the Word.

... It is not radicality that characterizes man as separated by a primal abyss from all that is merely animal, but it is his potentiality. If we put him alone before the whole of nature then there appears embodied in him the character of possibility inherent in natural existence and which everywhere else hovers round dense reality only like a haze.[177]

Ernst Cassirer writes:

All that which befalls man from without is null and void. His essence does not depend on external circumstances; it depends exclusively on the value he gives to himself.[178]

Lewis Mumford quotes Tolstoy as having said:

Every man bears within himself the germs of every human quality[179]

Hence it is the duty of the state to unlock and develop the full potential of this 'germ' and make it grow like a sturdy tree. Indeed only a state or society can bring this about. In Mumford's words:

To create a man of truly human dimensions, one needs the co-operation of a universal society ...[180]

Nicolas Berdyaev writes on the subject of the relation between individual and society:

---

[177] Buber, Martin (1947) *Between Man and Man* (trans. Ronald Gregor Smith) London: Kegan Paul, p.43, 45, 77-8 (quotation marks added for clarity). Of course this truth emerged from the 'haze' some 1400 years ago, but we Muslims are guilty of not having passed it onto others. Indeed, we ourselves hid the truth behind religion's shroud like it was 'non-existent, not even mentioned' (Qur'an 76:1).
[178] Cassirer, Ernst (1944) *An Essay on Man: An Introduction to a Philosophy of Human Culture* 1972 reprint, New Haven: Yale University Press, p.7
[179] Mumford, citing Tolstoy, *The Conduct of Life*, p.254
[180] Op. cit. p.275

Man, human personality is the supreme value, not the community. ... Personality is connected with memory and certitude; it is linked with the whole of a man's fate, and with his whole life history. ... Every personality has its own world. Human personality is the potential of all, all world thought, all world history. ... Of all the forms of slavery to which man is liable the greatest importance attaches to the slavery of man to society. ... it is difficult for him to set his freedom in opposition to the despotic claims of society, because the social hypnosis, through the lips of sociologists of various schools of thought, convinces him that he has received this very freedom from society and society alone. Society, so to speak, says to man: You are my creation; everything that is best in you has been put there by me, and therefore you belong to me and you ought to give your whole self back to me. ... [Personality] is not part of society ... As a personality, the 'I' never enters into society as a part into the whole, as an organ into an organism.[181]

Berdyaev finds it strange that the individual, who himself is the creator of society, should also allow himself to become wholly subordinated to it. Hence he also writes:

It is a question of fixing the scale of values. Not only is the existence of the state not the highest value, but even the existence of the world, of this objectivized world, is certainly not the highest value. The death of one man, of even the most insignificant of men, is of greater importance and is more tragic than the death of states and empires. ... Liberation from slavery is in the first place liberation from all will to power, from all power as a right. The right of power belongs to no-one. Nobody has the right to power but a burdensome obligation to power as an organic function for the protection.[182]

Professor Cassirer writes on the same subject:

Man cannot find himself, he cannot become aware of his individuality, save through the medium of social life. But to him this medium signifies more than an external determining force. Man, like the animals, submits to the rules of society but, in

---

[181] Berdyaev, Nicolas (1943) *Slavery and Freedom* London: G. Bles/Centenary Press, p.28, 40, 102, 103
[182] Op. cit. p.144, 150

addition, he has an active share in bringing about, and an active power to change, the forms of social life.[183]

In a state that doesn't recognise the value of an individual (and in line with what we have already observed), we find that though it may well provide for the individual, this is ultimately done only in the interest of the state (since all the state really wants is to improve individual working capacity and thus productivity); and at the same time, the individual becomes like an animal or a machine, leading a life of blind obedience to the state, and his will is crushed. In such a situation, the self can never become actualised. In order to perfect the self, it is imperative to both improve physical capacity and nurture a strong will. Hence the psychologist Wilhelm Stekel states:

> Whenever will and capacity harmonize we have the picture of a strong personality.[184]

We can see clearly that Western thinkers of the modern age are beginning to acknowledge the value both of the physical human being and his personality.

These are the foundations upon which the Qur'anic system of *Rabbubiya* is based, and these foundations also provide the incentive for its establishment. Neither are these mere abstract concepts that people cannot relate to, nor is there any doubt as to their practical implications. The results of following the programme can be seen and felt, and they become the solid proof of the system's veracity. At this point we should also reiterate that the higher purpose of the Divine system of sustenance is not just to meet the physical needs of people. Indeed, meeting physical needs is only a rudimentary and superficial aim. From the Qur'anic perspective this is only a step in the direction of life's true purpose, which is to develop and perfect the self, and this can be achieved only by enacting the principle of universal sustenance. Caird has written on this point:

---

[183] Cassirer, *An Essay on Man*, p.223. Further details on the relationship between the individual and the state can be found in on of my lectures which was published by *Tolu-e-Islam* in December 1974.

[184] Stekel, Wilhelm (1943) *Peculiarities of Behavior: Wandering Mania, Dipsomania, Cleptomania, Pyromania and Allied Impulsive Disorders* (trans. James Samuel Van Teslaar) New York: Liveright, Vol. II p.325-6. Emphasis in original.

If there is an escape from selfish isolation when the individual identifies himself with the larger unity of the family, or again, if his spiritual life is still more expanded and enriched when his happiness is implicated with the welfare and progress of the wider organism of the state, then most of all will the individual nature become enlarged when the love of kindred and of country expands into an affection yet more comprehensive, the love of humanity, and the life and happiness of the individual becomes identified with the spiritual life and perfection of the race. ... To be personally interested in the moral progress of the race, or in the welfare of men and nations connected with us by no bond save the bond of common humanity would, to many men otherwise good and virtuous, seem but a fantastic cosmopolitanism, at best a humanitarian enthusiasm which only exceptional natures can be expected to feel. Nevertheless it is the indication of a true moral progress when nationality has ceased to be the limit of individual sympathy, when the oppression or degradation of nations however remote begins to appeal to us with a sense of personal injury; or when, as has sometimes happened in modern times, the story of a great act of cruelty or injustice done to a single human soul breaks down for the moment the barrier of national and individual exclusiveness, and evokes from all lands a cry as of pain and indignation for a universal wrong. In such incidents there is a witness to the capacity of a universal life which every human spirit contains, and to the slow advance of mankind towards that ideal of goodness which all Christians have recognised in One who loved all men with a love more intense than the love of kindred and country, and who offered up life itself a sacrifice for the redemption of the world from evil.[185]

In other words, establishing a Qur'anic system of *Rabbubiya* requires conviction both in this 'universal life' and in the permanent values as a means to this destination. In short, the aim of the Divine system is not merely to manage the economy, but to make this management a part of the path to a higher goal.

Note that so-called 'economic management' or 'distribution' in Qur'anic terms does not literally entail making everyone live in exactly the same way. Humans are not to be treated exactly alike, as though they were prisoners, receiving the exact same nourishment, the same clothes, the same living quarters and the same furniture. This type of

---

[185] Caird, John (1880) *An Introduction to the Philosophy of Religion: The Croall Lecture for 1878-79* Glasgow: James Maclehose, p.279-80

'equality' or uniformity is obviously a hindrance to individuality and creativity, and indeed destroys all that is beautiful in human life. Russell aptly comments:

> There is justice where all are equally poor as well as where all are equally rich, but it would seem fruitless to make the rich poorer if this was not going to make the poor richer. The case against justice is even stronger if, in the pursuit of equality, it is going to make even the poor poorer than before.[186]

The Qur'an's purpose is to give humanity as much freedom as possible, and since the prerequisite of authentic freedom is to be free of anxiety, the Qur'an makes it the responsibility of the state to provide for the needs of all people. The implication of this (insofar as everybody has individual taste in general) is to allow for variety, i.e. there are no restrictions placed on the choices that people might make for the things that they need. The only exception to this rule would be the things that are prohibited in the Qur'an. Interestingly, the term *halal* (permissible) appears alongside the word *tayyab* (good or pleasant) in the Qur'an. This means that the Qur'an places special emphasis on the protection of the right of individual taste. Furthermore it emphasises a particular feature of heaven:

> They will abide in all that their souls have ever desired. 21:102

The above verse makes it clear that what we get in heaven will be down to our own individual taste. A 'heaven' that fails to account for individual tastes and preferences is really more like a hell.

Communism versus Islam

Before we end, let us remind ourselves that communism is an entire way of life, although it cannot be denied that economics is central to it. Islam is also a way of life, but it does not make economics its central subject. Rather it pervades every other aspect of human life as well.

---

[186] Russell, Bertrand (1949) *Authority and the Individual* 2010 reprint, London: Routledge Classics, p.61. (*Authority and the Individual* was originally part of a series of radio broadcasts titled *The Reith Lectures*, produced by the BBC (1948-49)).

Communism as an ideology is thus totally opposite to Islam's philosophy of life. Hence it is clear that any advocate of communism cannot ever be a Muslim, and no Muslim can be a communist. Any surface similarities between communism and Islam do not make the two the same. To believe otherwise is a misconception. Islam is a unique system of life and there is no better alternative. Nor can Islam compromise with any other system.

CHAPTER 9
Conflict

The Messenger Muhammad was sent with the Qur'an in order to establish the system of Islam and to invite the whole world to adopt it. He was born in a society that was based entirely on manmade law and so there was inequity and corruption everywhere (30:41). Under these conditions the invitation to Islam was nothing short of a call for a major revolution. The Messenger's earliest addressees were highly successful merchants of the tribe of Quraish who worked in all seasons (106:1-2). These people had mixed their business with their religion. The Quraish at the time were the proud custodians of the Ka'bah in Makkah, and they commanded much respect in their society. The situation was such that whilst no ordinary person was safe from robbers and bandits in the deserts, the Quraish could go anywhere without any fear of harassment. The Quraish merchants were also the chiefs of the land. As it is, political, economic, and religious forces are so powerful that they each have the capacity to strangle humanity. Thus we can imagine how tyrannical, oppressive and arrogant these forces become when they are combined. This was the state of the Quraish when the Messenger began preaching the lesson of equality, i.e. that every human is born equal and is equally worthy of respect.

The Messenger's revolutionary message

The Messenger invited people to join a way of life in which no one has the right to rule another. All human beings would be subject to only one law, one which is not manmade but which is ordained by the Almighty. It would no longer be permissible for anyone to pile up their wealth and thus acquire all the means of production as private property, because of the principle that these have been given freely to humanity by God. Priesthood would be declared a falsehood and thus abolished, since there are no intercessors between the individual and God. The only link between the individual and God would be the *Wahi* (Revelation) that was sent via the Messenger, which would be the universal code of guidance for all.

We can imagine how adversely the Quraish must have reacted to this revolutionary invitation, as they foresaw the consequences that a Divine system would have on their present society. At first they didn't take the threat very seriously. Some suggested that the Messenger was a madman. Others said he was under a spell. Others still said such ideas were mere (idealistic) poetry which would be forgotten with time, and thus there was no need to pay any attention to them. It was only when the Messenger gained a following and the early implications of the system became apparent that the Quraish sat up and took notice. Thereafter they began a campaign against the Messenger, and this campaign intensified as his movement gained momentum. The campaign reached its zenith at around the time of the Hijrah (the Messenger's emigration to Madinah, at that time called Yathrib). At the time, all the forces of the land were closing in on him. The Quraish had wealth, power, influence and armies at their disposal. They also had full control of the Ka'bah and were the chieftains of the land. Against them was a tiny band of people comprised of the poor, who had no influence and no force of power. It had taken the Messenger thirteen long years to rally just these few in his cause. It seems that only a tiny minority of people from the Quraish had understood the import of the Messenger's invitation and accepted it, whilst the vast majority had become vehemently opposed to it. The Messenger's enemies intended to find any means necessary to destroy the movement, and it was in view of this fact that he and his companions left the area and sought a better environment in which to introduce the Divine system in practice. This marks the commencement of the Hijrah. There is no doubt that circumstances had become unbearable in Makkah, but even so, having to leave the land of their ancestors, their homes, community, livelihood and everything that was dear to them, and travelling to a place in which their future was uncertain, was very difficult for them. If they had anything at all in their favour, it was their conviction that the cause for which they had given up everything was based on truth, that it was bound to succeed, and that it was worth the struggle. Of course even having this kind of conviction required much courage. It was a movement unlike any before in history. It would abandon the ancient traditions that its people had clung to for centuries, and replace them with values that they had never enacted before. They were about to create a new society. They had a 'conviction in the unseen' – that is, they trusted in the long-term implications of Qur'anic values. Again this required determination and courage. Such were the circumstances of the early Muslim period.

Reassurances

During this period, this small and weak society was in need of much encouragement to keep up its morale. If we look at the brief surahs (chapters) at the end of the Qur'an, we can see the full picture of the struggle. At one place the Quraish are told that their military might, wealth and power have intoxicated them and they think they are invincible; but that they should remember the fate of their powerful adversary, the Yemen 'Army of the Elephant'.[187] They had plotted against the Arabs, but their plans had come to naught and they were totally destroyed (105:5). In another verse the new society is told not to fear, but to persevere and establish the Divine system of sustenance (87:1). The Messenger's people were assured of God's support and were promised that their efforts would bring them success (110:1). With the establishment of the system, their sustenance and indeed abundance of resources would be guaranteed (108:1-3).

The Almighty also reassured them that the Quraish were headed to their doom. The Qur'an states that whilst the exploitative system of the Quraish thrived on the blood of the poor, it would soon be burned down along with those who ruled over it (104:1-9), and that nothing the Quraish had amassed in terms of wealth would save them (111:1-5). They were about to witness for themselves the consequences of living a life of falsehood (102:1-8). They were guilty of restricting the God-given resources (i.e. diverting the course of the local rivers), thereby depriving the poor of much-needed water for their crops and

---

[187] **Translators' note:** (Adapted from M. Asad's introduction to the 105th surah): The 'Army of the Elephant' alludes to the Abyssinian campaign against Makkah in the year 570 of the Christian era. At that time Yemen was ruled by the Abyssians, and Abrahah, their Christian viceroy, built a cathedral at Sana, with the intention of diverting the annual Arabian pilgrimage from the Kabah to the new cathedral. When this attempt failed he led a vast army (including some war elephants) to Makkah in a bid to destroy the Kabah. This terrifying army, the like of which the Arabs had never seen before, inspired the designation of that year as 'the Year of the Elephant'. Abrahah's army was totally destroyed, probably (according to historical sources) by an extremely virulent outbreak of either smallpox or typhus.

general living (107:1-7). Elsewhere the Qur'an emphatically states that there was no need for the new *jamaat* to fear for the future, since, it was only a natural law that:

> And, behold, with every hardship comes ease: / Indeed, with
> every hardship comes ease! 94:5-6

Thus God assured them of a bright future (93:4). They were asked to take the workings of nature, in which daylight always follows the night, as a sign (92:1-2); how the sun fills the world with its light (91:1); and how this light spreads far and wide (93:1-2). If the new Muslims feared the enemy, then the best course of action was for them to draw nearer to God and His Divine system. They would soon see how God would protect them from evil forces (113:1-3, 114:1-4). Their apprehension was understandable to some extent, since they were about to set up a system that had never been tried among them before, and they were perhaps uncertain that they would receive what was promised to them. In fact, they were told, this was not the first time that the world had witnessed the advent of the Divine system. It had been introduced countless times before. The Messenger's people were told to look at history and consider what had happened to previous oppressive societies that resembled the Quraish. All of them without exception had met their end. Likewise they were told to consider the fate of those who had brought the Message and established the Divine system before. History had recorded its verdict in their favour. Hence the Messenger's people were assured of the same success (103:1-3). Hence this movement for a Divine system was not really 'new' at all. Noah invited his people to the Divine system, and similarly Jesus made his invitation through his sermons at the Mount of Olives. The same movement was initiated at the Mount of Sinai under Messenger Moses' leadership, and the same legacy was now in the hands of the new Muslims under the leadership of Messenger Muhammad. God reminded them that whenever and wherever in the past the invitation to the truth had been made, those in power had opposed it and said:

> 'Richer [than you] are we in wealth and in children, and [so]
> we are not going to be made to suffer!' 34:35

God asked them to look at the ruins and other archaeological evidence left behind by former civilisations, and to consider what had happened to them all in the end. Compared with the Quraish, these civilisations were mightier, with larger populations and greater abundance of resources (30:9-10). As an example, some of these nations went to the extent of building fortresses in the mountains, believing that these buildings would always offer them protection (26:128-9). They lived in areas with plentiful natural resources, such as springs, forests and the means of cultivation (26:147-9). But since they were also creating economic inequities, every aspect of their lives was also unstable. They were creating chaos from falsehood (53:52). As a result, the edifice of their respective societies fell down (26:158).

> Those before them did also plot [against God's Way]: but God took their structures from their foundations, and the roof fell down on them from above; and the Wrath seized them from directions they did not perceive. 16:26

The outstanding characteristic of all these societies was their obsession with immediate gains, and their lack of long-term vision. No matter how progressive and attractive these societies may have seemed, their time was always limited. They soon vanished from the earth like a field mowed to the ground (10:24).

> And how many populations have We destroyed, which indulged in their life [of ease and plenty]! Now those habitations of theirs, after them, are deserted, all but a [miserable] few [remain]! And indeed We alone are their heirs! 28:58 (see also 28:78)

The fate of past nations

We have already mentioned that the same invitation had come from every messenger including Moses and Jesus. The new Muslims were given the example of numerous nations that had failed to change their ways. These include the people of Noah (11:38-44, 23:33, 26:120, 54:9-13); the tribe of 'Ad to whom the Prophet Hud was sent (26:139, 41:16, 46:26, 89:6); the people of Sheba who had strayed from the Divine system some time after Solomon's death (34:16); the nation of Midyan whose Messenger was Shoaib (26:189, 29:37); and the ancient Egyptians under the tyrannical rule of Pharaoh (43:51, 54:44) and Qaroon (Korah) (28:76, 39:49, 40:83, 41:50) to whom Moses was sent. Each of these nations failed to heed the warnings of their respective Messengers and thus all were destroyed in accordance with the Divine law of *mukafat* (requital) (65:8). They persisted for a while, but the consequences of their false way of life eventually caught up with them; and even with all their wealth and power, they were unable to prevent their destruction. The revolution of God overthrew them. They fell and were unable to stand again (51:45). Each of these nations had believed that they possessed great dignity and self-respect, but they were eventually disgraced (29:25). Indeed they were lost in history (29:40, 53:54). Eventually all that remained of them were stories and legends (23:44) that together served as a warning to others not to make the same mistakes (51:37).

The new Muslims were encouraged to travel and verify these facts for themselves (30:42, 35:44, 40:21). If they looked, they would find plenty of evidence of these nations' former glory and subsequent destruction (22:45, 46:25, 53:54).

In light of the examples we have listed above, the members of the new *jamaat* were asked: could their opponents, the Quraish, really expect to escape the grip of God? Was their unjust economic system immune to the law of requital? The Quraish were indeed deluded if they thought this was the case:

> Or do they think – they who do evil deeds – that they can escape Us? Poor indeed is their judgment! 29:4

The Quraish were short-sighted. They failed to see that any system based on miserliness invariably has the same outcome:

> And they should not think – they who niggardly cling to all that God has granted them out of His bounty – that this is good for them: nay, it is bad for them. 3:180

A doomed way of life

These people, states the Qur'an, stealthily prey upon the earnings of others, and they devise laws designed expressly to legitimise this thievery (9:67). But they don't understand that this will inevitably lead to their fall from grace.

> Indeed, God does not love any of those who, full of self-conceit, act in a boastful manner; / [nor] those who are niggardly, and bid others to be niggardly, and conceal whatever God has bestowed upon them out of

His bounty; and so We have readied shameful suffering for all who thus deny the truth. 4:36-7

Say: 'Those who invent a lie against God will never prosper.' 10:69

Do then those who devise evil [schemes] feel secure that God will not cause the earth to swallow them up, or that the Wrath will not seize them from directions they little perceive? 16:45

No matter how well these societies establish themselves, and no matter how clever their contingency plans to forestall disaster, they cannot persist, as this would contravene Divine law. In the words of Briffault:

[A society] in which disregard of right is habitual and accepted, inevitably deteriorates and perishes. However much the individual may temporarily benefit by iniquity, the social organism of which he is a part, and the very class which enjoys the fruits of that iniquity, suffer inevitable deterioration through its operation. They are unadapted to the facts of their environment. The wages of sin is death, by the inevitable operation of natural selection.[188]

The Qur'an warned that all the scheming of the Quraish could not save them from God's universal law (8:59, 24:57, 29:22, 34:5, 34:38). They couldn't escape it (29:4) and they couldn't do anything to obstruct it (52:8). The Divine revolution had been decreed and nothing could stop it.

Those of a selfish mentality do not oppose the Divine revolution merely with words; they are so wicked that they actively try to make life difficult for the *jamaat*. They insult or mock the believers in an attempt to put off anyone who might otherwise join the *jamaat*, and also to compel the existing believers to leave it. The aim is to divert the believers from their objective. At this point it becomes imperative for the members of the *jamaat* to protect themselves from these tactics, to evade them, and to keep forging ahead with their own program. Hence the Messenger was told:

---

[188] Briffault (1919) *The Making of Humanity*, p.262

> And the Hour is surely coming [when this will be manifest]. So [O Muhammad] overlook [any human faults] with gracious forgiveness. 15:85 (see also 15:3, 43:89, 52:45, 54:6, and 70:42)

God stated in no uncertain terms that the Divine revolution must and will come to pass, and that none could prevent it. The Quraish were making every effort to distract the Messenger's people from their mission. Hence the best recourse for the *jamaat* at that point was to avoid them.

> And endure with patience whatever people may say [against you, O Muhammad], and avoid them with a comely avoidance. 73:10

> And leave Me alone [to deal] with those who deny the truth – those who enjoy the blessings of life [without any thought of God] – and bear with them for a little while. 73:11 (see also 68:44 and 74:11)

> And you shall certainly know the truth of it (all) after a while. 38:88

Elsewhere the Qur'an states:

> Then turn away from them, and you shall incur no blame 51:54

> Endure then, with patience [all that the rejecters may say] – always remembering that no one but God gives you the strength to endure adversity – and do not grieve over them, and neither be distressed by the false arguments which they devise / For indeed, God is with those who are conscious of Him and do good! 16:127-8

Again it is stated:

> And extol His glory at night, and at the time when the stars retreat [i.e. keep working through the period of darkness and remain united] 52:49

> And pay no heed to anyone whose heart We have rendered neglectful of all remembrance of Us 18:28

According to the Divine law of requital, there is a brief period of time between an action and its consequence. When we sow a seed, a period of time passes before we see it grow and produce fruit. The period of time between action and consequence is termed the law of 'respite'. The same law comes into effect whenever steps are taken to establish the Divine system of sustenance.

Law of respite

It was during this period of 'respite' that the members of the *jamaat* were instructed by the Almighty not to allow themselves to be caught up in the schemes of their foes, but to remain focused on their goal at every stage. Since the results of their efforts did not immediately become manifest, the believers were constantly reminded not to become disheartened or impatient. The revolution was bound to succeed, but only in due course, and the results would become apparent step by step, almost imperceptibly, just as a plant grows and blossoms before our eyes. This is what the Qur'an means by a conviction in the 'unseen', i.e. the conviction that the system we put into action must bear fruit. Hence the *jamaat* are told that they need not waste their energy arguing with those who have no faith in the system. Such people would be dealt with in accordance with the dictates of Divine retribution:

> Hence, leave Me alone with those who deny this tiding. We shall bring them low, step by step, without their perceiving how it has come about. / For, behold, though I may give them rein [respite] for a while, My subtle scheme is exceedingly firm! 68:44-5

The incredulous Quraish believed that the idea of giving away one's wealth in order to achieve prosperity both on earth and in the hereafter was utter madness. They were given the reply:

> And soon you will see, and they [who presently mock you] will see / which of you was afflicted with madness. 68:5-6

The believers (*momineen*) were assured that they had nothing to fear, since Divine retribution was surrounding the enemy on all sides:

> But all the while God encompasses them [the rejecters] without their being aware of it. 85:20

The Divine law can neither be weakened by the grand schemes and falsehoods that the rejecters might devise; nor can the passage of time diminish this law and make it irrelevant to the age. This is because the Divine law is protected and impervious to the effects of time.

> Nay, this is a Glorious Qur'an, / (Inscribed) in a Preserved Tablet! 85:21-2

As for those who were proud and arrogant because of their material successes, God told the believers:

> Leave Me alone [to deal] with him 74:11

They believed that they would continue to prosper and become ever-richer:

> Yet is he greedy, that I should add (yet more); 74:15

But such people would never have their way.

> No, indeed he knowingly, stubbornly sets himself against Our messages / Soon will I visit him with a mount of calamities! 74:16-17

Whilst the Quraish failed to take the warnings seriously, they were actually headed towards their own destruction:

> Behold, this is indeed a word that distinguishes between truth and falsehood, / and is no idle tale. 86:13-14

The Quraish were conspiring against the Messenger's people, but this had not escaped God's notice (86:15-16). It was only a matter of time before the consequences of their actions would catch up with them (86:17). The Quraish didn't realise that they were being watched (96:14). God warned that if they did not mend their ways they would bring destruction upon themselves (96:15-18). He gave them a period of respite (7:183, 16:61, 35:45) to give them a chance to change. Of course this was a limited period; and once it passed, nothing would prevent their annihilation (34:30). The Messenger was hence told:

> But God did not choose to chastise them when you [O Prophet] were still among them, nor would God chastise them when they [might still] ask for forgiveness. 8:34

Eventually the Messenger left Makkah for Madinah, marking the point at which the Quraish had no hope of redeeming themselves. The tables were turned, and they would soon discover what happens to those who wilfully withhold the means of production that are given freely by God (68:12-16). The wealth they hoarded would offer them no security or protection (69:28, 92:11, 111:2). Their destruction was inevitable (70:17). Their death (figuratively speaking) would surround them on all sides. In fact theirs would be a fate worse than death, for they would live to see their humiliation (14:17). At this stage they would be abandoned even by friends and loved ones.

> For on that Day you will see all who were lost in sin linked together in fetters, / clothed in garments of black pitch, with fire veiling their faces. 14:49-50

> Then can they who devise evil schemes ever feel sure that God will not cause the earth to swallow them, or that suffering will not befall them without their knowing where it came from? / or that He will not take them to task [suddenly] in the midst of their comings and goings without their being able to elude [Him]? 16:45-6

Wrong impressions

When the Messenger's opponents were warned about the period of respite, they mocked him and accused him of fear-mongering. They asked him: 'When will our promised [destruction] come?' (27:71) Of course giving them a response was futile. Instead the Messenger asked his people not to allow themselves to be upset by the derisive remarks of the Quraish (27:70). God's promise was true, and was bound to be fulfilled; hence the Messenger's people were told to have patience and not weaken their resolve (30:60).

> Those who behave arrogantly on the earth without any right, these will I turn away from My Messages: for even if they see

all the Signs, they will not believe in them; and though they may
see the way to redeem themselves, they will not adopt it; but if
they see the way of error, that is the way they will adopt. For
they have rejected Our Messages, and have remained
heedless of them. 7:146

The Quraish had created a system that was designed to maintain
inequity in society, but this very scheme would lead to their downfall.
God's law of requital has always acted to restore balance, without
exception. If anyone has any doubts about this, said the Almighty, then
they should review history and ask themselves whether a system
based on inequity has ever prospered in the long term.

[Despite the warnings, they continue] their arrogant
behaviour on earth, and their devising of evil. Yet [in the end]
such evil scheming will engulf none but its authors; and can
they expect anything but [to be made to go] the way of those
[sinners] of olden times? Thus [it is]: no change / Have they
never journeyed about the earth and seen what happened in
the end to those [of a similar mentality] who lived before their
time and were [so much] greater than they in power? God can
never be foiled by anything whatever in the heavens or on
earth, for He is all-knowing, infinite in His power. 35:43-4

We have already mentioned that for every action there is a
reaction and that this reaction will come after a certain amount of time
has passed:

Every tiding [from God] has a term set for its fulfilment: and
in time you will come to know [the truth]. 6:67

After this 'term' (of respite), the system of falsehood will be
severed at its root (108:3). Since the new Muslims were founding their
society upon truth, God guaranteed them success.

It is God who sends forth the winds, so that they raise a
cloud – and then He spreads it over the skies as He wills [i.e.
nature operates as He set it to do so], and causes it to break up
so that you see the rain issue from within it: and as soon as He
causes it to fall upon whomever He wills of His servants – lo!
they rejoice 30:48

This guarantee was decreed and put on record:

[For] God has so ordained: 'I shall most certainly prevail, I and My apostles!' Indeed, God is powerful, almighty! 58:21

God decreed that if a false system and a true system could meet the same fate, then this was as good as saying that His law of requital was not in force anywhere in the universe. According to the Qur'an, the notion that might is right is a falsehood. The outcome of these two ways of life could never be the same:

Would We treat those who have attained to faith and do righteous deeds in the same manner as [We shall treat] those who spread corruption on earth? Would We treat the God-conscious in the same manner as the wicked? 38:28 (see also 45:21)

By refusing to change their ways, the Quraish were merely awaiting their fate, just like those in history who had fallen before them.

Do they then expect (anything) but (what happened in) the days of the men who passed away before them? Say: 'You wait then: for I too will wait with you.' 10:102 (see also 18:55, 32:30, 43:89 and 52:31)

The final outcome

In the end, the final Messenger left them with the words:

O my people! Do whatever you can: I will do [my part]: soon you will know to whom the future belongs: certain it is that the evildoers will not prosper. 6:135 (see also 11:93, 11:21, 20:135 and 39:39)

The Qur'an makes similar statements:

But those who are lost in sin will never prosper. 10:17

Indeed, such rejecters of the truth will never prosper. 23:118

God does not further the works of spreaders of corruption. 10:81

Note that God proposed a scientific means by which to verify His *deen* (way of life), rather than simple debate or philosophical argument through the Messenger. The Divine system was being put to the test in history's laboratory. They needed only to wait for the result. They were asked to be patient, for the results of their efforts would not become manifest immediately; but in any case they would see the results here on earth (hence, '*soon* you will know to whom the future belongs' – 6:135).

Cutting all ties

The Quraish were too arrogant and set in their ways to heed the warnings. In fact they were so filled with hatred that they decided to eliminate the man who was extending the invitation to the Divine system, once and for all. It was at this point that the *jamaat* was advised to formally dissociate from the Quraish and to leave, since the two groups had no common ground. The Messenger took his people and parted with the words:

To you be your Way (*deen*), and to me mine. 109:6

The Messenger Muhammad was actually following in the footsteps of other Messengers in history:

[Lot said]: 'I will leave home for the sake of my Lord (*Rabb*): for He is Exalted in Might, and Wise.' 29:26

[Abraham] said: 'I will go to my *Rabb*! He will surely guide me!' 37:99

Of course those with vested interests among the Quraish could hardly be expected to tolerate the establishment of the Divine system anywhere, whether it be in their own backyard or anywhere else. They were well aware that in the long term the effects of this new way of life would be felt far and wide, and so would threaten their very existence. Hence they tried to thwart the movement with the force of the sword.

The new Muslims now had to make a decision once and for all. Either they would give up the movement, leaving the fate of humanity in evil hands, or they would fight in the name of freedom, for the good of humanity. God obviously supported their decision to fight. They were prepared, if necessary, to lay down their lives to defend the

Divine system of sustenance. This was total commitment, and in tune with the Qur'anic principle that the self can only develop by giving. Broadly speaking humans have two things they can give: the material possessions that they earn, and their God-given lives. Material possessions usually can be replaced; life cannot. Thus if a human being sacrifices his life, his self gains immortality. It follows that the decision of the new Muslims to take to the battlefield was inevitable.

Taking up of the sword

Let us briefly review those verses in the Qur'an that mention the taking up of arms (or 'iron'):

> [God does not love] those who are miserly [with God-given resources] and bid others to be miserly! 57:24

In other words (as we have mentioned earlier in this chapter), the Qur'an tells us that those who prey upon others' possessions and find ways to legitimise their thievery will find no favour with God.

> [Through this Divine guidance We gave you] a balance [with which to weigh between right and wrong] so that men might behave with equity; 57:25

In other words, God has provided Divine guidance through Revelation and hence the means to establish the Divine system of *Rabbubiya* for the benefit of humanity. The verse continues:

> ... And We provided [the ability to make use of] iron, in which there is awesome power as well as benefit for man: and [all this was given to you] so that God might mark out those who would stand up for him and His Apostle ... 57:25

Here the Qur'an raises the important point that God provides (a sword of) iron, which is both a source of power and benefit for humanity. Thus it essentially refers to iron as a means of defence. When selfish elements try to destroy the Divine system, or prevent its establishment in the first place, and neither argument nor reason convinces them to desist, and they won't respect the teachings of the Revelation, there is no choice but to take up arms against them. Furthermore, when the supporters of the Divine system decide to defend it with their lives, this becomes living proof of how much their inner selves have developed, and their total conviction in the as yet 'unseen' results of the system.

> ... even though He is beyond the reach of human perception. 57:25

The Qur'an places much stress on the 'sword' (power) and when it can justly be used. Here we will not go into further detail on this point.[189] Suffice it to say that in light of the Qur'an (and to paraphrase Dr. Iqbal), power that is not tempered by *deen* is deadlier than poison; and power that is in the guardianship of *deen* is the antidote to all poisons. We have already seen that according to the Qur'an, the meaning of *deen* is to provide material sustenance for humanity and also nurture and strengthen the self (*nafs*). This system is established in order to reflect the Divine attribute of *Rabb-il-aalameen*, and is the only means by which the self can be perfected. The Qur'an is the constitution of this system, and the 'sword' is its defence. The Qur'an is the custodian of the sword in order to ensure that it is never raised unjustly, and the sword protects the Qur'an against those who would like to see it vitiated and turned into a mere recital.

The Quraish raised its military might against the *jamaat* for a number of years, but with time the Quraish began to fall one by one.

> ... And [in the end,] the last remnant of those folk who had been bent on evildoing was wiped out. 6:45

As a result, the *jamaat* looked forward to a brighter future (39:69).

An aside

Note that in everything we have written over the last few pages (and as we will continue), our only source of reference for the history has been the Qur'an. We have not referred to either written accounts of history or oral traditions. Nor have we delved beyond any surface details of how the final Messenger went about establishing the Divine system, and how long it survived after his death. It is not that there is a

---

[189] Further details can be found in three of my publications, *Jihad* (1967), *Miraaj-e-Insaaniat* (Ascent of Humanity) (1949), and *Shahkaar-e-Rasaalat* (Masterpiece of Prophethood)

lack of relevant information to be found in these sources. A thorough study of these sources will of course reveal much of these details. However the problem is that for every instance of evidence in a book that supports a particular viewpoint, there will be at least one instance in the same book that contradicts it. None of the historical resources are in consensus on even minor details. Subsequently Muslims cannot agree on whether they should pray with their hands over their chests or over their navels, or whether they should utter the word 'Amen' loudly or in a whisper. There is endless debate over the reliability of the historical resources.

As an example, there was once a debate on television (in Pakistan) over the division of crop produce between the cultivator and the landowner (since in Pakistan the system of feudalism still exists, and landowners take a sizeable portion of the crop produce by virtue of the fact that they own the land). Those involved in the debate looked to early Muslim historical sources to try and discover how the Messenger might have handled the issue. One party argued that it was wrong to divide the crop between the cultivator and the landowner. The other party claimed it was perfectly legitimate. Both sides referred to the *hadith* (traditions and narrations of the final Messenger) to corroborate their respective positions, and both claimed that their *hadith* was more reliable and authentic than that of the other side (and in fact arguments for and against feudalism continue in Pakistan on and off to this day). This problem arises whenever *hadith* are discussed, for whatever reason. In *deen* however, the highest authority belongs to the Qur'an, which God has taken upon Himself to protect for all time, and in which there is no contradiction. It follows that this is the only truly reliable source we can refer to, and hence I have used only the Qur'an as my point of reference.

Since we accept that the Qur'an is free of contradiction, and since we have quoted solely from the Qur'an on these pages, we can safely assume that the historical events occurred as we have described them (and it goes without saying that the Messenger's mission in life was to build his society expressly in accordance with the teachings of the Qur'an). The fact is that the Messenger would never say or do anything that went against the Final Revelation. With this in mind, we can easily test any historical material in light of the Qur'an. Any material that is in agreement with the spirit of the Qur'an can be said to be correct or reliable in principle. Otherwise it should be rejected. So reliable historical sources tell us, for example, that the Messenger never hoarded any wealth; that he never left any inheritance to his family;

that he reportedly said: 'Whoever has more horses for riding than he needs, should give the surplus horse to others', and that he encouraged those travelling with surplus supplies to share them with others. The companion of the Messnger, Abu Saeed Khidri, in fact noted that the Messenger mentioned many things that ought to be shared. Reflecting upon this, the companion realised that the point of these utterances of the Messenger was to stress that the Qur'anic teaching 'keep only what you need' applied not only to money, but to every material possession.[190] But in any case, not all historical evidence is reliable. If we take the traditionalist view, according to which we are expected to accept all that has been handed down to us through the ages without question, and to even use it to interpret the Qur'an, then we can see that this is wrong, since history is open to dispute whilst the Qur'an is not. Our history was compiled at the time when Muslim civilisation was already slipping away from the Qur'an's guidance. This was the time during which the Caliphate was being turned into a monarchy and those with vested interests were taking back control of every department of human life (monarchy and capitalism are two sides of the same coin). Obviously with such leaders now at the helm, we can hardy expect them to provide an objective (let alone accurate) depiction of events during the time of the Messenger. Even during this early period, these vested interests couldn't afford to tell the truth, since it would only expose their false setup. How could the emerging tyrannical monarchy allow anyone to see that its system flew in the face of God's teachings and the practice of the Messenger? Thus it is quite reasonable to presume that the written history of the Messenger we have today is corrupted, especially in light of the fact that it was compiled in a much later period, when the Caliph was being hailed as the 'Shadow of God' in every sermon at every mosque. Obviously if the 'Shadow of God' is un-Qur'anic, then it follows that any institutes declared *halal* (permissible) under this corrupt system (in particular those of the capitalist and other vested interests) are really un-Qur'anic as well. Therefore it is not surprising that we find few signs of the Divine system of sustenance in the pages of history compiled during the period of the monarchical Caliphate. We may find a few scattered clues here and there that give us a vague idea at best.

---

[190] In my book *Shahkaar-e-Rasaalat* (Masterpiece of Prophethood) I have noted other similar examples found in numerous other narrations of the Final Messenger's companions.

Yet some people demand to see historical evidence of the Divine system of sustenance in operation during the time of the Messenger. They argue that the lack of such evidence itself proves that the Qur'anic system we have outlined in this book is a falsehood. It goes without saying that this argument is both flawed and misleading.

Others may argue that what we have outlined in this book contradicts the traditional beliefs of Muslims that have been handed down through the ages, and according to which private ownership is perfectly legitimate. But with respect, it is common knowledge that the Caliphate lasted only a short period and Muslims have been ruled by kings for over a thousand years. We have tolerated monarchy even though it is acknowledged by all that Islam totally opposes it. Likewise, the fact that capitalism has persisted in Muslim society does not mean that it is acceptable in Islam.

Note that neither history nor traditions are the final authorities on matters of *deen*. The only authority is the Qur'an, and this is why I have attempted to describe the Divine system from a strictly Qur'anic point of view. It is up to the reader to decide whether or not my findings are in accordance with its teachings.

A fundamental objection

Now we come to an issue which, if not adequately addressed, has the potential to raise unsettling questions in the mind. We might ask: If hoarding and private acquisition is forbidden in the Divine system, then what becomes of precepts such as *sadaqaat* and *zakaat* in the long term, or the commands to take care of orphans, poor relatives, the weak and vulnerable sections of society, and the poor? Indeed, what of the laws of inheritance? Will these teachings, all of which appear frequently and are given much attention in the Qur'an, not become obsolete? Does the fact that these teachings are preserved in the Qur'an not suggest that God does allow private acquisition and hoarding after all? This question is important, and so we must weigh up the facts carefully.

First of all we should bear in mind God's claim that had the Qur'an not come from Him, but from some other source, then it would have contained contradictions (4:82). Thus if we take the established practices of any (Muslim) society or system *in toto*, and find that they conflict even slightly with the Qur'an's teachings, then it can be safely said that the society does not reflect the spirit of the Qur'an. A society can only be said to be Islamic if it is in total harmony with the Qur'an.

The Qur'an completely forbids the hoarding of wealth. Nowhere do we find a single verse that denotes otherwise. With this in mind, can we justify the claim that we are permitted to hoard as much as we like and then give a small fixed amount as *zakaat* in order to sanctify it?[191] Does this practice really accord with Qur'anic teachings? Obviously it does not. It contradicts the Book that claims to never contradict itself. For an example of how the Qur'an has been misinterpreted, we should take a look at the narrations that have been fabricated for the purpose. In the Qur'an there is a verse that states:

> But as for all who lay up treasures of gold and silver and do not spend them for the sake of God – give them the tiding of grievous suffering [in the life to come] 9:34

The next verse states that the hoarded wealth of such people will be melted in the fires of Hell and used to brand them (9:35).

Hence, according to the Qur'an, those who hoard their wealth are destined for Hell. This verse alone is sufficient to show that the traditional understanding of *zakaat* is completely wrong. According to the traditional view, we can hoard as much as we wish, but if we give 2.5% of it annually to charity, then this makes the rest of our wealth *halaal* (permissible). According to one *hadith*:

> Ibn-e-Abbas says that when this verse [9:34] was revealed to the Messenger, the believers were confounded. They became heavy-hearted.[192] Umar Ibn Khattab said to them, 'I will take your troubles away and ease your hardship.' Thereupon Umar went to the Messenger and beseeched him: 'Oh Messenger of God! This verse has troubled your Companions.' The Messenger replied: 'This is why God has made *zakaat* obligatory, so that the rest of your wealth will become purified; and [similarly], inheritance laws have been made obligatory to ensure that those you leave behind after death will receive your

---

[191] **Translators' note:** One of the root meanings of the word *zakaat* is 'purify'; hence, the implication (in traditional Islam) that giving some of it away as *zakaat* may in some way cleanse or sanctify this hoarded wealth.

[192] **Translators' note:** Numerous Qur'anic verses testify that the believers' hearts would never become 'heavy' at hearing a Divine command. See 8:2, 13:28, 16:22, 22:35, 23:60, 48:4, 58:22. In fact it is the hypocrites whose hearts became heavy at hearing Divine commands (e.g. 47:24, 9:125).

wealth.' Ibn-e-Abbas says that upon hearing the Messenger's reply, Umar happily declared: 'God is great!'[193]

It is quite clear from the tone of the above passage that it was invented to protect capitalist interests. The capitalism thriving in today's Muslim world owes its very existence to *hadith* of this type, in spite of the clear injunctions of the Qur'an that oppose this position. Yet not only do modern Muslims ignore the Qur'anic injunctions, but they have also made it obligatory to accept these *hadith* as true.

Moving on, and as we have already mentioned, the Qur'an likens the establishment of the system of *Rabbubiya* to a climb up a 'steep uphill road'. We know that it is inadvisable to run up a steep hill or mountain. A climber must take his time and ascend gradually, and even then he or she will become breathless. We don't know exactly when the concept of private ownership first infected human society, but since that time it seems to have become accepted that the desire to possess is in 'human nature'. In fact, it is also commonly accepted that if the right of ownership is taken away then this diminishes the incentive to work. From a traditional religious perspective, banning private ownership (and hoarding) also makes it impossible to practice *sadaqaat* or *zakaat* ('alms giving' and 'charity' respectively), as no one will have any surplus to give away, and so the opportunity of doing a good (religious) deed will be lost. Hence, so say the critics, any system that abolishes private ownership is doomed to fail and is impractical in any case. As such they are not wholly wrong. If we are told that tomorrow we must voluntarily give up our property and possessions or they will be taken from us, then indeed this is unrealistic. After all, in the 'selfish' systems that we live in, every individual accepts that he and his offspring must have possessions in order to survive. In times of hardship no one will take care of him and so he must depend upon himself – i.e. his own savings. When this is the accepted norm, we can understand why the idea of giving up possessions would seem totally unrealistic and impractical.

This is why the Qur'an adopts a gradualist approach to reforming human society to bring it in line with its ideal. On one hand, as we have already shown, it brings about a psychological change in the people; and on the other, it creates an atmosphere in which the individual feels

---

[193] Abu Daud, citing from *Mishqaat*, chapter: *'Kitab al- Zakaat.'* Urdu translation (date unknown), Karachi: Noor Muhammad Kar Khanna Tajaarat, p.309-10 (Publication details are as provided in Parwez's original text)

increasingly secure in the knowledge that giving away his possessions will not put him in danger. All Qur'anic instructions on subjects such as alms-giving and charity, trade, lending, borrowing, inheritance, etc. may be considered part of the first phase. As society begins to change and new circumstances and challenges arise, the laws pertaining to the first phase are obviously no longer applicable, and they effectively recede into the background. The fact is that these laws are conditional, i.e. they are concerned with the specific condition of a given society.

For example, the punishment for adultery is clearly ordained in the Qur'an (24:2). The underlying principle is to create a culture in which adulterous behaviour gradually decreases and then becomes unheard of. Obviously in such circumstances there will no longer be any need to enforce the Qur'anic punishment for adultery, since this behaviour itself will have become outmoded, although of course the law itself will remain preserved in the Qur'an, just in case. As another example, the Qur'an states that anyone who wilfully breaks a promise should feed ten impoverished people, or clothe them, or free a slave (5:89). We know that the Qur'an abolishes the institute of slavery, but since slavery still existed during the time of the final Messenger, these instructions were designed to help integrate the existing slaves into society. Once the existing slaves were integrated into society, and the acquisition of replacements was banned, then the institute of slavery was automatically abolished. From that point onward, the Qur'anic option to free a slave to atone for a broken promise no longer applied. In the same way, if a society becomes so self-sufficient that there is no longer a poor or needy citizen to be found, then the Qur'anic option to feed an impoverished person no longer applies. At this point it will be left to the administration to decide a suitable penalty for a broken promise. As yet another example, if an administration makes arrangements to provide loans to people, then private lending will obviously become obsolete, and so the Qur'anic instructions regarding individual loans will no longer be enforced. Similarly, if an individual has nothing to leave in his estate upon death, then the laws regarding inheritance cannot be implemented. From these examples we can see that these Qur'anic injunctions are conditional; that is, they may or may not be actively in force depending upon the circumstances of a given time. In any case however these injunctions are never *abrogated*. They are conditionally *inoperative*. The Qur'anic injunction allowing the individual to use fine sand for ablution instead of water before prayer may become inoperative in a city where water is easily available, but the injunction is never abrogated, in case it becomes necessary to apply it again in the future.

Summary

In this chapter we have observed that according to the Qur'an:

1) In an Islamic society the administration is responsible for ensuring that all the needs of the people are met (and the exact means for doing so is also left up to the society in accordance with its particular circumstances)

2) No one can own anything that is surplus to his needs. The surplus – whether money or produce – must be left open for the benefit of society. (Again how this surplus is collected is left up to the society)

3) In an ideal Islamic system, the meaning of 'private ownership' will become restricted to the things that we use every day, but have neither the desire nor the need to sell. These 'private possessions' may not even remain in the hands of those who inherit them, as their needs will already be met by the system.

We can imagine that in such a society, Qur'anic laws on such matters as charity, trade and inheritance[194] will no longer be

---

[194] With regards to inheritance, the Qur'an explains in detail that merely inheriting wealth from the father (i.e. not having earned such wealth through one's own labour and effort) is a basic feature of capitalism (since it goes a long way towards creating and perpetuating the rich-poor divide). Hence the Qur'an states: 'And you devour inheritance with greed' (89:19). This verse clearly shows that according to the Qur'an, the laws relating to inheritance were applicable in the early phase of the Divine system. Given that inheritance is identified with selfishness or greed, and the Qur'an condemns it, how can we expect it to persist among people whose very *raison d'être* is to *provide*, rather than *take*, in accordance with the principle of *Rabbubiya*? In any case Muslims proudly declare (and justly so) that one of the fundamental principles of Islam is human equality. All men are born equal. There is no difference between a Brahmin (highest caste Hindu) and a Shudra (lowest caste Hindu), or a king and a peasant, and this is why there is no concept of caste and creed in Islam. And yet in practice we also accept divides in every department of human life, as though they were natural and inevitable. Hence, for example, whilst we say that the son of a man with the title 'Syed' should

applicable as such, but will forever apply to any Islamic society that is still in its early stage. As society evolves ever closer to the ideal system of *Rabbubiya*, the laws pertaining to the early phase will recede further into the background and so the system will be manifest in its full glory. It will change the world and indeed the heavens.

> One day the Earth will be changed to a different Earth, and so will be the Heavens, and (men) will be marshalled forth, before God, the One, the Irresistible 14:48

The human values of today will be replaced by God's values. When that time comes, human beings will no longer operate on principles for personal gain but will stand only for the law of *Rabbubiya*.

> A Day when (all) mankind will stand before the Sustainer of the worlds 83:6

Here we must address an important point. Looking at history we find that those individuals who gave their all for the betterment of humanity are revered and remembered throughout the ages. Neither are such individuals motivated by self-interest or personal gain, nor do they leave anything material behind. The history of the Messenger tells us that he never accumulated any wealth, and he left nothing behind in his estate. This being the case, then obviously he could not have given *zakaat* (as traditionally understood), since *zakaat* is only given annually in order to 'purify' accumulated wealth. God made the Messenger's life an example for the *ummah*; and since we know that this was the way of the Messenger, the *ummah* should follow his example, which is at any rate in accordance with the teachings of the

---

not expect to be treated differently just because the title implies he is descended from the Final Messenger's family, we never think to apply the same rule to a millionaire's son. Simply by virtue of being born in a millionaire's house, the son receives all the privileges that come with such wealth, even though he has done nothing to contribute to those millions. He can buy anything, including status, and this is perfectly accepted. How can this be tolerated, when in Islam all men are supposed to be equal regardless of birth? The Qur'anic laws on inheritance thus only apply until the Divine system of sustenance is fully established. Once this system is fully established, we will find that just as the Messenger never left anything behind as inheritance, the society that follows his example will likewise not continue the tradition of inheritance.

Qur'an. Other than the Messenger, the defining quality of any *Wali Allah* ('friend of God') is his/her selflessness; indeed, such individuals have always been celebrated for giving whatever they received to hungry and impoverished people. It is universally accepted that such selflessness is a sign of greatness. However when it is suggested that Islam teaches this as the norm, critics are quick to raise objections. Remember that Islam offers a way of life in which it becomes possible for every individual to confidently give his surplus away to help meet the needs of others. In other words it creates a community in which every single individual is a 'friend of God'. This is the reason that the Qur'an has not mentioned any special group comprising 'friends of God'. Instead it states that all *momineen* (people of conviction) are friends of God.

CHAPTER 10
Resolution

As we discussed in the previous chapter, the final Messenger (with the support of his companions) continuously struggled for a period of around 23 years before he finally succeeded in establishing a Qur'anic system which was ideal for its time, and which took human society to its peak.

Later Muslims

However later Muslims neglected the Qur'anic programme and reverted back to a way of life in which they could indulge their self-interests. In making this choice Muslims ended up just as the Qur'an had forewarned; living in hunger and fear, and in disgrace. Muslims have dwelled in this self-inflicted hell for centuries and subsequently the rest of the world is also suffering. Had Muslims remained true to the Divine programme then their legacy would have spread and encompassed the whole of humanity. In short, we would all have been spared from the problems of today.

So how did these failures occur, and what forces were responsible for resurrecting falsehood? To answer this question requires a detailed examination of history and there is insufficient room to go into it here.[195] However the immortal Qur'an makes the following pertinent statement:

> And tell them the story of the man to whom We send Our messages, but he discards them: so Satan catches up with him, and he strays. / If it had been Our Will, We should have

---

[195] A detailed examination of the subject is given in the last chapter of my book *Shahkaar-e-Rasaalat* (Masterpiece of Prophethood)

elevated him with Our messages; but he inclined to the earth, and followed his own vain desires. 7:175-6

Likewise Muslims abandoned the truth and reverted to falsehood.

His similitude is that of a dog: if you attack him, he lolls out his tongue, and if you leave him alone, he [still stubbornly] lolls out his tongue. That is the similitude of those who reject Our messages; so relate the story, that they may reflect. / Evil is the example of people who reject Our messages and wrong their own selves. 7:176-7

We should also take a look at what the Qur'an says about the laws governing the rise and fall of nations. The Qur'an provides details on many nations, but has also succinctly stated the root cause of their decline, thereby revealing the bigger picture:

Behold, you are the ones invited to spend freely in God's cause: but among you are some that are miserly. Yet any who is miserly is but miserly at the expense of his own self: For God is indeed self-sufficient, and you stand in need [of His God-given sustenance]. If you turn back [from the Path], He will cause another people to take your place, and they will not be like you! 47:38

The Qur'an has thus shown us that the overwhelming early success of Muslims was down to the Divine system which they had established for the sustenance of humanity. Once they reverted to old habits and reinstated manmade selfish systems, everything that they had accomplished was lost. Note that when the Qur'an refers to a nation's destruction, this is not a literal statement that every member of that nation is wiped from the face of the earth. In fact their destruction takes a far worse form. The nation physically remains in existence, but loses its dignity and status in the comity of nations. It is considered a 'dead' nation. Hence the Qur'an states:

[Theirs is a hellish existence] in which they will then neither die nor live. 87:13

Careful consideration of these facts will surely lead us to the realisation that this has been the plight of Muslims for centuries.

The story of Adam

The question now is: Do dead nations remain disgraced forever, or is there a way to revive them? The Qur'an replies in the affirmative. The one and only way is to wholeheartedly adopt the Divine system and thereby earn its benefits once again. As long as they do not take this step they will continue to remain in hell.

> He whom God guides, he alone is truly guided; whereas those whom He lets go astray – it is they, they who are the losers! 7:178

> ... God does not change a people's condition unless they change their inner selves; and when God wills people to suffer evil [in consequence of their own evil deeds], there is none who can avert it: for they have none who could protect them from Him. 13:11 (also 8:53)

Here we should revisit the story of Adam. The Qur'an tells us that Adam was living in heaven, where he never had to worry about his means of sustenance. Everything he needed was available in abundance. This was so that Adam could get on with working towards the greater purpose for which he was created, without socioeconomic worries getting in the way.

Adam was deceived by Satan, and subsequently the children of Adam began to pursue self-interests. They became increasingly divided due to jealousy, hatred and grudges, and became mutual enemies. Abundance turned into scarcity. Adam suffered from hunger and exposure, and he lived in fear of failing to secure his means of sustenance. Hence his former heavenly existence was left far behind. Now all his energies were spent on finding food, shelter, etc. and taking care of his offspring. He forgot the higher purpose for which he was created.

Adam seemed to be without hope,[196] and he despaired of his present existence. He had no idea what to do. God reassured him and told him that he could atone for this mistake. Adam needed only to follow His Path, and he would find himself on a fast route back to heaven. And since this heaven would be built through Adam's own

---

[196] Note that the word *Iblees* (used for Satan in the story of Adam) means despair or hopelessness.

efforts, he would never have to leave it again. It would be of Adam's own making, through his own deeds.

> For such will be the paradise which you shall have inherited by virtue of your past deeds: / fruits [of those deeds] shall you have in abundance, [and] thereof shall you partake! 43:72-3

This in short is the story of Adam according to the Qur'an, and it is likewise an analogy for the rise and fall of nations. In the period of the Messenger (when the Qur'anic programme was being implemented), Muslims were living in a heavenly existence with 'rivers of milk and honey' (47:14). Later the 'children of Adam' once again destroyed their heaven with their own hands, and again fell into despair. That state of despair is at its peak today. There is only one solution; and it is the same as the one that was given to Adam:

> We said, 'Down with you all from this [state],' [but] nonetheless, We shall send you Our Guidance: and those who follow My guidance need have no fear, and neither shall they grieve. 2:38

But the question arises: How can we reform the society of today? Where do we begin? Who will lay the foundations? This is the question that has confronted every individual who is aware of the truth, and it has been a stumbling block for many. It is important that we fully understand the issue at hand, and we can do so with the following analogy. Two farmers live in an area affected by drought, and grain is scarce. They each possess the same amount of wheat. At the time of year when farmers are supposed to cultivate the fields, one farmer chooses to grind his grain into flour to feed his family, while the other plants his grain. For a while, the first farmer and his family have food to eat, and the family of the second farmer go through hardship since they have a lack of available food. However, the following year the situation is reversed. The first farmer runs out of flour and has nothing to eat, while the second farmer not only has plenty from his newly-grown crop, but he also has enough surplus to replant more grain, thereby ensuring that his family will be taken care of during the following year as well. The first farmer obviously thought only in the short term and so he prospered only in the short term, leaving nothing for himself and his family in the long term.

> There are men who say: 'Our Sustainer! Give us (Thy
> bounties) in this world!' But they will have no portion in the
> Hereafter. 2:200 (see also 3:77)

The second farmer however was more farsighted and thus he prospered in the long term.

> And there are men who say: 'Our Sustainer! Give us good in
> this world and good in the Hereafter, and defend us from the
> torment of the Fire!' 2:201

So what was it about the second farmer that made him ignore his short-term needs even as he watched his neighbour happily feeding his family? The obvious answer is his conviction that for every seed he planted he would get back several hundred. This was his reason for ignoring his short-term needs. Had he not been utterly convinced of this outcome, he would never have planted his grain. He had conviction in the *sunnat-Allah* (lit. the 'habit of God'), i.e. His absolute natural law. The farmer had of course witnessed this process many times during his life and so he had the experience to know what to expect when he cultivated the land.

Conviction in the unseen

But what would be the case if this man had never seen this process? If someone were to simply tell him that burying the seed would magically turn it into a crop, then it would be extremely difficult for him to accept. Even if he was willing to try, those around him would call him mad and mock him and knock his confidence. Even as he was waiting for the crop to grow, he would be in a state of anxiety. But if he bore this period with patience, then with time he would receive the proof that indeed planting the seed creates an abundance of produce. This is what is termed 'conviction in the unseen'.

The believing pioneers

From the above analogy we get a good idea of what the pioneers of the Divine system come up against. The concept of life presented in the Book is not presently in operation anywhere in the world. In fact it is totally at odds with all systems currently operating in human society. Humanity in general accepts the mentality of 'taking' as a means of survival, in accordance with the demands of the intellect. The outcome of such a lifestyle is plain to see in today's inequitable world. Humanity is much like that first farmer of our analogy, who is grinding his grain into flour and feeding his family in the short term. Contrary to this, the Qur'an teaches any would-be pioneers that the secret to protecting life lies not in taking but in giving. Obviously taking will lead to immediate gain, but the gain that comes from giving does not manifest itself in the short term. Hence a *jamaat* of believers will readily try the Qur'an's experimental 'alternative' way of life, based on their conviction that it is the true way (*haqq*); and that following its programme will, in time, guarantee constructive (*tayyab*) results and so their efforts will never fail. This is their unshakeable 'conviction in the unseen'. A conviction in the unseen thus forms the very foundation of the Divine system. The later generations living under this system will get to see the result of the programme with their own eyes (9:100); but of course those who pioneered it had a conviction in the *unseen*. According to Bertrand Russell, the difference between civilised and uncivilised peoples is:

> The civilized man is distinguished from the savage mainly by *prudence*, or, to use a slightly wider term, *forethought*. He is willing to endure present pains for the sake of future pleasures, even if the future pleasures are rather distant.[197]

The Qur'an opens with the following introduction to the Divine system of *Rabbubiya*:

> All praise is due to God alone, the Sustainer of the worlds 1:2

A little later the Qur'an describes the distinctive features of the pioneers who endeavour to establish the Divine system. It states:

> This is the Book in which is guidance, let there be no doubt, for all the God conscious 2:2

In other words, the Qur'an states that there should be no anxiety about the Divine guarantee (*rayba* in the above verse means both

---

[197] Russell, Bertrand (1946) *History of Western Philosophy and its Connection with Political and Social Circumstances from the Earliest Times to the Present Day* London: George Allen & Unwin, p.33. Emphasis in original.

'doubt' and 'anxiety'). But God states that He will only guide those who are firmly convinced of the Divine system's unseen results.

[They are the ones] who believe in the Unseen ... 2:3

In the same verse the Qur'an presents two principles upon which the entire system must necessarily rest (and which we have already covered in earlier chapters):

[They] establish *salaat*,[198] 2:3

And:

[They] spend freely out of what We provide for them as sustenance. 2:3[199]

The Qur'an tells us that a close study of its practical programme will reveal the truth of what it has to offer. In addition, a proper assessment of history will reveal that the Divine programme has been offered to humanity before. Once we see the results that this programme has produced before, along with the fate of those nations that opposed it, we will become totally convinced of our potential future and immortality:

And [they are the ones] who believe in the Revelation sent to you, and sent before your time, and have the assurance of the life to come [in their hearts]. 2:4

Any *jamaat* (group) that develops this level of conviction and thereafter dedicates itself to the establishment of the Divine system is guaranteed long-term success.

It is they who follow the guidance [that comes] from their Sustainer, and it is they who will prosper. 2:5

Therefore their conviction in the unseen is the driving force behind their revolutionary movement. Accordingly the Qur'an states

---

[198] **Translators' note:** As a reminder: *Qiaam-e-salaat* is to 'establish *salaat*', i.e. the Divine system. See Chapter 8.
[199] See Chapter 6.

elsewhere that the only people receptive to God's warnings will be those who are truly aware of the difference between truth and falsehood, and who can recognise the unseen potential of the Divine law of sustenance:

> You can warn only those who are conscious of their unseen Sustainer and establish the system of *salaat* 35:18

These people are also convinced that in establishing a system designed to benefit the collective, they are in fact benefiting (and 'purifying') their own selves. The same verse thus continues:

> And whoever purifies himself does so for the benefit of his own self; and the destination [of all] is to God. 35:18

Trying times

Hence only those who have conviction in the unseen can establish the system of sustenance, but in any case their path is a difficult one. Every step is fraught with danger and may lead to self-doubt and anxiety for the new community. Hence the Qur'an addresses the pioneers of the movement with these words:

> [But] do you think that you could enter paradise without having suffered like those [believers] who passed away before you? Misfortune and hardship befell them, and so shaken were they that the Messenger, and the believers with him, would exclaim, 'When will God's succour come?' Oh, indeed God's succour is [always] near! 2:214

Hence the pioneers must have patience:

> In the case of those who say, 'Our Lord [*Rabb*] is God,' and then steadfastly pursue the right way, the angels [*malaika*][200] often descend on them [saying]: 'Fear not and grieve not, but receive the glad tidings of the Garden (of Bliss), that which you were promised! / We are your protectors in this life and in the Hereafter, where you shall have all that your souls may desire, and where you shall have all that you ask for!' 41:30-31

---

[200] **Translators' note**: *Malaika* (usually translated as 'angels' as above) are better understood as simply 'forces', since they include the forces of nature.

It goes without saying that every attempt to establish the Divine system will be met with opposition from those who habitually live off the blood of others. As we discussed in Chapter 5, the spirit of competition seems to run in our blood but it has a tendency to lead to exploitation. It is commonly said that once a lion tastes human blood it will never be satisfied with the flesh of any other animal again. The lion of course doesn't know better; but in the human world we see the disastrous consequences of this psychology every day, and our history is replete with examples of greed and exploitation.

The Qur'an warns us of the consequences of living by exploitative means as follows:

> A fire kindled by God, / which will rise over the [guilty]
> hearts 104:6-7

It is true that human beings appear to have covetousness in their hearts; that is, they envy others and would like to possess others' belongings. Thus it should hardly come as a surprise that when a group attempts to establish a system rewarding hard work and outlawing exploitative living, another group tries to rise against it. We find that capitalists and religious leaders are at the forefront of such opposition for the obvious reason that they exploit others in order to fatten themselves.

Opposition from vested interests

Capitalists will come up with rational arguments to justify their claim that this sort of system is at odds with the dictates of human nature. They follow the logic that once everybody's needs are met, and people discover that they are not allowed to keep more than they need regardless of how much they earn, there will remain no incentive to work. Mandeville thus states:[201]

> To make the society happy and people easy under the
> meanest circumstances, it is requisite that great numbers of
> them should be ignorant as well as poor. Knowledge both

---

[201] **Translators' note:** The next two citations (fn 202, 203) were originally taken (by Parwez) from EH Carr's *The New Society* (referenced below, fn 204) but we are inserting the original sources.

enlarges and multiplies our desires, and the fewer things a man wishes for, the more easily his necessities may be supplied.[202]

Townsend meanwhile writes:

The wisest legislator will never be able to devise a more equitable, a more effectual, or in any respect a more suitable punishment, than hunger is for a disobedient servant. Hunger will tame the fiercest animals, it will teach decency and civility, obedience and subjection, to the most brutish, the most obstinate, and the most perverse.[203]

Defoe's position is summed up adequately by EH Carr as follows:

In 1704 Defoe published a pamphlet entitled *Giving Alms no Charity and employing the Poor a Grievance to the Nation*. He argued that if the poor were relieved they would remain idle, or alternatively that, if they were set to work in public institutions, the private manufacturer was equally deprived of his source of labour, the conclusion – expressed in modern terms — being that they should be thrown on the labour market and allowed to starve if they failed to find a place there.[204]

Hence, according to this logic, keeping people hungry actually keeps them working day and night, and thus improves productivity. The Qur'an however states that those whose focus is on short-term gains lack true knowledge, and have little scope for improvement:

Therefore shun those who turn away from Our Message and desire nothing but the life of this world. / That is as far as their knowledge goes. Indeed your Sustainer knows best those who stray from His Path, and He knows best [about] who receives guidance. 53:29-30

---

[202] Mandeville, Bernard (1732) *The Fable of the Bees, or, Private Vices, Publick Benefits* (sixth edition) London: J. Tonson, p.328

[203] Townsend, Joseph (1786) *A Dissertation on the Poor Laws: By a Well-Wisher to Mankind* 1971 reprint, London: University of California Press Ltd., p.23, 27

[204] Carr, Edward H. (1951) *The New Society* 1957 reprint, Massachusetts: Beacon Press, p.41

The religious leaders meanwhile will issue fatwas to claim that whoever gives *zakaat* out of his capital will sanctify the rest of it, and that every man has the right to own his land, his possessions and his inheritance. There is no limit (they will say) as to how much an individual may acquire and own, nor can he be deprived of his possessions. The rich-poor divide has come from God. Any attempt to change the status quo is to go against the will of God. They believe that without this divide, without a poor class, and without estates to pass onto offspring, all the Qur'anic injunctions regarding charity, alms-giving and inheritance will become meaningless.[205] Therefore the call for universal sustenance is heretical, contrary to *deen*, and against all traditions. Most people will be silenced and/or satisfied with these arguments because they accept the ways of the world as they are at present. They are the victims of the present paradigm and can see no other way to live. Indeed, they are used to their hell and furthermore they are happy in it. Since they cannot change themselves inside, they are incapable of taking practical steps to change their world.

> [They are the ones] We have made for Hell: they have hearts that fail to understand, eyes that fail to see, and ears that fail to hear. They are like cattle, nay, more misguided: for they are heedless [of the warning]. 7:179

Indeed such people are worse than cattle, for cattle will stop consuming once their bellies are full, but the human hunger for more is insatiable. The Qur'an states that these people invent arguments against the Divine system in order to protect their vested interests. The basic premise of the Divine system is to make all resources and means of production universally available. Its goal is to make life easy and pleasant for the whole of humanity:

> O humanity! Partake of what is lawful and good on earth 2:168

But Satan seeks to divide humanity and lead people to ruin:

---

[205] **Translators' note:** This again highlights that if we accept the limited traditional meaning of the word *zakaat* as 'charity', this also falsely implies that we can or indeed *must* necessarily accept the concept of a perpetual poor class.

> And follow not Satan's footsteps: for indeed, he is your open foe / and [Satan] bids you only to do evil, and to commit deeds of abomination 2:168-9

We are warned not to naïvely accept the present realities of life as though this is God's will:

> And to attribute to God something of which you have no knowledge 2:169

Indeed, says the Qur'an, we must challenge those who would have us believe that their satanic ideas are God's decree, by demanding that they turn to the Book:

> But when they are told, 'Follow what God has revealed,' some answer, 'No, we shall follow the ways of our forefathers.' Why, even though their forefathers were devoid of reason and guidance? 2:170

According to the Qur'an, if the advocates of the Divine system remain firm in their stance in the face of all opposition, then in time God's absolute law of respite will guarantee that the constructive programme of the believers will overcome the opponents' destructive programme. This is part and parcel of the Qur'anic revolution.

Rise of the revolution

Of course the believers begin the preparations for this 'revolution' long in advance (through long-term education), but once it takes off, it takes the enemy completely by surprise.

> Those who treat their inevitable meeting with God as a falsehood are lost indeed, until all of a sudden the Hour comes upon them, and they say: 'Ah! We despair that we disregarded [the truth of it]; for they shall bear their burdens on their backs, and evil indeed are the burdens that they bear. / What is the life of this world but a play and passing delight? But best is the life in the Hereafter, for those who are conscious of God. Will you not then use your reason? 6:31-2

Once the revolution has taken off, it will be too late for the opponents to make amends. Hence the Qur'an states that our intent and focus should be to strive for restoring balance in society in accordance with the true way, before it becomes too late to turn back.

> But set your face to the only true *deen*, before there comes from God a Day which cannot be averted. On that Day men shall be divided [in two]. 30:43

At this stage the difference between the two sides will become abundantly clear from the results of their actions. The group that has rejected the truth will see the results of their rejection, whilst the group that adhered to Divine guidance and brought about balance in the society will likewise see the result of their actions as well. The opponents of the truth will be left behind and will go without (30:44).

> Those who reject [the truth] will suffer from that rejection: and those who work righteousness will have made goodly provision for themselves: / So that He may reward those who believe and work righteous deeds, out of His bounty. Indeed He does not love the rejecters. 30:44-5

This will not happen spontaneously or by accident; it is inevitable, in accordance with the Divine decree. Hence the Qur'an states:

> Would We treat those who have conviction and do righteous deeds the same as those who spread corruption on earth? Would We treat the God-conscious in the same manner as the wicked? 38:28

It would be hardly fair if the two were to share the same fate. Hence the Qur'an states:

> The blind and the seeing are not alike; / nor are the depths of darkness and the light; / nor are the [cooling] shade and the [scorching] heat: / And neither are those that are living and those that are dead [of heart] alike. God can make any that He wills to hear; but you cannot make those hear who are [dead inside like those who are dead] in graves. 35:19-22

Why then should we expect these two parties to be treated alike?

> Is then the man who believes no better than the man who is rebellious and wicked? They are not equal. 32:18

Now as for those who indulge in sinful ways – do they think that We place them, both in their life and their death, on an equal footing with those who have conviction and do righteous deeds? Poor indeed is their judgment. / God created the heavens and the earth for just ends, and in order that each soul may find the recompense of what it has earned, and none of them be wronged. 45:21-2

And never will God grant to the unbelievers a way [to triumph] over the believers. 4:141

And do not think that the rejecters are going to frustrate [God's Plan] on earth: their abode is the Fire, and it is indeed an evil refuge! 24:57 (also 8:59)

And it was due from Us to aid those who had conviction. 30:47

The Qur'an also states:

God has decreed: 'It is I and My Messengers who must prevail': for God is One full of strength, able to enforce His Will. 58:21

True success is thus only possible by adhering to Divine guidance:

He who desires might and glory [ought to know that] all might and glory belong to God [alone]. To Him all good words ascend, and it is He who exalts the righteous deed. But as for those who devise evil deeds, a terrible penalty awaits them; and all their devising is bound to come to nought. 35:10

In other words: Not only must a society have a clear understanding of the Divine principles that will bring true prosperity ('to Him all good words ascend'), but its people must act on them ('He exalts the righteous deed'). However a society that adopts falsehood and operates on selfishness and exploitation ('devise evil deeds') is destined to destroy itself.

This is the end of those who deny people their basic rights:

The last remnant of the wrongdoers was wiped out. Praise be to God, the Sustainer of the worlds (*Rabb-il-aalameen*). 6:45

All traces of falsehood will be eliminated thanks to the Sustainer's Divine decree.

> Then Praise be to God, Sustainer of the heavens and Sustainer of the earth, Sustainer of all the worlds! 45:36

His universal and absolute sovereignty – on earth and beyond – will be acknowledged by all.

> To Him be Glory throughout the heavens and the earth ... 45:37

His law is firm, dominates everything and is perfectly logical (i.e. every cause has an effect):

> ... and He is Exalted in Power, Full of Wisdom! 45:37

Hence 'God's will' means that whether we come to power, or become weak, or have a place of honour, or are disgraced, is all down to His law of *mukafat* (requital):

> Say: 'O God! Master of Power [and Rule], You grant power to whomever You will, and You strip power from whomever You will: You give honour to whomever You will, and You bring disgrace to whomever You will: in Your hand is all good. Indeed, You have the power to will anything.' 3:26

Here the law is that every action has a result which in turn has consequences which will become manifest in time:

> Every tiding has a term set for its fulfilment: and in time you will come to know [the outcome]. 6:67

This is the period of delay or 'respite', which represents the term of a nation or society before its inevitable destruction. The length of this term is determined not by random external factors but by God's law, which takes into account the strength of every positive action and that of every negative action.

> God annuls or confirms whatever He wills – for with Him is the source of all Revelation. 13:39

> For all people a term has been set: when the end of their term approaches, they can neither delay it by a single moment, nor hasten it. 10:49

No action, however large or small, is exempt from this law, and it all goes on record:

> What a record is this! It leaves out nothing, be it small or great, but takes everything into account! 18:49

> Indeed, your Sustainer's grip is exceedingly strong! 85:12 (see also 44:16 and 73:16)

Verses 22:1-7 declare that the 'Final Hour' – the ultimate outcome – is bound to come. At this time the rejecters who are presently in power and who oppose the truth will fall (14:45-52). In fact even as they begin to see the consequence of their wrongdoings they will look for ways to escape it; but they will be unable to either escape or find refuge (21:12-14, 75:11). It is at this stage that they finally will see the outcome of their actions, and the destruction it has brought them, as decreed in the Book (45:28-9). At this time they will become like a field that has been mowed down, and still and burned out like ash (21:14). They will not be missed, and it will be too late for them to turn back and make amends (44:29). This will all have occurred as a natural outcome of the law of requital. Thus the Qur'an's warnings must be taken seriously (53:60).

The Qur'an's clear and indisputable evidence helps to create a strong sense of conviction in the hearts of those who become the pioneers of the Divine system; and, as we have stated already, it is this conviction alone that can prepare them for the Divine revolution. Therefore, should any Muslim today become convinced of the veracity of the Divine system of sustenance and the Qur'anic aim to create an ideal society; and if there is no doubt in his mind that a group formed for the purpose of bringing about the Divine revolution is bound to succeed, then there is only one course of action. He must seek out other individuals who likewise possess a living conviction in these truths, and bring them together on one platform so they can work together to promote the Qur'anic invitation far and wide. At this time the world is trapped in its own self-made hell, and can see no way out of its troubles. Humanity has tried and tested every one of its manmade systems, and with each new experiment have come new problems. The whole world seems to be in a state of despair. Every time someone comes up with a new idea, humanity is filled with hope for a while that this will offer the solution we desperately seek; but sooner or later we find that our new guides are not saviours but robbers, and so we become disillusioned. Yet if any Muslim country today were to establish the Divine system and become an example for others to emulate, then rest assured it would soon lead the world; and the Adam who fell from grace and lost everything would find himself back in heaven.

At this stage it is of the utmost importance to understand that the system of *Rabbubiya* can neither be established by an individual, nor through a political party. It can only be established by a nation, one that introduces the economic principle of leaving not a single individual deprived of the basic necessities of life. This nation must comprise of people who have a strong conviction in the law of the Qur'an and its permanent values, and who thus dedicate themselves to making this way of life (*deen*) a practical reality. As a nation-state, it will become the laboratory in which to test the system of sustenance. Thereafter the brilliant results of the system will attract the attention of the whole world.

God's universal programme

This is the method by which the system of sustenance can be enacted through human agency. But even if humanity chooses not to try this system, God's universal programme dictates that the revolution will certainly happen naturally at some point in the future. However in human terms this programme is extremely slow, moving at an evolutionary rate. We know that even a minor change in a species takes thousands of years if not longer. Hence the Qur'an states that a 'day' in Divine terms is the equivalent of thousands (or even fifty thousands) of solar years (22:47, 32:5, 70:4). Goodness knows therefore how long it will take for the system of sustenance to become established at an evolutionary rate. In the present age humanity is bound to continue suffering and experiencing hardships and improving only very gradually. However, if humanity willingly takes Divine principles as its guide, then this process will speed up and the results will be manifested much sooner.

In the Qur'an, those with vested interests mocked the Messenger's warnings that their time was limited, and kept asking why the Divine revolution he predicted wasn't coming about.

Yet they ask you to hasten on the punishment! But God will not fail in His promise. Indeed a Day in the sight of your Sustainer is like a thousand years of your reckoning. / And to how many populations did I give respite, which were given to wrong-doing? In the end I punished them. To Me is the destination [of all]. 22:47-8

Thus in accordance with the universal programme, systems based on falsehood will be destroyed in the distant future. But since the Messenger adopted the Divine principles and made them the basis of his society, his opponents among the Quraish saw the promised revolution with their own eyes. Hence the Messenger's answer to the mocking questions of his people was:

All that has been promised to you will come to pass: nor can you thwart it [at all]. / Say [O Muhammad]: 'O my people! Do whatever you can: I will do [my part]: soon will you know to whom the future belongs: certain it is that the evildoers will not prosper.' 6:134-5

In other words, the revolution was bound to come sooner or later. Left at the natural evolutionary rate, the universal programme would take millennia, and in the meantime humanity would continue to suffer needlessly. However if any nation decided to take control of its own destiny in accordance with the Divine programme, then the revolution would come about swiftly and without bloodshed. Leslie Paul thus writes:

Man is an anti-evolutionist in his living. He does not wait for events to proceed in his direction or for time to function on his behalf. He proceeds to compel events: he wills that which he wants and transcends his circumstances by creative acts. He does not wait for the raspberries to evolve into jam, or for the bricks in the course of years to form themselves out of clay and build him a house. There is an absolute affinity between raspberries and jam, between clay and bricks, yet no possibility of an evolution of one into the other, however much one is 'potential' in the other. Corn gives us bread, yet not in a million years does corn become bread. What is needed to produce one from the other is manufacture, a gross and violent intervention upon the part of man with the processes of nature, but one which is above all his normal procedure for grappling with the problems of his existence. Inherently these are acts of creation, or the repetition of them. What is incorrectly described as the evolution of man is full of these dramatic, self-revealing acts against his environment and even against himself – acts which cannot be inferred from what has gone before but deny or upset what went before. If they are not predictable as the acts of an inviolable law, they transcend law. They are their own law. For man discovers and uses fire, which no animal has ever done. He makes tools. He invents an articulated language which, with its arbitrary associations and infinite combinations, is so unlike the unformed cries of animals as to deserve to be considered a miraculous birth. He caps this by an altogether inconceivable development, the association of arbitrary written signs which tally with spoken signs which stand for things. Not in a million, million years could these things have occurred by an evolution.[206]

Now let us consider the message of the Qur'an. As a matter of fact it was a revolutionary message against all false and destructive ideals upon which humans have been building their societies. The Qur'an identifies each false ideal and clearly shows why it is false. In addition it explains in detail the ideals of truth upon which human society should be based. The Messenger strove against a false system and replaced it with a system that was based on truth, in accordance with the needs of his time. In other words, a revolution that ordinarily would have taken thousands of years to come about was brought to fruition within a mere few years. After some time the same nation abandoned the truth and once again reverted to false ideals. People no longer took Divine principles as their guide. Subsequently it has been left to the natural processes of the Divine programme to bring about the revolution at an evolutionary rate. And yet, over the last fourteen hundred years we have nevertheless witnessed that humanity is gradually letting go of false ideals. As an example, the Qur'an condemned monarchy as a falsehood fourteen hundred years ago. It explained that no human had the right to rule another, and that people should adopt the principle of mutual consultation to manage their everyday affairs.

The Qur'an verified

We can see that humanity is gradually beginning to accept the same truths that the Qur'an has propounded all along. Though it has not yet

---

[206] Paul, *The Meaning of Human Existence*, p.157-8

reached the ideal stage that the Qur'an can take us to, we have nevertheless abandoned the idol of monarchy and are advancing towards mutual consultation.

Along with monarchy the Qur'an has also denounced the institute of priesthood, which again has a false basis. It tells us that there is no need for an intercessor between people and God. Today priesthood has lost much of its former grip on humanity. The Qur'an has likewise taught that slavery is a blot on the face of humanity. It declares that all humans are created equal and everyone is equal by virtue of having a common origin (4:1). In this century we have taken strides in eliminating slavery across the world. The Qur'an states that division by colour, caste, language and ethnicity is utterly unacceptable and all human beings belong to one family and one *ummah* (nation). Today the world's people are accepting this as a universal truth.

All of these changes are happening gradually and automatically. This is the law that the Qur'an terms *sunnat-Allah* or 'habit of God' (or, in the words of Iqbal, the subtle signs of Nature). It is this law that determines which ideas and systems will persevere, and which of them will be terminated (13:39). In short, the law dictates that those who live by falsehood will forge the instrument of their demise with their own hands, whilst the truth will out. In the words of the Qur'an:

> That He might justify truth and prove falsehood false, distasteful though it be to the guilty ones. 8:8

> Nay, We hurl the truth against falsehood, and it knocks out its brain [i.e. psychology], and behold, falsehood perishes! Ah! woe upon you for the [false] things you ascribe [to Us]. 21:18

All that is of universal benefit to humanity will persevere, and that which is not universally beneficial will perish and be set aside (13:17).

> See how God presents a parable? A goodly Word like a goodly tree (*shajar-e-tayyab*) firmly rooted, [reaching out] with its branches towards the sky, / yielding its fruit at all times by its Sustainer's leave. 14:24-5

The exploitative system called capitalism is based on falsehood, and so it cannot remain forever. A system can only persist if it guarantees the total sustenance and prosperity of humanity, i.e. it meets the needs both of the physical body and of the self. Hence it will guarantee humans success both in this world and in the hereafter. Just as some of the falsehoods mentioned in the Qur'an have already been exposed in the course of history, a revolution to end economic falsehood is bound to come.

We can see an early acknowledgement of this fact today. In Chapter 8 we quoted Jack Belden's book, *China Shakes the World*, which reviews the Chinese revolution. It has received critical acclaim among political thinkers in the West. Belden has written in his foreword to *China Shakes the World* that the world was surprised at how suddenly the Chinese revolution took place. The 'Emperor of China' (Chiang Kai-shek) held absolute power in his time, and the US had been supporting him, supplying weapons and ammunition in abundance. How, with all this power and wealth, was Chiang Kai-shek defeated, and why did the strategy of the US fail? Belden writes that the world is anxious to know the answer, but in any case:

> Neither the American government, the American press, nor the American people, nor many of their representatives in the Far East in the embassies, the military establishments and the business offices sought to look beyond narrow or personal interests toward the heart of the admittedly ignorant, but terribly emotional, bitter men and women of China.[207]

Belden adds:

> To all such people, one could justly address the words Mohammed used to denounce the Meccan merchants:
> But ye honour not the orphan
> Nor urge ye one another to feed the poor.[208]

Note that this non-Muslim American writer agrees with the truths that the Qur'an mentioned over a millennium ago. In fact we can see subtle hints of the inevitable economic revolution in the Qur'an itself. The current system of economy in which earning potential and inheritance is unrestricted has of course existed for centuries. Since it has been around for so long, people have come to believe that this is the way it is meant to be, and indeed they will even defend it with the argument that it has a long tradition:

---

[207] Belden, *China Shakes the World*, p.5
[208] Ibid.

Nay, We gave the good things of this life to these men and
their fathers until the period grew long for them 21:44

But the Qur'an states (and in our time this statement is
most pertinent):

[Do they] see not that We gradually reduce the land [in their
control] from its outlying borders? 21:44

The verse continues:

Is it then they who will succeed? 21:44

(In other words: Will their belief system bring them success, or
will Divine law defeat them?)

The time of an unjust economic system is coming to an end, and we
are heading towards a new period that will stand for justice.

We shall set up scales of justice for the Day of Judgement,
so that not a soul will be dealt with unjustly in the least. And if
there be [no more than] the weight of a mustard seed, We will
bring it [to account] 21:47

In practice, this means that neither a capitalist nor a landlord will
be responsible for deciding how much a given individual can earn. The
administration – the one established in accordance with Divine law –
will take on this responsibility. Elsewhere the Qur'an states:

Those before them did [also] devise plots [to
preserve their manmade systems]; but in all things the
master-planning is God's. 13:42

Hence, the Divine system of *Rabbubiya* must inevitably come to
pass. But just as humanity generally progresses at an evolutionary
rate, it follows that the Divine revolution, if left to Nature, will also
arrive at the evolutionary rate; and since it will advance at the
evolutionary rate, in the meantime humans will continue to suffer
unnecessarily. (Nevertheless there are signs at present to suggest that
the time of this revolution is not far off). If humanity accepts the
teachings of Revelation and adopts its programme willingly, not only
will we save time but we will also spare ourselves from a more bloody

revolution. Conversely, if humanity continues to choose its own way and waste time on fruitless social experiments, then it will take much longer to reach its higher destination. In the words of Iqbal, 'Revelation creates ease for human effort'. The Adam who wished to lead his life his own way without Revelation's guidance was the one that angels feared would bring much destruction and bloodshed. But the other 'Adam' is the one who takes Revelation as his guide in life. The Qur'an says about this new Adam:

> Thereupon Adam received words [of guidance] from his Sustainer, and He accepted his repentance ... / ... Whosoever follows My guidance, on them shall be no fear, nor shall they grieve. 2:37-8

It is also true that when humanity makes mistakes it usually learns from them, and yet the full picture of the truth continues to elude us; hence we continue to feel our way through the dark, always unsure which of our choices will take us in the right direction. We will look at this problem in detail in the Afterword.

As we have already stated, the Divine revolution is inevitable. If we don't choose it ourselves, then we must be prepared for more suffering and chaos. In the words of the Qur'an:

> O humanity! You [that] are ever striving towards your Sustainer, painfully striving – but you shall meet Him! 84:6

The Qur'anic legacy

However if humanity chooses to adopt the Divine programme, then prosperity and success is guaranteed in the near future.

> Then he who is given his Record in his right hand, / Soon will his account be taken by an easy reckoning 84:7-8

Such a society will be able to withstand every challenge and obstacle it faces. Obviously every system of the world, including the capitalist democracy of the West, and Russian communism, presently stand in the way of the Divine system's establishment. This is because neither the West nor the East bloc is guided by the light of Revelation. Hence it will be necessary to reject both these systems in order to establish the Divine system of *Rabbubiya* in their place. The Divine system cannot meet with these systems halfway because it is a unique system in its own right, it is based on truth, and truth can never compromise with falsehood. But this system will surely be established, and no power on earth can prevent it.

CHAPTER 11
Riba and *zakaat*

Translators' note: In the 1978 edition of *Nizam-e-Rabbubiyat* Parwez added a number of appendices (see Editor's Foreword for details). Although these have not been translated for this edition, we have nevertheless translated some important sections from the appendix titled *Riba ke Behs* (*The Debate over Interest*) as an additional chapter.

I - RIBA

We have already touched on both the issues of *riba* (interest) and *zakaat* in this book. In Pakistan in 1978,[209] there was much talk of abolishing interest in commerce and banking and replacing it with an economic system based on *zakaat*, with the aim of resolving all contemporary economic issues. At this point it would be appropriate for us to review *riba* and *zakaat* in more detail.

What is *riba*?

Let us begin with *riba* or interest. The Qur'an gives the fundamental meaning of *riba* as follows:

> O you who have conviction! Fear God, and give up
> what remains of your demand for interest[210] (*riba*), if you are

---

[209] **Translators' note:** Here Parwez has written in the present tense, since this article was originally written in the late 1970s. We have converted it to past tense.

indeed people of conviction. / If you don't, take notice of war from God and His Messenger: but if you turn back, you shall have your capital sums; do not deal unjustly [with others], and you shall not be dealt with unjustly. 2:278-9

From this we can see that:

1) If a lender takes back only the exact amount that he loaned to the borrower, then this will be just and fair to the borrower
2) If a lender takes even a small amount as interest, this is unfair to the borrower

This in short is how the Qur'an defines *riba*. It means 'to take more', no matter how small that amount may be. This definition is clear and unequivocal. Generally it is said amongst Muslims that *compound* interest is prohibited (*haraam*) whilst regular interest is permissible. This is an erroneous belief, and they usually derive this view from the following verse:

O you who have conviction! do not devour *riba*, doubled and multiplied; but fear God; that you may [really] prosper. 3:130

However they have misinterpreted the meaning of the verse. Imam Raghib has said that in this verse, the word *moza'afatun* is actually derived from the root *zafun*, meaning, 'to reduce', and not *zefun*, which means 'to accumulate'. Therefore the real meaning of this verse should be written as:

O you who have conviction! do not devour *riba*, which [despite what you think] will diminish and reduce [in the long term]; but fear God; that you may [really] prosper. 3:130

Hence the verse is really telling us that in the long term *riba* actually serves to *reduce* people's prosperity (that is, it reduces the viability of an economy) and those who consume interest become increasingly unproductive, both in their abilities (out of a lack of need

---

[210] **Translators' note:** Most translations use the word 'usury' but we have changed it to 'interest' since 'usury' implies excessive interest, whilst *riba* means interest of any amount.

to work) and in their capacity (as they become lazy). In the long term this shrinks the economy as a whole. It is a self-evident fact that in capitalist systems those at the top become completely unproductive, and the overall national economy suffers.

Generally Muslims tend to identify *riba* only with interest on loans, but again this is a misconception. The term *riba* should be understood holistically and indeed this is how the Divine system of sustenance treats it. The real question is: Is a return legitimate *only* on labour, or is a return on capital legitimate as well? According to the Qur'an:

Man can have nothing but what he strives for 53:39

Hence the former is a legitimate form of return, and the latter (return on capital) is not. This means that any type of loan involving interest (and in which the lender will profit without making any physical effort on his part) will be deemed *riba* and thus *haraam* or forbidden in the Qur'an, and is effectively an act of rebellion against 'God and His messenger' (2:279).

The many faces of *riba*

Let's suppose a farmer asks for a loan so he can purchase some land where he can cultivate crops for his livelihood, and with which he intends to gradually pay off his debt to you. Instead of loaning him the money, you decide to purchase that land on his behalf and become his landlord. Thereafter the farmer works throughout the year, and you take half of the proceeds from his produce. This is an on-going annual arrangement and furthermore, he remains in debt to you in principle because he owes you for the price of the land that you purchased. Is this not *riba*?

As another example, a shopkeeper asks for a loan so he can purchase and expand his available stock. You agree to give him the money not as a loan, but as an investment in his business (and thereby you become his business partner). He is responsible for the day-to-day running of the business but you take an equal share from his profit. Yet the investment is never deemed to have been repaid. Is this not *riba*?

Now another example: you deposit some money in a bank, and the banker lends that money to a businessman. When the businessman pays interest on his loan, a small portion of that interest is given back to you, since you deposited your money at the bank. Meanwhile your original deposit remains safe in the bank and you see your money grow. Is this not *riba*?

Of course all of these examples count as forms of *riba* and the Qur'an counts them all as unjust, whether the interest takes its regular form or whether it is compounded.

Whatever we take

If we consider the facts carefully we will soon realise that 'taking' comes in a number of forms, and is not necessarily tied to just the concept of a loan. The following are all forms of 'taking':

1) Gifts. You neither work for a gift nor pay towards it monetarily. The person who gives the gift does not generally expect it to be returned. Therefore gifts do not fall into the category of loans. Similarly, *sadaqaat* can be considered a 'gift' since the person giving it does so in the path of God. In light of the Qur'an the needy person can claim *sadaqaat* as a matter of right, and so again this does not fall into the loan category

2) Wages. You earn your wage as a result of giving time and effort to your work. You do not invest your own money (as with business) towards that work. You simply work and receive the wage

3) *Riba* (interest). You give money to another with the expectation that your return will be greater than the value of the original loan. You contribute nothing in terms of effort, but you profit from the effort of the other party (the borrower)

4) Profit from trade. Here you invest both your money and your time.

5) Gambling. Here you do not put in any physical effort but merely risk your money in the hopes of a quick return

Return solely on effort

Bearing in mind that the Qur'an accepts 'taking' as legitimate only if it involves personal physical input, we can see that only the second and fourth item of the above list is really permissible (and we will ignore the first item on the list, 'gifts'). In the Messenger's time, people were as yet unfamiliar with the Qur'anic principle and so they were confused about the true difference between *riba* and trade. If someone buys a product and then sells it for 10% more than the original purchase price to someone else, how is that different from lending someone some money and taking back an extra 10% as interest?

They say: 'Trade is like *riba*' 2:275

Since both the examples result in a profit of 10%, they were treating *riba* and trade as the same. But they were answered in the Qur'an as follows:

God has permitted trade and forbidden interest (*riba*). 2:275

They are forgetting that trade and interest are not the same. Business involves both money *and* effort. Hence trade is permissible. But *riba* generates a return solely on capital and no direct effort is involved on the part of the investor. Therefore it is not permissible. However if a trader charges more for a product than it is worth (in terms of the effort involved in its production) then it is a 'rip off' in laymen's terms, and thus falls under the category of *riba*. This is because his profit is not coming from his effort. Ultimately it will be up to society (the customers) to decide what counts as a fair price. It is generally said that trade involves 'risk' to some extent, because there is a possibility of both profit and loss, whilst *riba* involves no risk. This raises the question of whether the seemingly safer option ought to be permissible. But this is essentially semantics and is misleading. If 'risk' is the main factor in determining whether profit is permissible, then would gambling not also be permissible? After all, gambling is the riskiest money-making method of all. Yet we already know the difference between trade and *riba*. In trade, profit comes from effort plus capital. In *riba* profit comes from money plus money. The Qur'an teaches that profit derived from effort is permissible and profit derived solely from capital is not.

Why the difficulty?

The Qur'an makes the issue of *riba* easy to understand. The reasons humanity faces such enormous economic problems are:

1) There are many forms of *riba* that are prohibited in the Qur'an, but unfortunately our current *shari'ah* has declared them permissible. These include business agreements in which one party seeks to profit purely on the basis of capital investment (yet mutually agreed *riba* is prohibited in the Qur'an – see 4:29)

2) People in the wealthy classes have become so accustomed to making money easily through capital that they baulk at the very idea of trying to make money through physical effort. This is also the main reason that they are not prepared to return to the principles of the Qur'an

3) The greatest problem of all is that our present economic system is not Islamic. Instead of wholeheartedly transforming our system to make it Qur'anic, we actually just want to adopt a few token laws that appeal to us and then delude ourselves by saying that our system has become Qur'anic.[211] But in reality the two are incompatible and cannot fit together, and so any efforts to this end always fail

A holistic approach

The Divine system is a complete concept that cannot be broken down into parts, and so un-Qur'anic ideas can never be successfully introduced into it. According to the Divine system of sustenance:

a) The land and its resources (crops, oil, minerals, etc.) are a free gift to humanity from the Almighty (just as light and air are free to everyone, so should be all other resources). Thus there is no question of private ownership. The distribution of all resources is entrusted to the administration (as representative of the *ummah* or society) and it is their duty to ensure that every single person's needs are met

---

[211] **Translators' note:** Here Parwez is referring to attempts made in the 1950s to fuse Qur'anic injunctions and capitalism into Pakistan's constitution. For a detailed critique of the first Constituent Assembly's failed attempt to create a 'compromise' constitution during this period, see Karim, Saleena (2010) *Secular Jinnah & Pakistan: What the Nation Doesn't Know* (Paramount Books, Karachi and CheckPoint Press, Co. Mayo (Ireland)), Chapters 3 and 4.

b) In the Divine system no one can possess more wealth than he needs. Hence the question of capital-based investment and acquisition of property never arises

c) The system is responsible for ensuring that all members of the society receive everything that they need for their sustenance. Subsequently no one is compelled to beg, nor does anyone try to exploit the vulnerable or desperate through any means involving *riba* (e.g. through interest-based loans)

d) The Divine system will automatically render the concept of private enterprise obsolete, and shopkeepers will merely become the agents of distribution. They will not be motivated by profit. Their wages will come from the administration

Hence *riba* itself will become obsolete.

Summary: Two opposite systems

To reiterate, *riba* means more than simply 'interest'. It is the singular factor that makes all human systems exploitative and thus contrary to the Qur'an. In the Divine system every citizen works to full capacity and happily keeps a minimum for him/herself whilst giving most of it to society. In a human system every individual seeks to do as little as possible and simultaneously maximise his profits through the work of others. The two system-types are so fundamentally different that the Qur'an even terms human systems as a 'revolt against God and His Messenger' (2:279). In practice this means that human systems stand in opposition to the Divine system. Knowing all this, can we really expect to find a way to eliminate *riba* whilst living in a human, un-Qur'anic system?[212] During the Abbasid period Muslims tried (and failed) to allow for capitalism and landlordism, and to declare the acquisition of unlimited wealth lawful. Likewise if we try to retain the present capitalist system as it is and try to eliminate *riba* only half-heartedly, then we too will fail. At best we might succeed only in changing its face a little. The Divine system of sustenance however eliminates *riba* altogether, automatically and painlessly.

---

[212] **Translators' note:** Here Parwez is evidently addressing Pakistan's system, but his words apply broadly to all human systems.

II - ZAKAAT

Before we look at the Qur'anic definition of *zakaat*, it is necessary for us to understand how present-day Muslims define it. In contemporary Islam, a certain percentage (usually 2.5%) of an individual's annual earnings are supposed to be set aside and spent 'in God's path'. The threshold above which *zakaat* becomes mandatory is called *nasaab* and the portion to be levied as *zakaat* is called *sharha*. For example, the threshold for various commodities may be as follows:

1) Silver 52.5 oz
2) Gold 7.5 oz
3) Camels 5
4) Cattle 30
5) Goats 40

Furthermore it is said that in an Islamic state the government is responsible for collecting *zakaat* from the people, while Muslims living in secular countries may give *zakaat* individually to worthy causes. But whether collections are made through governmental institutions or individual communities, the *zakaat* collections will be spent only on certain causes that are predetermined under *shari'ah* law.

There is no doubt that the Qur'an ordains the collection of *zakaat* (and we will describe the Qur'anic position shortly). However we should note that nothing that we have just described on *zakaat* (being taken from contemporary Islam) actually exists anywhere in the Qur'an. It is generally said in traditional Islam that the Qur'an tells us where to spend *zakaat*, as in the following verse:

> Alms [*sadaqaat*] are for the poor and the needy, and those employed to administer the [funds]; for those whose hearts have been [recently] reconciled [to the truth]; for those in bondage and in debt; in the cause of God; and for the wayfarer: [thus is it] ordained by God, and God is full of knowledge and wisdom. 9:60[213]

---

[213] **Translators' note:** Here in the original Urdu text Parwez referred to the well-known Urdu translation by Shah Rafi-ul-Din which also used the Urdu equivalent of 'alms'. As such all widely known translations make the same error in this verse.

Note that here the Qur'an uses the word *sadaqaat* and not *zakaat* (a word that is also usually translated as 'charity'). Hence it is erroneous to claim that *zakaat* applies to the subjects of this verse – i.e. the poor, the needy, etc. The Qur'an differentiates between the two words. As far as *zakaat* is concerned, exactly how it should be spent is mentioned nowhere in the Book. Hence the contemporary Muslim concept of *zakaat* cannot be corroborated from the Qur'an. Since *nasaab* (threshold) and *sharha* (portion) are the crucial part of the contemporary view, we shall focus on them now. For example, say that silver has a value of 5 rupees per ounce, and the price of gold is 600 rupees per ounce. An individual who own 270 Rs. worth of silver (or 54 oz) jewellery must pay *zakaat* on it because he has reached the threshold (based on our earlier list of figures). But the individual who owns gold jewellery worth 4200 Rs. (7 oz) will not have reached the threshold and so will not be expected to pay *zakaat*. In other words a man will have to pay *zakaat* on something worth only 270 Rs. but not on something worth a significantly greater amount. And yet this is a relatively minor example of the injustice that occurs. To give another example, we already know that 270 Rs. worth of silver is eligible for *zakaat*, yet a man with 29 cows, which are worth thousands of rupees, will not have to give *zakaat* just because his number of cattle falls one short from the threshold of 30. In short, the poorer man of the two is more likely to be paying *zakaat*. Hence we can easily see the implications of this law on other forms of wealth and property.

Zakaat in light of the Qur'an

Now let us see what the Qur'an has to say about *zakaat*. The word means 'growth' and 'development'. The phrase 'establish *salaat*, and give *zakaat*' (22:41) appears numerous times in the Qur'an. In fact *salaat* and *zakaat* are the two pillars of the Divine system of sustenance. We will return to *salaat* later, but for now we will focus on *zakaat*. To 'give *zakaat*' ultimately means 'to provide all means of sustenance and development'.

In a Divine system the implication of this Qur'anic phrase is that the central administration must fulfil God's responsibility to humanity on His behalf[214] – that is, to sustain and develop humanity. The

---

[214] **Translators' note:** Whilst Alllah could fulfil this responsibility Himself, this would negate the concept of human free will, a gift that enables us to choose how to lead our lives.

opening verse of the Qur'an declares that God is the 'Sustainer of the worlds' – meaning that He is responsible for the *Rabbubyiat* or total sustenance of the universe. *Rabbubiya* means taking something from the very first phase of its creation all the way to its perfection. This includes everything in the natural universe, as well as the universal sustenance and development of humanity (physical body *and* self). The Qur'an thus describes His responsibility as follows:

> And there is no living creature on earth whose sustenance does not depend on God; and He knows its time-limit [on earth] and its resting-place [after death]: all [this] is laid down in [His] clear decree. 11:6

And regarding humanity the Qur'an states:

> It is We who shall provide sustenance for you as well as for [your children] 6:151

The purpose of establishing the Divine system therefore is to fulfil God's stated responsibility and thus ensure that every single human being receives all that he requires for his development. The Qur'anic phrase for this is *eeta-e-zakaat*, i.e. to 'give *zakaat*'.[215]

> Those who, if We firmly establish them on earth, will establish *salaat*, and give *zakaat* 22:41 (also 20:55)

Note that according to the above verse it is the duty of the Islamic administration to give *zakaat* to humanity (or, at least to begin with, a single society), and not the other way round. In other words, the entirety of the central administration's revenue is to be treated as *zakaat*. Whilst this revenue will have been collected from the public, the administration will redistribute it immediately back to society and eventually to humanity as well. The amount of *zakaat* that is collected from the public at any time will of course be dependent on how much is needed to raise the living standards of the people as a whole. Ultimately therefore, it is the *administration* that does the giving and *not* the people, because the administration's only job is to raise the living standards for all, and not to keep anything for itself. Thus we can

---

[215] See also Chapter 8.

describe this process of collection and redistribution of *zakaat* as 'a means of universal development'.

During periods of crisis for which there are insufficient funds in the general budget, e.g. during a natural disaster or war, the administration may appeal to the people for voluntary contributions as aid. The Qur'an calls such contributions *sadaqaat*. Hence, as we mentioned earlier, the verse 9:60 uses the word *sadaqaat*, and not *zakaat*, for such contributions. From this it becomes clear that:

1) Charity that is presently given in the name of *zakaat* is not actually *zakaat*
2) The institute of *zakaat* cannot actually exist without the establishment of the Divine system
3) The Islamic administration ultimately gives to the people and provides for every aspect of their development
4) The process of the circulation of *zakaat* (as described above) may be properly termed the 'means of universal development'. It is not something to be collected at a fixed rate, but will vary according to the needs of the time. (The final Messenger and the early Caliphs no doubt determined the rate in accordance with their needs)
5) Anything contributed voluntarily by the public in times of crisis is called *sadaqaat*

Leaving aside the minor details and considering the issue of *zakaat* in general terms, it doesn't take much to see that the present concept of *zakaat* has no place in the Qur'anic system of sustenance. As we have observed in earlier chapters, the fundamental principle of the Divine system of sustenance is that people do not hold onto their money and hoard it. Contrary to this, today's concept of *zakaat* holds that the individual can hang onto his money through the whole year, and at the end he is expected only to set aside a fixed percentage (2.5%) for *zakaat*. The remaining 97.5% can remain in his possession and thereafter he may collect as much as he likes.

The background history of how we came to the current concept of *zakaat* is both interesting and serves as a tale of warning. To quote a verse that we referred to earlier in this book:

> But as for all who hoard up treasures of gold and silver and do not spend them for the sake of God – give them the news of grievous suffering [in the life to come]: / on the Day when that

[hoarded wealth] shall be heated in the fire of hell and their foreheads and their sides and their backs will be branded with it [those sinners shall be told:] 'These are the treasures which you have laid up for yourselves! Taste, then, [the fruit of] your hoarded treasures!' 9:34-5

How zakaat became mandatory

The above verses make it clear that the hoarding of wealth is a heinous crime. Abu Daud states:

> Ibn-e-Abbas says that when this verse [9:34] was revealed to the Messenger, the believers were confounded. They became heavy-hearted.[216] Umar Ibn Khattab said to them, 'I will take your troubles away and ease your hardship.' Thereupon Umar went to the Messenger and beseeched him: 'Oh Messenger of God! This verse has troubled your Companions.' The Messenger replied: 'This is why God has made *zakaat* obligatory, so that the rest of your wealth will become purified; and [similarly], inheritance laws have been made obligatory to ensure that those you leave behind after death will receive your wealth.' Ibn-e-Abbas says that upon hearing the Messenger's reply, Umar happily declared: 'God is great!'[217]

It doesn't take much to see that this account is a spurious fabrication, and was created in the period when capitalism had reasserted itself in Muslim civilisation. In the first place, this historical account claims that the Companions received God's decree on *zakaat* with reluctance and anxiety. Yet in the Qur'an the final Messenger was told in no uncertain terms:

> But no, by your Sustainer (*Rabb*), they can have no conviction (*eiman*) until they make you the judge in all disputes between them, and find in their souls no resistance against your decisions, but accept them with the fullest conviction. 4:65

---

[216] **Translators' note:** See our comment in Chapter 9, fn 192.
[217] Abu Daud, citing from *Mishqaat*, chapter: '*Kitab al- Zakaat.*' Urdu translation (date unknown), Karachi: Noor Muhammad Kar Khanna Tajaarat, p.309-10 (Publication details are as provided in Parwez's original text)

Is it even possible that these Companions of the Messenger would become heavy-hearted at hearing a Divine decree? These are the same people whose strength of conviction is recorded in the Qur'an as:

> Behold, God has bought of the believers their lives and their possessions ... 9:111

And yet, according to the *hadith* we have quoted, we are supposed to believe that Umar – who famously wore patched clothing even during his reign as Caliph – actually complained to the Messenger to protect the Companion's selfish interests. And we are also expected to believe that the Messenger circumvented the Divine decree on *zakaat* with the excuse that we can in fact keep 97.5% of our wealth, even though this is the same person who, as founder and head of the Islamic state never even kept a single surplus penny in his home. See for example, this *hadith*:

> When the Prophet was on his deathbed, he possessed only 7 Dinars. He gave the instruction that this money should be given away as *sadaqaat*. Then he suddenly fell unconscious and the people began running about to get him medical attention. When the Messenger regained consciousness, he again said: 'Bring those Dinars to me.' He took the money in his hand and said to those present: 'How will Muhammad feel if he goes to meet his Maker whilst still possessing these Dinars?' Then the Messenger gave the money away himself.[218]

Could this same Messenger make it permissible for people to hoard as much as they like and then have to spend only 2.5% on charity as a means to sanctify the rest of their wealth?

Changing the traditional stance

Up to the present day it has been said that the *nasaab* (frequency threshold) and *sharha* (rate) of *zakaat* have both been fixed by the Messenger himself, and that these are fixed for all time. However the demands of the present time have inevitably forced a rethink on this tradition. For example the Ahle-Hadith sect, whose followers adhere

---

[218] Cited in *As-h'ha al Seer* by Hakeem Dana Puri (Publication details are as provided in Parwez's original text)

most strictly to the *hadith*, have a weekly journal produced in Lahore of the same name. In their 16 August 1974 edition was an article in which it was stated:

> The fundamental aim of Islam is to create a happy and prosperous society ... [and] *zakaat* was made mandatory as part of that aim. But the conditions in which this [threshold and rate of *zakaat*] was fixed were different to those of today ... and so, we may reconsider [*zakaat*] on the basis of the 'law of expediency'. According to *shari'ah*, *zakaat* is mandatory on four items: 1) cattle 2) perishable goods (fruit, flour etc.) 3) capital (gold and silver) 4) trade. We can leave the first three as they are. But trade has changed and grown enormously, and therefore it has become necessary to review it. *Nisaab-e-zakaat* (frequency threshold of *zakaat*) is also fixed in Islam, but the ulama are in consensus that these amounts represent a *minimum* expenditure in the path of God. When the system of *zakaat* was originally implemented, it was fixed in accordance with the needs and supplies of the time. The purpose of *zakaat* is not merely to fix a percentage (of charity) irrespective of how few would actually benefit from it. *Zakaat* is meant to fulfil the needs of *all* poor and needy people. Therefore it is necessary that we review present-day needs and adjust the [rate of] *zakaat* accordingly.[219]

Moving on, the Kingdom of Saudi Arabia gives sanction to the legal application of *hadith*. The *Rabita al-Alam al-Islami* (Muslim World League) founded in Makkah (and largely funded by the Saudi government)[220] is an administrative organisation that has a formal function of interpreting *hadith* and *shari'ah* law. In the June 1978 (Rajb 1398 Hijri) issue of their journal was an article discussing whether it is possible to change the rate (2.5%) of *zakaat* that was supposedly fixed by the final Messenger. On page 66, the author writes that if the present *sharha* rate [2.5%] is insufficient to accomplish the aim of *zakaat* (namely, to meet the needs of the poor), then obviously the individual who is contributing this fixed amount has not really fulfilled his responsibility. It is the duty of those who arrange the distribution

---

[219] *Ahle-Hadith* journal (Lahore), 16 August 1974 (Publication details are as provided in Parwez's original text. Page unknown).

[220] **Translators' note:** The Muslim World League, founded in Makkah in 1962, is an international Muslim religious organisation which receives funds from a number of Muslim countries including the Saudi government (which is the largest contributor).

of *zakaat* and the government to collect a higher rate from the wealthiest sections of society. The author adds that although the original (2.5%) may have been sufficient to feed the poor during the time of the Messenger, the Qur'an itself has not fixed the rate, and so it is open to variation.[221]

Hence even our conservative religious class acknowledges that the rate of *zakaat* is not unchangeable. As we have already shown, it is the duty of the administration to meet the needs of society and moreover to sustain it. Whatever means it deploys to this end (in accordance with the dictates of the Qur'an) will be called *zakaat*. In light of the Qur'an therefore, 'giving *zakaat*' (*eeta-e-zakaat*) is the duty of the administration and not the people.

> Those [are the ones] who, if We firmly establish them on earth, will establish *salaat*, and give *zakaat* 22:41

---

[221] *Muslim World League Journal*, June 1978 (Rajb 1398 Hijri), p.66 (Publication details are as provided in Parwez's original text.)

AFTERWORD

In this book we have described the Divine system of *Rabbubiya* in detail. We deem it appropriate to end with a summary of its essential features in order to reiterate all that we have covered.

A human being is comprised of two things: His body and his self. His body is subject to physical laws, and in accordance with these laws it must one day perish. But his self is not subject to physical laws, so it does not die in accordance with these laws. It has the potential to live forever, but the only means by which it can act and reveal itself within the confines of time and space in this present universe is via a physical body. Therefore a human being can only develop his self and unfurl his hidden potential by first taking care of the needs of his body.

Meeting the physical needs of the body has been handed over to the intellect (or survival instinct). For this reason, intellect concludes that the best way to survive and grow strong is to hoard the means of sustenance. It must 'take'. However the development of the self is governed by a different law: The more we leave open the available resources for the benefit of everyone, the stronger the individual self will become. It must 'give'.

Conflict

Thus there is a conflict of interest between the intellect and the self. Resolving this conflict is the greatest challenge in human life.

Humanity so far has considered two solutions. One group advocates that the individual should focus all his energies on the self, and ignore the demands of the intellect in the process. According to this group, the secret to developing the self lies in destroying the physical body. This group is called spiritualist or religious.

The other group declares that the self doesn't exist, and that the true and only purpose of life is to look after the physical body. Hence the individual should be left free to follow the demands of his intellect. This group is called materialist or mechanist.

The Qur'an states that both these concepts of life are wrong. It asks humanity to listen to God's invitation and place their trust in Him, and in return He promises to resolve this conflict. The Qur'an teaches that choosing between the self and the body is itself wrong. We don't treat a headache by cutting off the head. Developing the self requires the ability to act, which in turn requires a healthy body. Hence the physical needs of the body cannot be ignored either. On the other hand the Qur'an also teaches that the ultimate purpose of life is to develop the self, and that the body is only an instrument to that end. To treat the *instrument* as the object of development is to make the grave error of avoiding the real object and shirk from reality. The true way therefore is to satisfy the demands of the intellect and simultaneously achieve the higher purpose of strengthening the self.

The Qur'an has stated that as long as humanity is divided and fails to unite, the intellect of every individual will be concerned only with protecting its self-interest. This will inevitably lead to clashes and perpetual chaos. The only way to end these clashes is to create an environment in which people are no longer anxious about meeting their material needs; and this can be accomplished only if the administration takes on the responsibility of meeting these needs, treating all citizens as members of one family.

Obviously such an environment can only be created if the means of sustenance are in the control of society and not subject to private ownership. Hence the Qur'an states that no one has the right to privately own the land (and all the natural resources it contains). When people feel secure that their needs and those of their children will be met, then of course the intellect will be satisfied that it need not resort to hoarding. Instead of worrying about the protection of so-called personal interest, the intellect will make decisions that are in harmony with the *true* needs of the self. Hence in practice the intellect will not think in individualistic terms but in terms of the collective, and indeed humanity. In accordance with a saying of the Messenger, Satan will have become Muslim. To 'give', therefore, also means that all our creative energies will be directed at benefiting and strengthening the whole. Obviously there will be no question of private ownership in such a society, since society will have taken care of the needs of every individual. The output of every individual will be effectively pooled to benefit everybody. Thus the Divine programme is the only way to satisfy the intellect as well as to attain the higher purpose of developing the self.

In order to ascertain how 'self-actualised' a given individual is, we can check to what extent his personal attributes correspond (within human limits) to those of God. In Qur'anic language this is called the 'hue of God' (2:138).

Hue of God

> [Say: 'Our life takes its] hue from God! And who could give a better hue [to life] than God?' 2:138

Knowledge of God's attributes can only be acquired through Revelation (*Wahi*). The Qur'an explains these attributes in detail, and so it follows that the standard by which to test our self-actualisation can only be found in the Qur'an.

The Qur'anic ideal

A Qur'anic society has the following characteristics:

1) Society will meet the needs of every individual
2) There will be no question of private ownership
3) Having satisfied the demands of the intellect, the individual will focus his entire creative energy on the betterment of humanity, which in turn will strengthen his self

This is the Qur'anic ideal, but the Qur'an takes us to this stage gradually and not overnight. In the early stages individuals are encouraged to give *sadaqaat* (alms) and charity; and laws governing lending and borrowing and wills and inheritance etc. are laid down. These laws are for a transitional period that will take society to the next stage. They exist to deal with the present state of affairs but they nevertheless aim at the Qur'anic ideal. Thus the Divine ideal of *Rabbubiya* – sustenance of the universe – will be manifested within the earthly sphere as the sustenance of all humanity. The Qur'an has provided a detailed programme for establishing this society, but the essential prerequisite is that its pioneers must firmly accept and have conviction in the following truths:

1) Human life is not limited to just the physical. The human self contains the potential for immortality. Life is a journey that doesn't end at death. Therefore human beings should not only take care of their short-term needs and desires, but should also fix their vision on the good things of the future (i.e. the Last Day)

2) 'Developing the self' essentially means the ever-increasing development of attributes that reflect those of God (within human limits)

3) The secret to developing the self lies in *giving* instead of taking, i.e. how much an individual contributes towards the sustenance of humanity and in retaining the balance (*husn*) and beauty of the universe

When the pioneers' hearts are fully convinced of the above truths this will be reflected in their general behaviour, since they will be acting in accordance with God's law. Their good example will obviously influence the wider community and eventually this will create a whole new society. The gradual establishment of the society in this fashion is termed *qiaam-e-salaat* (lit. 'establish *salaat*') in the Qur'an. This society exists to follow the laws of the Almighty. Regular congregations are a key feature of this system, and they also fall under the Qur'anic *qiaam-e-salaat*.

The inevitable outcome of 'establishing *salaat*' is 'giving *zakaat*' (*eeta-e-zakaat*), i.e. 'giving' to humanity for its benefit. Indeed the pivotal point of this system is *qiaam-e-salaat* and *eeta-e-zakaat*; and it is the meaning of Islam in practice. Thus the only 'praiseworthy' system is one that takes on the responsibility of providing sustenance for humanity in accordance with Divine directives (hence the opening line of the Qur'an: *Praise be to God, the Sustainer of the worlds*).

With the support of his companions the Messenger struggled for and eventually established the Divine system in a form consistent with the needs of his time. But after some time, vested interests regained their former control, and the system that the Messenger had established effectively vanished. Subsequently over the centuries their false ideals have become infused in Muslim culture. Our conservative class is the greatest supporter of this culture and it takes its authority from the idea of tradition, when in fact the authority of *deen* can only be found in the Qur'an, and God Himself has promised to safeguard it (and indeed every word of it remains intact to this day). As things stand at present the result of the Muslim adherence to traditions and customs speaks for itself. Muslims are trapped in their own hell, and so the rest of the world knows no peace either, since it has no shining example among the nations to follow.

The only way out of this hellish existence is for Muslims to quit their blind following of tradition, to turn their focus back to the Qur'an, and ask themselves: What sort of system did God decree, and what sort of system did we end up with? If we can answer this question honestly, then we might yet find our way back into the heaven that Adam lost. But if we don't change our ways, and we fail to adopt the Qur'anic system in our lives, then some other nation is bound to adopt it in our place; and the work that ought to be done by the present-day Muslim community will be completed by some other nation. This is because Divine law neither belongs exclusively to a particular nation nor is it bound by geography or culture.

> To God belong the East and the West 2:115 (see also 2:142, 26:28, 70:40, 73:9)

In the following verse, the Qur'an clearly states:

> Behold, you are those invited to spend in the Way of God: but among you are some that are miserly. But they are miserly at the expense of their own selves [nafs]. 47:38

Next the Qur'an challenges this 'miserly' mentality: Do they think that God *needs* them to establish the law? Or is He simply giving them guidance for their own good?

> God is free of all wants, and it is you that are needy. 47:38

Finally the Qur'an issues its warning:

> If you turn back [from the Path], He will substitute in your stead another people; then they would not be like you! 47:38

God's immutable law never compromises with those who follow falsehood, however well-intentioned they may be.

> Not your desires, nor those of the People of the Book (can prevail): whoever works evil, will be requited accordingly. Nor will he find, besides God, any protector or helper. 4:123

Conversely:

> If any do deeds of righteousness – be they male or female –
> and have conviction, they will enter Heaven, and not the least
> injustice will be done to them./ Who can be better in *deen* than
> one who submits his whole self to God, does good, and follows
> the way of Abraham who turned away from falsehood? For God
> did take Abraham for a friend. 4:125

The Qur'an thus refers to its *deen* (the system of *Rabbubiya*) as 'right and straight' (98:5). The ideal society established via this system is described in the Qur'an as 'Heaven' or the 'hereafter' (13:29). By 'Heaven', it means a heavenly existence both on earth and in the hereafter, representing the height of human achievement. The Qur'an describes the state of affairs in an earthly state of heaven as follows:

> [This will be] their cry therein: 'Glory to You, O God!' and
> 'Peace' will be their greeting therein! And the close of their cry
> will be: 'Praise be to God, the Sustainer of the Worlds!' 10:10

This verse tells us that in this 'heavenly' state, the people will hold fast to their conviction that not a single productive deed of theirs will go to waste. Hence their society will strive day and night to build the system of sustenance and make it an example for the rest of the world (hence, 'Glory to God'). Its people will be inspired by the idea that not only are they free to perfect their own individual egos, but they will desire to (and thus will) help others perfect theirs as well (hence, 'Peace will be their greeting'). In the end their convictions will have been proven in reality; and the world will come to know that the Divine system is indeed the only one that can be credited with sustaining the whole of humanity (hence, 'Praise be to God, the Sustainer of the worlds').

Opposition

Yet I am convinced that most Muslims will not heed this message and instead will oppose it. Their greatest objection will be that this is a new call – a new religion, even. The problem is that they are subordinated to tradition and have followed it blindly for so long that their thinking faculties are paralysed. To the present-day Muslim, these traditions have been passed down over the centuries, so they must be right. Any attempt to introduce a new idea or practice or system is deemed *haraam* (prohibited) in his religion. Every innovation is deemed an attempt to corrupt religion and lead its followers astray. To quote a *hadith*: 'Every corruption [in religion] is to lead astray, and going astray takes you to Hell'. And yet at one time the Muslim nation was known for its innovation. It was this characteristic that made it a living nation. It was an ever-evolving society, taking on new ideas and making changes in accordance with the exigencies of the times. Now this same Muslim nation fears new ideas in the same way that a caged bird is afraid of open spaces.

However the concept of 'new' versus 'old' is strange in itself. Whatever is unfamiliar and not widely accepted is considered 'new'; but once it is widely accepted (however quickly), it is deemed 'old'. At present the Qur'anic system of sustenance seems novel and unfamiliar, and hence new. But let us consider the numerous Qur'anic concepts which at the time of its revelation were completely novel to the world, but which are now the norm in the modern age. For one, the idea that monarchy is inhumane, whilst accepted in today's world, was wholly alien at the time of the Messenger. And the idea that we are equal at birth and division by caste and creed is unacceptable, when introduced by the Qur'an, was also totally new. The idea that there is no need for a mediator between man and God was again totally new. So was the idea that nationalist or racial division is inhumane and humanity is actually one race, subject to one and the same moral law. These 'new' ideas have become accepted by the whole world, one at a time; and now they are neither new nor unfamiliar to anyone, Muslim or not. Of course there are many Qur'anic concepts that remain new, unfamiliar and thus impractical or unacceptable. Among these remaining 'unacceptable' concepts in the Qur'an is the one that denounces private ownership as the root of societal chaos. According to the Qur'an a true society makes the universal sustenance of humanity its *raison d'être*. Today this idea is deemed new and impractical, so we presently fail to accept and adopt it. But once adopted, this idea too will become accepted as the norm.

Today's Muslims are in a very sorry state indeed. They were duty-bound to adopt the true way of life immediately and make it an example for the world. They were not supposed to simply stand by and wait for the Divine decree to gradually fulfil itself in accordance with the exigencies of the time (i.e. at the evolutionary rate). Indeed, today's Muslims are the first to object whenever the world wishes to test a new concept in accordance with the exigencies of the time. When the world disregards the Muslim view and adopts the new idea nonetheless, Muslims have no choice but to eventually follow and also come to accept it. Muslims seem destined to follow instead of lead! Long ago the West heeded the signs of the times, revolted against monarchy, and finally banished kings from their society. In that very same period Muslims continually supported monarchy as a diehard tradition, and prayed for the king's long life in every mosque, until the exigencies of the time naturally overturned these kingdoms in the early twentieth century. As another example, the West raised a voice of protest against the religious dictatorship of its clergy and gradually saw to it that this inhumane institute was eliminated from their lives. But Muslims continue to revere their holy men and priests to the present day. Of course these Muslim holy men too are losing their power with time. And again: Whilst the West has formally abolished slavery, this curse is still alive in Muslim culture; and furthermore, today's Muslims are feeling the shame of this practice as the world sits in judgement against it and them.

This then is the present condition of the nation that was supposed to lead by example. As we have mentioned above, when some other nation decides to adopt a concept that happens to exist in the pages of the Qur'an, Muslims are the first to oppose it. Incidentally, this was the mentality of the 'People of the Book' (Jews and Christians) when the Qur'an was revealed. Subsequently the first people to accept the teachings of the Qur'an were the unbelievers and idolaters from among the Arabs, whilst the People of the Book, despite being the recipients of earlier Revelation, were its foremost opponents. The Qur'an addressed them with the warning:

> Be not foremost among those who deny its [the Qur'an's] truth. 2:41

The Qur'an denied their claim that it was introducing a 'new' religion. It declared that it was only repeating what had appeared in the very earliest Revelation onward, including the Books of Abraham and Moses (87:18-19. See also 53:36-40). In fact the followers of this earlier Revelation had cast it aside, forgotten it and adopted manmade religion instead, which was why they no longer recognised the original truth. Only a few from among the People of the Book were willing to pay heed to the Qur'an.

Like the People of the Book before them, today's Muslim world is stuck in the same closed-minded mentality. The concepts of the Qur'an are plain to see as they always have been, but since Muslims have put the Book aside and have adopted manmade religion, they no longer recognise these concepts, and think that they are 'new'. As a result, Muslims are also the first to object to them.

Some may also be tempted to say that in this book we are interpreting the Qur'an in light of communist ideas. Insofar as interpretation is concerned, it is extremely important to bear in mind the following. The Qur'an contains a code of life from God addressed to all humanity and is valid to the Last Day. Therefore it exists in its perfect and complete form. There is no human or social issue for which the Qur'an has not provided guidance. Obviously these issues and challenges don't present themselves all at once, but appear over time. History is witness that some issues that were considered unimportant in the past will later become critically important and receive universal attention. The Qur'an is designed such that thinking people easily recognise the merit of the guidance it has provided for every potential issue. Hence it states:

> In time We shall make them [those who think] fully understand Our signs in the utmost horizons [of the world] and within themselves [their own nation], so that it will become clear unto them that this [Revelation] is indeed the truth. 41:53

In other words, with time thinking people will come to appreciate the merit of Qur'anic guidance and its application both at home and abroad.[222] These 'signs' thus serve to substantiate the truth of every single law in the Qur'an, as reflected in the positive effects of the Qur'anic programme in every sphere of life.

Since we don't consult the Qur'an in resolving the issues of our time, we fail to receive the benefit of its guidance. We are presently living in an economic age; that is, the question of resolving the economic problem is the main focus of our time. As I understand it, if we study and learn from the Qur'an as it directs us to, we will soon find that its Divine system of *Rabbubiya* will give us much-needed insight into resolving our present economic difficulties. The suggestion

---

[222] The phrase above 'utmost horizons (*aafaaq*) and within themselves (*anfas*)' can be understood in terms of external/physical vs. the internal (self), since the word *anfas* is derived from *nafs*, the self. However the two words can also be understood in sociological terms – i.e. domestic/national (*anfas*) versus international (*aafaaq*). I (Parwez) have chosen the latter interpretation for this reason, but as such both meanings are equally valid.

therefore that my understanding of the Qur'an has been inspired by Russian and Chinese communism is a shallow accusation. Such an accusation could only be made by someone who has studied neither communism nor the Qur'anic system of sustenance in detail. Whoever makes an in-depth comparative study of the two will find that at heart they stand in total opposition to one another. Indeed we have critically analysed communism throughout this book so that those with a superficial understanding of the subject will not jump to the wrong conclusion. As we have already explained, communism was certainly conceived as an attempt to resolve the modern economic question. It sought to create heaven on earth, but instead it led humanity to hell. Its fatal flaw was that it focused its entire ideology on the issue of 'bread' (of course such a flaw was inevitable given that Marx was inspired by mechanistic thought). This theory treated humanity as nothing more than a steam engine that requires only fuel and water to keep it running. As long as these requirements are met, the driver can take the train along any track he chooses and the train will run blindly on. The train has no will of its own; it doesn't know where it is running or why. Eventually when the train can no longer function and becomes useless, it can be replaced, since all it had ever worked for was fuel and water. According to this view of life humans are not really alive, but are like parts of a machine. We can imagine what it takes to turn a living human being endowed with free will into a cog within a machine or to make him run blindly on a railway track. It obviously requires an iron fist. Communism cannot be established without tyranny, and so communists are left with two options. The first is to suppress the first generation so completely that they cannot do anything to resist it. The other option is to brainwash the second generation via an education programme that will teach them to accept this ideology blindly, and so destroy their free will in the process. Humanity thus pays the ultimate price for its 'bread': It has to give up its life.

Of course neither Marx nor the others from his school of thought intended to oppress the poor and the working class for just their material sustenance. They were in fact doomed to fail simply because they were utilising their limited intellect, when the intellect is incapable of conceiving a system of life that will simultaneously fulfil *all* human needs (which after all are interlinked and cannot be separated from each other) in perfect balance and 'just proportion'[223].

---

[223] **Translators' note:** See explanation of the word *husn* (lit. just proportion) in Chapters 1, 5 and 6.

Intellect might adequately deal with these issues one at a time, but it certainly cannot deal with them holistically. Every attempt made by the intellect to resolve any single issue has untold repercussions in all spheres. Conversely, since Revelation treats human life holistically the Divine system can fulfil its every need. It is not that humanity is unaware of these issues. Of course throughout history humanity has faced all manner of issues which are all on record, and which can therefore be compiled in one place for analysis. But human intellect cannot make sufficient sense of this data to create a system that will resolve all issues simultaneously. Nor has the Qur'an claimed that it will provide a blueprint the likes of which we have never seen before. It has simply offered a system designed to verify the truth of the ideals that have been presented to humanity many times before:

> A Messenger comes to you confirming the truth that is already with you ... 3:81

Humanity has long been searching for such a system and to date it has failed spectacularly. The Qur'an however offers its matchless Divine system along with the claim that it is beyond human capability to come up with an equivalent. Only the Divine system can guarantee it will meet the physical needs of every individual, as well as his 'spiritual' needs. Indeed this is the meaning of life. Such a system cannot be found anywhere but in the Qur'an.

The fact remains that human intellect constantly endeavours to resolve the issues before it, in accordance with the exigencies of the time; but solutions are never found easily. Humanity takes only small steps forward, and it is only after a long struggle and bitter experience that intellect happens upon a solution that is in line with the Divine 'straight path' (*siraat-e-mustaqeem*); and even then the human solution is imperfect. It is limited in scope and may deal at best with one issue at a time, without taking into account the repercussions it may have elsewhere. Conversely, the guidance of Revelation is holistic in its approach and it takes us directly along the straight path. And whereas human intellect left on its own is in constant danger of losing its way, Divine guidance is guaranteed to prevent such a possibility.

> We shall send you Our Guidance: and those who follow My guidance need have no fear, and neither shall they grieve. 2:38

This is why human intellect has been unable to separate the truth from the falsehood within whatever system it has chosen to adopt. For example the thought of Rousseau et al rejected monarchy and chose to pursue democracy. Their endeavour was no doubt a step in the right direction. But their democracy did not take them where only Revelation could have taken them. As a result the Western concept of democracy is far removed from *true* democracy and so presently we find that there are several versions of it being tested in various nations. If, instead of Rousseau, someone had come forward with a concept of democracy inspired directly from the Qur'an and with his vision fixed on its ideal, then the world would have immediately set itself on the path to its higher destination; and unlike the defective and false human democracy, the Qur'anic form would not have neglected life's other issues, but instead would have resolved them all.

Similarly, the circumstances of the time compelled Marx et al to resolve the economic question. Again their intent was genuine and their best intellectual efforts did reveal a vague way forward. But they couldn't find their way onto the true straight path. Their sight was fixed solely on bread, and they failed to see that they were neglecting numerous other issues relating to the self. If at that time someone had come forward with a Qur'an-inspired solution to this question, then the modern world would have adopted the Divine system of sustenance. Of course it was the duty of those who claim to be the custodians of the Final Revelation to come forward with this solution. However if Muslims fail to lead by example in light of Revelation, what choice does humanity have but to continue to struggle using its limited intellect? Of course, a nation that at least utilises its intellect is still better than the nation that neither takes its guidance from Revelation nor utilises its intellect.

In order to reach the Divinely-ordained straight path, we must humbly accept that our intellect is indeed limited. If we adopt this attitude, then the light of Revelation will ensure that our intellect is adequately equipped to take us to a heavenly state.

> But give glad tidings to those who believe and work righteousness, that their portion is Gardens, beneath which rivers flow. 2:25

In this heavenly state, in the words of the Qur'an, the people will have 'no fear, and neither shall they grieve' (2:38).

In this book I have attempted to delineate the features of a system that can deal with human issues together as a whole. I have presented it here for the people of today with the hope that they might put aside their own ideas and consider it carefully in light of their knowledge, insight and historical experience. Should humanity reach the conclusion that this system contains a solution to all of humanity's problems, we should test it in practice. After all we cannot know for certain whether or not a system will have fruitful results without testing it. Incidentally the Qur'an urges humanity to put its Divine system into practice, in order that its results will speak for themselves:

> [This Book has been revealed] to the end that it may warn everyone who is alive [of heart], and that the [Divine] word may be proved against all who deny the truth. 36:70

The Qur'an thus tells us that only those who are 'alive' – that is, those who have a zest for life and can envision the limitless possibilities offered in the Qur'an – will heed its message and strive to make the Divine system of sustenance a reality. As for those who are 'dead' – those who have no appetite for life and have become mere men of clay – they are not even worth addressing. Indeed, neither does the Qur'an address this latter group, nor does this author have any expectations from them.

As we have stated earlier, the Qur'an emphasises that the establishment of an ideal human society is inevitable. This is Nature's decision, and it is final. No force on earth can stand in the way of the Divine system of sustenance.

> And they will ask you about the mountains. Say, then: 'My Sustainer will uproot them and scatter them like dust, / and leave the earth smooth and level, / [so that] you will see no curve on it, and no ruggedness.' 20:105-7

Having cleared all the obstacles in its path, those countless human beings who once suffered from oppression will suddenly have the way clear for them to rise up:

> And you shall behold the earth void and bare [i.e. free of obstacles] 18:47

And so when the system of *Rabbubiya* is widespread, humanity's suppressed qualities and neglected potential will be free to develop in full. Humanity as a whole will finally become strong enough to stand on its feet. The Qur'an states that this awesome revolution must and will come to pass.

Let us reiterate this point once more: This revolution *must* come to pass. We have repeated this on a number of occasions in this book. The question now arises: What will it take to make this revolution happen?

What it takes

The general reply to this question is that it is in the hands of God. After all, He is the Almighty, and everything is in His control. He can do whatever He wills. He answers to no one. So if He says that this revolution *must* occur, then surely it will.

No doubt God has all the power and none can change His decision. But God Himself has told us that everything He creates does not appear spontaneously or immediately like magic, but comes into being over a given period of time, in accordance with a fixed law. Earlier in this book we described this as God's universal programme. Therefore this revolution will manifest itself in accordance with the universal programme. But the difficulty is that we don't appreciate just how powerful this law is.

Force of law

When we hear the word 'law', we immediately think of courts of law because the word is generally associated with all that is legal. However 'law' in our context is not restricted to the judicial, but in fact encompasses the whole of reality. All that happens in the universe is in accordance with this law. All the celestial bodies throughout the universe move in precise orbits in accordance with this law. The sun rises and sets in a predictable pattern. The lunar phases are similarly fixed. The tides are controlled by this law. It allows huge heavy ships to float on the seas as easily as a duck. The winds are subject to this law, as is the rain. This law causes tiny acorns to grow into giant oaks and fields to produce crops for our subsistence. Electricity, the power source that has changed the face of this world, is also governed by this law. Even our physical bodies live and operate thanks solely to this law. In short there is nothing in existence that is not subject to it. 'Universal law' follows the logic of 'if ... then ... always': *If* you fulfil a certain condition, *then* there will be a certain result, and it will *always* be so. Whoever understands this universal law will thus always be confident in saying: '*If* this is the case, *then* this will happen, and it will *always* be the case.' When a doctor diagnoses a disease, he knows which treatment applies, and furthermore he will be absolutely certain of what effect it will have. Hence he can say with confidence that it will certainly work. He trusts in the predictable nature of the universal law. Similarly an astronomer can accurately predict which given date and time that a solar eclipse will next occur. He is so absolutely certain of this that he would bet his life on it. And as a domestic example, we have absolutely no doubt that the perfect boiled egg is ready seven minutes after we begin boiling. This is what is meant by a 'universal' law.

Certainty and the universal law

The Qur'an tells us that just as God's law operates throughout the universe it also applies to human life and society as well. This is where we can differentiate between a *momin* ('believer' or person of conviction) and a *kafir* ('rejecter'). It tells us also that the majority of people may accept that the physical universe is subject to an external law, but when it comes to the human equation they don't accept or acknowledge that the same law applies here as well. By 'external law' we mean that this law is controlling the universe, and not the other way round. For example, this law dictates the temperature at which water becomes steam, but the water itself does not decide this temperature. Again, the majority of people accept the existence of this law as far as the natural universe is concerned, but they will not accept it at the human level. Instead they say that every individual has the right to *decide* the laws that he will abide by. The Qur'an tells us that this attitude is erroneous:

> If indeed you ask them [the majority of people] who has created the heavens and the earth and subjected the sun and the moon [to His Law], they will certainly reply, 'God.' How are they then deluded away [from the truth]? 29:61

After this the Qur'an challenges them: If they accept that an external law is operational throughout the universe, then why, when it comes to human socioeconomic questions do they look to other (manmade) sources of law? And why don't they accept that our times of abundance and shortage occur not because of human laws, but rather they occur in accordance with the same external law that is in operation throughout the universe (29:62)? Those who accept the existence of an external law and yet openly deny that it applies to human life as well are called *kafireen* (plural of *kafir*) in the Qur'an. Those who recognise the existence of the external law in the natural universe (and even quietly acknowledge that it applies to the human equation), and yet choose to live under manmade systems are *mushrikeen* (lit. 'polytheist'[224]). For example the nations of the West recognise the existence of an external law operating throughout the physical universe, and so they study it and exploit it for their material progress. However when it comes to human society, they do not accept Divine law and so, instead of sharing the benefit of their study of nature with the rest of humanity, they utilise it to their own ends. As a result this earth has become a veritable hell. Yet if the West accepted and abided by Divine law, then we would witness a heaven on earth.

The natural universe differs from human society as follows:

1) Divine law is universal and automatically controls everything in the universe
2) Nothing in the natural universe has free will and so nothing can do anything that contravenes Divine law

Conversely, when it comes to human society:

1) These laws are not innate in us, but are made available to us via Revelation
2) Humanity has free will. We can choose to obey Divine law, or we can devise and live by laws of our own making

But just as nothing in the physical universe can supersede the dictates of natural law, no human system can hope to compete against Revelation. And just as we can do nothing to change the physical laws of the universe, we cannot do anything to circumvent Divine law in our socioeconomic existence. Hence:

---

[224] **Translators' note:** *Shirk* means 'to make someone a partner' and implies dividing or sharing, whether of property or authority (so a *mushrik* is someone who chooses to obey more than one authority). In the Qur'an it means a partner sharing in the authority that belongs to God, and so it is also a reference to polytheism. See Lane, *An Arabic-English Lexicon*, Book I (Part 4), p.1541.
Online: http://www.laneslexicon.co.uk Last retrieved 29 June 2012

> Not *on earth nor in heaven* are you able to frustrate [His Law], nor have you any protector or helper besides God. 29:22 (see also 24:57)

Hence we should not even presume that anyone could ever change or escape from the effect of Divine law, or that those who spend their lives in pursuit of selfish ends will progress in the long term (as compared to those who have conviction in Divine law):

> What! do those who seek after evil [i.e. manmade] ways [of life] think that We shall hold them equal with those who believe and do righteous deeds, that equal will be their life and their death? Ill is the judgment that they make. / God created the heavens and the earth for just ends, and in order that each soul may find the recompense of what it has earned, and none of them be wronged. 45:21-2

History as witness

The Qur'an urges us to study our own history, and observe that every great civilisation eventually fell and new nations took their place:

> How many were the populations We utterly destroyed because of their iniquities, setting up other peoples in their place? 21:11

Such was the state of these civilisations that when the consequences of their actions inevitably began to catch up with them, they panicked:

> Yet, when they felt Our punishment [coming], behold, they [tried to] flee from it. 21:12

> Flee not, but return to the good things of this life which were given you, and to your homes, in order that you may be called to account. 21:13

In other words, Divine law gripped them and they had nowhere to hide. They had no choice but to face the consequences of their ill-gotten wealth. They had exploited and benefited from the work of others; they had hoarded, and built extravagant monuments to their material success. And so they stood exposed.

Called to account

Let us briefly consider the final line of the above verse more closely: 'that you may be called to account'. This is the Qur'an's way of telling us that all people without exception will eventually answer to Divine law. As things stand at present, when a group of people becomes extremely powerful, it does whatever it feels like, and its members feel supremely confident that they will never have to answer to anyone. Whether this powerful force takes the form of a singular tyrant like Genghis Khan, or whether, as in the modern age, it takes the form of the tyranny of the majority, the resultant attitude is the same: 'No one can question us'. As far as they are concerned, once they take a decision it becomes law and no one can challenge it. The Qur'an tells us that this attitude is false. The fact remains that the outcome of every decision they take is actually determined by Divine law. Even if a ninety-nine percent majority *decides* that from today poison will be good for you, their decision will not change the fact that it is poison and it will never be good for them. Poison will not change its nature just because the majority says so. It will retain its nature in accordance with the dictates of Divine law. Likewise the majority may decide that it is fine to exploit and live off others' efforts, but this does not mean that they will get away with it. They can decide or believe whatever they like, but they will still be subject to Divine law. This is what the Qur'an means when it says that they will be called to account:

> But stop them, for *they must be asked*: 37:24

Again, they are deluded in thinking that they will never have to account for their actions. Indeed they are subject to Divine law and cannot escape it. Their unjust actions have not gone unnoticed; in fact, the consequences will surely engulf them sooner or later:

> They ask you to hasten on the punishment: but, of a surety, Hell will encompass the rejecters! 29:54

> They shall not [be able to] evade [the consequences]. 82:16

The Divine law of requital

When nations of 'rejecters' (*kafireen*) devise a law that serves their interests, they gloat: 'See? No one can touch us!' But they don't realise that the law of requital has already surrounded them on all sides.

> And yet, they who are bent on rejecting the truth persist in doing so: / but all the while God encompasses them without their being aware of it. 95:19-20

Divine law dictates therefore that no matter what they do, the consequences must and will catch up with them. Accepting (as we do) that history corroborates this reality and the power of the law of requital, we can say with a full sense of conviction that the Divine revolution for an ideal state will certainly occur.

This is a Divine guarantee:

> The Hour will certainly come: of that there is no doubt: yet most men have no conviction in it. 40:59

The mistake that most people make is they expect an immediate result of the type we frequently observe in the physical universe. For example, we know that putting one's hand in fire is bad for us, since the consequence is immediately apparent. But when we defy Divine law in our social life, the consequences of doing so do not materialise in the short term. Subsequently we make the mistake of thinking that there was no consequence. Hence, in the above verse, 'yet most men have no conviction in it'. Thus it is in our social existence that a sense of conviction is absolutely necessary. We must unequivocally accept the fact that the universe does not operate on blind forces, but upon a law behind which is the Personality that is Wise, the All-Aware, the All-Knowing, the All-Hearing, and the All-Seeing.

The need for conviction

The external law that exerts its influence throughout the natural universe similarly exerts its influence on socioeconomics. It is simply not possible for any human law to supersede Divine or natural law, because it is impossible for any manmade system to benefit humanity as Divine law does. Only a system that is established in line with the

Divine decree is beneficial to humanity, since it is also in harmony with the natural order. Any system not established in accordance with the Divine decree is bound to lead to chaos and destruction. And yet if Qur'anic ideals are introduced to a manmade system, they will transform it from a chaotic force to a beneficial one. This is what we might call a Divine or heavenly revolution.

Human versus Divine law

By 'revolution', we mean change, i.e. the replacement of manmade laws with a true system. To make a comparison of the differences between manmade systems and the Divine system would require a book of its own; but we can list the general major differences as follows:

1) In human systems there will always be an inequitable distribution of labour, i.e. there will always be a class that is wholly unproductive and is a burden on society. Yet strangely, rather than being recognised for what they really are, this class of people either sit in positions of political and economic power or they sit in the pulpit where they can live off the blood of others (9:34). However in the Divine system of *Rabbubiya*, the formation of such a class is impossible, since no one bears the burden of another (53:38)

2) In human systems there is a class that profits solely from investment, and not from labour. Others do all the work, and they take the lion's share of the earnings. This is what the Qur'an calls *riba* (lit. 'increase'), and it can take any form. In the Divine system (barring those who for whatever reason are *unable* to work) everyone must work. Anyone who tries to avoid work without a valid reason will be immediately prevented from sharing in the benefits of the society. The basic principle of such a society will be that we can earn only that which we strive for (53:39)

3) The basic principle of a human (capitalist) system is that whatever an individual earns by using his intellect becomes his rightful property and none can take it from him. Hence a single household might acquire excessive wealth whilst others are left without enough to get a daily meal. In the Divine system every individual works to full capacity, but keeps only what he needs, whilst leaving the

remainder of his earnings open for the benefit of society (2:219). In this system hoarding will be considered a grave crime with dire consequences (9:35)

4) In human systems some people take the land (including its potential for produce) into private ownership and restrict others from utilising its resources. In the Divine system however neither the land nor its resources can be taken into private ownership. These are left open for the benefit of all (41:10)

5) In human systems the tax collector's only duty is to receive the people's dues; but no one is responsible for ensuring that these taxes are put to good use in helping everyone to meet their needs. In the Divine system the responsibility of ensuring that sustenance reaches each and every member of society falls on the administration (11:6). It will take care of their children as well (17:31). Not only will the system ensure that no one goes hungry, but it will also ensure that all other physical needs are met as well (20:118-19). In a human system the focus is solely on bread and defines its success in terms of its ability to meet just this form of sustenance; but in the Divine system 'sustenance' goes beyond bread and includes everything needed to unlock humanity's hidden potential. The pioneers of this ideal society work to establish a system of *salaat* and thereby arrange for the sustenance and development of humanity (22:41). The subject of this 'development' will be the human 'self', because in a true system success is defined in terms of how developed the human personality becomes (91:7-9). Thus the purpose of establishing this system is to perfect the self. The individual does not sacrifice himself for society; rather society exists for the benefit of the self. Since the human self will continue to exist beyond death and continue with its evolution, the Divine system not only provides everyone with the good things on earth, but also ensures that the self will receive the good things of the life after death as well (2:201)

6) In human systems humanity has become divided into conflicting nations and groups, and every nation exploits

and deceives others in order to protect its interests. In the Divine system all manmade divisions are eliminated and humanity becomes united as one family. This system aims to serve the interests of the whole of humanity and not just one particular section of it. This is because it is founded upon the principle that the only true system of life is one that benefits the whole of humanity. It is the only one that will persist or 'remain on earth' (13:17)

7) In human systems, the criterion for respect and honour is based upon one's social background. Those who are born into wealthy households and thus are able to purchase power are automatically treated with respect. This class also tends to view all other people as being below them in status. In the Divine system however, every single person is equally worthy of respect simply by virtue of being a human being (17:70). Here the criterion for respect is based upon how much an individual does for humanity. He who fulfils his duty to the utmost will have the greatest position of honour (49:13)

8) Finally, it has always been the case that whatever system the human intellect might conceive of, it has ultimately created a class of rulers and a class of the ruled. This has been true in every system, from the monarchy of old to present-day democracy. No matter what form the government takes, this class divide always exists. Conversely there is no concept of rulers versus the ruled in the Divine system, because the laws that govern how human beings should lead their lives have been predetermined by God and not humans, and thus they are fixed into the constitution. Subsequently no one will be able to declare his own authority over another, since this would be a subversion of the Divine authority (3:79). All everyday affairs of the state will involve the people in what the Qur'an calls 'mutual consultation', and all subsidiary laws will be enacted accordingly. Such laws will be followed by all, starting with those who work directly in the administration, since they will lead by example (6:163)

The members of this ideal society will themselves bear witness to the fact that here there is no one begging and no one deprived; there is no master and no slave. The Divine system is one in which there is no oppression and coercion (2:256). It is designed to bring humanity to its peak and is the one that will certainly come into being, in accordance with the decree of the Qur'an.

Human revolution

Just as the Divine system is incomparable to any other in the world, likewise the revolution to establish it is unlike anything seen in human revolutions. Generally speaking a human economic revolution is driven by a desire to create a society in which everyone's material needs are met. We know that the vast majority of the world's people do not have enough to meet their needs, whilst a tiny percentage of people control the vast majority of the world's wealth. Obviously under these circumstances any revolutionary cry for equity will receive the support of the majority, since the majority are poor. It doesn't take much to incite rebellion against the wealthy elite and to take everything from them without fear of consequence. The fact is that needy people are always quite willing to steal from the rich; it is only the force of law that prevents them from doing so. If someone tells them to break their shackles and rise up, and promises them that he (as instigator of the rebellion) will take responsibility for any fallout, then a violent revolution can occur overnight. This was the call that Marx made to the proletariat. His slogan was: 'Workers of the world, unite! You have nothing to lose but your shackles.'

But let us consider the aftermath of this 'revolution'. You call out to the desperate and the needy. They heed the call. They snatch the wealth from the rich and see change happen in front of their eyes. They quickly gain much and lose nothing in the process. But before they have even finished looting you suddenly order them: 'Now get back to work'. It goes without saying that the people do not like to hear this. They respond: 'What's the point of a revolution if it ends with us returning to hard labour again?' Nevertheless they may reluctantly return to work, but then you tell them that the surplus of their earnings must come back to you (i.e. the government) so that it can be distributed to those who cannot earn for whatever reason. Will the people agree to it? They will say: 'You had called us to revolt with the promise that we will lose nothing, and gain everything. But now, not only do we have to work, but most of what we earn has to be given away as well! We supported you in order to *gain*, not to *give!*'

Mark the underlying problem. This was the same class that was never happy to give in the first place. They supported the revolution only for its gains. Now you have little choice but to deal with this class as you did with the capitalists: You have to take their wealth by force. Without force neither can you get the people to work to full capacity, nor can you get them to give up any of their wages. If a person knows that no matter how much he produces – even if he produces a tonne – he will only receive a tiny portion of it to fulfil his basic needs, then what incentive does he have for being fully productive? The fact is you will have to make the people productive by force, and you will have to take their wages from them by force as well. The final resort is the 'iron curtain' of the type Russia adopted after its first generation in order to hide its shameful situation from the world. Of course, a system in which people *willingly* give to one another will be productive and successful, its society will be happy, and so there will be no need for a curtain of any kind, let alone an iron one. In fact its people will be anxious to share their success with the rest of the world, and will be acting as an example for others to follow.

And you see the people enter God's *deen* in crowds 110:2

Divine revolution

A revolution for the Divine system of *Rabbubiya* does not employ the above aggressive methods that communism does. In reality, our present understanding of revolution is not really a revolution at all; it is mere rebellion and chaos. The person who advocates the system of sustenance does not direct his call at the poor, nor does he promise nothing but gain. Instead he addresses those who already have plenty and are in a position to give their surplus away. He invites them to help create a system whereby their surplus will be used to raise the living standards of all. The Qur'an shows us that all the messengers addressed the wealthy class for this reason. They were invited to help establish a system in which everyone would work to their full capacity and leave their surplus earnings open to society. The Qur'an thus sets up its system through those who are in a position to give. It asks nothing of those who will receive. In fact the opening pages of the Qur'an state that the pioneers of the revolution will be those who:

Who believe in the unseen, establish *salaat*, and spend out of what We have provided for them 2:3

No one compels or forces these pioneers to do this. They willingly act upon the truth that they have seen in the Qur'an and which they have wholeheartedly accepted. In short, they recognise that the secret of life lies in giving, not taking. It is with this in mind that they take the steps to establish the Divine system and they also work as hard as they can, so that they will be in a position to give more and thereby develop their selves further. Of course not only wealthy people but also poor people support the Divine revolution, and indeed the poor are the first to be drawn to its ideals. However they don't join the revolution in order to take from the rich; rather, they join it with a view to eliminate the injustices caused by false human systems in operation throughout the world. Indeed they are prepared to give up their lives for it. Ultimately all who join the revolution do so with the intent to give to humanity – whether that 'giving' is in the form of time, energy, talents, or even life. The method of revolution for the Divine system thus begins in the heart, and the external revolution that occurs is its natural outcome. It goes without saying that bringing about this kind of revolution requires much effort and hard work.

Surplus wealth

Bernard Shaw has said (and to an extent rightly so):

> When we have examined the possibilities of this apparently simple matter of spare money, *alias* Capital [*sic*], you will find that spare money is the root of all evil[225]

In fact the entire economic problem comes down to surplus wealth. Those with surplus wealth tend to hide it to prevent anyone from stealing it. And those who would like to take it are constantly following wealthy people around. If a man keeps his surplus wealth in his wallet, someone is always ready to pickpocket him. If he puts it in a safety deposit box, a thief will find a way to break in. If he puts it in a safe, armed robbers will come for it. If he puts it in a bank, the taxman will demand it. And finally, Heaven's salesmen have their eye on whatever is left and seek to take it by 'collection'. All this happens in order to try and take an individual's surplus. But the Qur'an does not

---

[225]   Shaw,   Bernard   (1928)   *The   Intelligent   Woman's   Guide   to Socialism,   Capitalism,   Sovietism   and   Fascism*   1949   reprint, London: Constable & Co., p.128

take surplus wealth by force. It brings about a change in hearts and minds; and so whoever has a surplus will constantly be looking for somewhere to spend it on humanity.

> And they ask you as to what they should spend [in God's cause]. Say: 'Whatever is surplus to your needs.' 2:219

They do so because they know that their expenditure will benefit the whole of humanity and enable every individual to perfect his or her 'self'. Hence they will not only live in dignity on earth, but they will also be entitled to receive the good things of the hereafter. This is the kind of revolution that the Qur'an decrees for humanity. It is also called Islam, and those who establish it are 'Muslim'.

Here the question arises as to how we can bring about the change in people's hearts, minds and outlook that will make the external change a reality. The obvious answer is education. The Qur'an addresses this point as follows:

> It is He Who has sent to the unlettered people a messenger from among themselves, to rehearse to them His messages, to sanctify them, and to instruct them in Scripture and wisdom 62:2

In other words, here the Qur'an shows us that the Messenger's role in instigating the Divine revolution was that of a teacher. He introduced them to the Revelation, and showed them the implications of its teachings. He also explained the basis of these teachings and the results its followers should expect to see from implementing them in practice. Likewise, any pioneers of the Divine revolution today would need to go ahead and pass on what they have learned to others, and thereby change their hearts also. These disseminators of the message thus act as *rabbani* (i.e. human agents of *Rabb* – Divine sustenance):

> 'Become men of God [*rabbaneeyena*][226] by spreading the knowledge of the Divine writ, and by your own deep study [of it].' 3:79

---

[226] Asad explains his use of the expression 'man of God' for *rabbani* (singular of *rabbaneeyena*) as follows: 'According to Sibawayh (as quoted by Razi), a *rabbani* is "one who devotes himself exclusively to the endeavour to know the Sustainer (*ar-Rabb*) and to obey Him": a connotation fairly close to the English expression "a man of God".'

They remind each other that they will always participate in positive work in accordance with Divine law, and will remain committed to the Divine programme:

> [They] do righteous deeds, and enjoin upon one another the mutual teaching of truth, and [enjoin upon one another] patience in adversity. 103:3

Hence these pioneers become so dedicated that they have the ideal in mind at all times (3:191) and indeed it becomes as natural to them as breathing. Their children, being born into this environment, also naturally pick up the truth as they grow and take it for granted; and furthermore, when they go out into the world they will find proof everywhere of all that they have learned at home, and this will serve to strengthen their conviction. This is how the Qur'an makes clear that the secret to developing the self at the individual level lies in actively working towards the development of humanity; and that the purpose of life is to develop the self. Those who fully comprehend this point are the ones who ultimately lay the foundation for the Divine revolution. As we have already discussed, neither is anyone compelled to join this programme nor is anyone prevented from leaving the system should he so desire. Since the system is dedicated to freeing and developing the self, obviously there can be no room for compulsion. Nevertheless if any force attempts to hinder the Divine system, or tries to thwart the propagation of its ideals by force, then it will be incumbent on the *momineen* (people with conviction) to stand against it.

> And fight them [the oppressors] until there is no more oppression, and justice and God's *deen* prevail; but if they cease, let there be no hostility except to those who practise oppression. 2:193

Even in war, the members of the Divine system will never commit deceitful acts, and will never be involved in any conspiracy; there will be no breach of trust on their side, nor will they commit any crimes against humanity. This is because they obey Divine law and their ideals are freedom and the betterment of humanity.

We might wonder whether it is indeed possible for a mere education movement to instigate such a momentous change across this vast world. But we mustn't forget that in today's world with its modern technology and ease of travel, the world has essentially shrunk and become a global village. Communicating an idea across the world is much easier today than at any previous time in history. But of course whoever wishes to spread a new idea must have the power of the media at his disposal. If any country today comes to accept and then implement the truth, it is not difficult to imagine that the rest of the world will be inspired by its success and prosperity. For this reason, today's conditions are ripe for the Divine revolution.

Now consider the following: If this system is established, it will automatically resolve the socioeconomic issues that presently seem irresolvable. With the establishment of the Divine system, economic slavery will come to an end, and so will the war between wealthy landlords and poor farmers. The never-ending conflict between industry workers and bosses which presently wastes enormous time and energy will cease, as will the conflict between home proprietors and their tenants. The lender and borrower will be no more. There will be no more haggling between shopkeepers and customers. There will be no more fighting over estate and inheritance. The parasitic institutes of interest and profit will be eliminated. Crimes that people have always committed out of desperation and poverty will be no more, whilst the chaos that ensues with economic inequity will cease to be an issue. There will be no more wealthy classes that are free to do as they please. All homes will be sanctuaries of peace and happiness. People will be free to roam through the markets without fear of being robbed or attacked. People will be able to trust all businesses and services. In short, every member of society will be dedicated to following Divine law and to working for the betterment of everyone; and so we will witness a heaven on earth.

Conclusion

Remember that this is not merely the vision of a poet, or a utopian dream. This is a reality which must and will come into being; a revolution that will happen. Time itself is waiting to see which fortunate nation will take up the torch of truth and light the way for the rest of the world. This nation will lead and take the whole of humanity towards the heaven that Adam lost so long ago. This – the Divine system of sustenance – is humanity's beautiful destination:

> [And so it is that] they who attain to conviction and do righteous deeds are destined for happiness [in this world] and the most beauteous of all goals [in the life to come]! 13:29

BIBLIOGRAPHY

[Some books and journals for which the bibliographic details are incomplete have been omitted.]

Ali, Abdullah Yusuf (1934) *The Holy Qur'an* 2000 reprint, Hertfordshire: Wordsworth Editions Ltd.

Asad, M. (2003) *The Message of the Qur'an* Bristol: The Book Foundation

Belden, Jack (1940) *China Shakes the World* New York: Harper & Brothers

Bentham, Jeremy (1838-43) *The Works of Jeremy Bentham, published under the Superintendence of his Executor, John Bowring* Edinburgh: William Tait Vol. X

Berdyaev, Nicolas (1943) *Slavery and Freedom* London: G. Bles / Centenary Press

Berdyaev, Nicolas (1949) *The Divine and the Human* (trans. R.M. French) London: Geoffrey Bles

Bergson, Henri (1935) *The Two Sources of Morality and Religion* (trans. R. Ashley Audra and Cloudesley Brereton) London: Macmillan & Co.

Briffault, Robert (1919) *The Making of Humanity* London: George Allen & Unwin

Briffault, Robert (1930) *Rational Evolution (The Making of Humanity)* New York: Macmillan

Buber, Martin (1947) *Between Man and Man* (trans. Ronald Gregor Smith) London: Kegan Paul

Caird, John (1880) *An Introduction to the Philosophy of Religion: The Croall Lecture for 1878-79* Glasgow: James Maclehose, p.279-80

Carr, Edward H. (1951) *The New Society* 1957 reprint, Massachusetts: Beacon Press

Cassirer, Ernst (1944) *An Essay on Man: An Introduction to a Philosophy of Human Culture* 1972 reprint, New Haven: Yale University Press

Darwin, Charles (1860) *On the Origin of Species by Means of Natural Selection: Or, The Preservation of Favoured Races in the Struggle for Life* (5th printing) London: John Murray

Department of Social Sciences, 1952. *The Race Concept: Results of an Inquiry* Paris: UNESCO, p.6. Online: http://unesdoc.unesco.org/images/0007/000733/073351eo.pdf Last retrieved 15 June 2012

Driesch, Hans (1914) *The Problem of Individuality* London: Macmillan

Dwight, Thomas (1911) *Thoughts of a Catholic Anatomist* New York: Longman, Green & Co.

Fineberg, J. (ed.) (1935) *V.I. Lenin: Collected Works* Vol. XI: The Theoretical Principles of Marxism New York: International Publishers

Frederick II, *Political Testament* as cited in Murray, Robert H. (1946) *The Individual and the State* London: Hutchinson

Fromm, Eric (1956) *The Art of Loving* (1995 reprint) London: Thorsons

Freud, Sigmund (1922) *The Pleasure Principle* (Authorised translation from the second German edition by C.J.M. Hubback) London/Vienna: The International Psycho-Analytical Press

Freud, Sigmund (1925) *On Creativity and the Unconscious: Papers on the Psychology of Art, Literature, Love, and Religion* New York: Harper

Hastings, Rashdall (1907) *The Theory of Good and Evil: A Treatise on Moral Philosophy* Oxford: Clarendon Press Vol. II

Hawtrey, Ralph G. (1944) *Economic Destiny* London: Longman, Green & Co.

Huxley, Aldous (1937) *Ends and Means: An Enquiry into the Nature of Ideals and into the Methods employed for their Realization* 1965 reprint, London: Chatto & Windus

Huxley, Julian (1945) *Essays in Popular Science* London: Chatto & Windus

Iqbal, Muhammad (1936) *Zarb-e-Kaleem* (*The Rod of Moses*). Translation online:
http://www.allamaiqbal.com/works/poetry/urdu/zarb/translation/0 7rod.pdf Last retrieved 21 May 2012

Iqbal, Muhammad (1938) *Armaghaan-e-Hijaz* (*The Gift of Hijaz*). Translation online:
http://www.allamaiqbal.com/works/poetry/persian/aramghan/tran slation/09gift.pdf Last retrieved 21 May 2012

Iqbal, Muhammad (1977) *A Message from the East: A translation of Iqbal's Payam-i Mashriq into English verse* (trans. M. Hadi Hussain) Lahore: Iqbal Academy Pakistan

Joad, C.E.M. (1940) *Philosophy For Our Times* 1941 reprint, London: Readers' Union

Joad, C.E.M. (1948) *Decadence* London: Faber & Faber

Jones, Frederic Wood (1942) *Design and Purpose*, London: Kegan Paul

Karim, S. (2010) *Secular Jinnah & Pakistan: What the Nation Doesn't Know* Co. Mayo: CheckPoint Press

Lane, E.W. (1968 reprint) *An Arabic-English Lexicon* in 8 parts Beirut: Librarie du Liban. Online: http://www.laneslexicon.co.uk Last retrieved 29 June 2012

Laurat, Lucien (1940) *Marxism and Democracy* (trans. Edward Fitzgerald) London: Gollancz

Lovedey, Alexander (1950) *The Only Way: A Study of Democracy in Danger* London: William Hodge & Co.

Machiavelli, Niccolo (1532) *The Prince* 1913 reprint, Oxford: Clarendon Press

Mandeville, Bernard (1732) *The Fable of the Bees, or, Private Vices, Publick Benefits* (sixth edition) London: J. Tonson

Mason, J.W.T. (1926) *Creative Freedom* New York: Harper & Brothers

Morgan, Conwy Lloyd, 'The Ascent of Mind' in Mason, Francis Baker (ed.) (1934) *The Great Design: Order and Progress in Nature* New York: Macmillan

Mumford, Lewis (1940) *Faith for Living* New York: Harcourt, Brace & Co.

Mumford, Lewis (1951) *The Conduct of Life* 1970 reprint, New York: Harcourt Brace Jovanovich

Murray, J.M. (1944) *Adam and Eve: An Essay towards a New and Better Society* London: Andrew Dakers

Niebuhr, Reinhold (1932) *Moral Man and Immoral Society: A Study in Ethics and Politics* 2005 reprint, London: Continuum International Publishing Group

Nietzsche, Friedrich W. (1891) *Thus Spake Zarathustra* English translation by Thomas Common 2007 reprint, Kansas: Digireads.com

Ouspensky P.D. (1922) *Tertium Organum* (trans. Claude Bragdon) 1970 reprint, New York: Vintage Books

Ouspensky, P.D. (1931) *A New Model of the Universe* 1997 reprint, New York: Dover Publications

Ouspensky, P.D. (1949) *In Search of the Miraculous* (2001 reprint) New York: Harcourt

Parwez, G.A. (1945) *Iblees-o-Adam* Lahore: Tolu-e-Islam

Parwez, G.A. (1949) *Miraaj-e-Insaaniat* (Ascent of Humanity) Lahore: Tolu-e-Islam

Parwez, G.A. (1952) *Asbaab-e-Zawal-e-Ummat* Lahore: Tolu-e-Islam

Parwez, G.A. (1953) *Letters to Saleem* Lahore: Tolu-e-Islam

Parwez, G.A. (1955) *Insaan ne Kya Socha?* Lahore: Tolu-e-Islam

Parwez, G.A. (1967) *Jihad* Lahore: Tolu-e-Islam

Paul, Leslie Allen (1949) *The Meaning of Human Existence* London: Faber & Faber

Planck, Max (1931) *The Universe in the Light of Modern Physics* (first English edition). London: Allen & Unwin

Russell, Bertrand (1946) *History of Western Philosophy and its Connection with Political and Social Circumstances from the Earliest Times to the Present Day* London: George Allen & Unwin

Russell, Bertrand (1949) *Authority and the Individual* 2010 reprint, London: Routledge Classics

Selsam, Howard (1943) *Socialism and Ethics* New York: International Publishers

Shaw, Bernard (1928) *The Intelligent Woman's Guide to Socialism, Capitalism, Sovietism and Fascism* 1949 reprint, London: Constable & Co.

Sheen, Fulton John (1948) *Philosophy of Religion: The Impact of Modern Knowledge on Religion* New York: Appleton-Century-Crofts

Simons, Yves Rene (1951) *Philosophy of Democratic Government* 1993 reprint, London: University of Notre Dame Press. Online (University of Notre Dame website): http://maritain.nd.edu/jmc/etext/pdg.htm Last retrieved 03 August 2012

Sorely, William R. (1921) *Moral Values and the Idea of God: The Gifford lectures delivered in the University of Aberdeen in 1914 and 1915* (second edition) Cambridge: Cambridge University Press

Spalding, H.N. (1939) *Civilization in East and West: An Introduction to the Study of Human Progress* Oxford: Oxford University Press / Humphrey Milford

Spencer, Herbert (1879) *The Data of Ethics* New York: Cambridge University Press 2012 reprint

Stekel, Wilhelm (1943) *Peculiarities of Behavior: Wandering Mania, Dipsomania, Cleptomania, Pyromania and Allied Impulsive Disorders* (trans. James Samuel Van Teslaar) New York: Liveright, Vol. II

Townsend, Joseph (1786) *A Dissertation on the Poor Laws: By a Well-Wisher to Mankind* 1971 reprint, London: University of California Press Ltd.

Whitehead, Alfred North (1926) *Religion in the Making: Lowell Lectures, 1926.* 2011 reprint, New York: Cambridge University Press

OTHER WORKS BY THE AUTHOR

- *Exposition of the Qur'an*
- *Islam: A Challenge to Religion*
- *The Book of Destiny*
- *Qur'anic Laws*
- *Reasons for the Decline of Muslims*
- *Letters to Tahira*

Publication details of the above titles appear over the following pages. For queries regarding availability, please contact:

UK, Europe:

Islamic Dawn Society
76 Park Road
Ilford, Essex

bazm.london@talktalk.net

Pakistan, international:

Tolu-e-Islam Trust
25-B Gulberg 2
Lahore – 54660
PAKISTAN

www.toluislam.com
trust@toluislam.com

EXPOSITION OF THE QUR'AN

The celebrated Urdu expositional translation of the Qur'an by G.A. Parwez, titled *Mafhoom-ul-Qur'an*, is now available in English. In 1983 Parwez began this translation himself, but managed to complete just over half the text (up to the 18th surah) before he passed away in 1985. Some time after his death, the Tolu-e-Islam Trust resumed the editing and publication of this work.

It is well known that translating the Qur'an into any language, let alone English, is a most challenging task. Many Qur'anic terms represent entire concepts and so are impossible to faithfully translate using one equivalent English word – and sometimes an English word doesn't even exist for it. For this reason Parwez did not translate word for word as with most traditional translations, but presented his as an 'exposition'. To avoid making the text cumbersome and repetitive, he also chose not to translate certain Qur'anic terms at all but instead retained them in the text, e.g. *deen, hamd, kafir, momin, mushrik, nabi,* etc. and explained their full meanings in a specially-prepared glossary.

This is a work of English translation quite unlike most efforts of the past, and a scholarly attempt to convey the pristine concepts of the Qur'an. However, as Parwez himself acknowledged, the original Arabic text of *Wahi* is eternal and so no human interpretation can be treated as the final word on the subject.

The book is complete with footnotes, Arabic and Biblical names, bibliography, index and a comprehensive glossary of around 140 important Qur'anic terms.

ISLAM: A CHALLENGE TO RELIGION

The very name of the book appears paradoxical, for it is universally accepted that Islam is one of the major religions of the world. So how could a religion challenge the very institution to which it subscribes? The author has indeed made a successful bid to prove this strange aphorism for the first time in the history of Islamic thought and his research deserves careful study. It is thought-provoking; it is revolutionary, opening new vistas and horizons for fresh intellectual endeavours. It is the outcome of a life-long study of one of the renowned Qur'anic thinkers of our times.

The author has not, however, taken a negative attitude towards Islam. Having proved his claim that Islam is *not* a religion, he has lucidly explained what it really is, and how it offers the most convincing and enduring answers to those eternal questions which even thinking man asks about the meaning and purpose of life and how it can be achieved. The book is thus a unique attempt at the rediscovery of Islam: Scholarly written and exquisitely presented.

THE BOOK OF DESTINY

Originally appearing in Urdu under the title *Kitaab-ut-Taqdeer* in October 1971, this scholarly work addresses a philosophical subject that has confounded Muslim thinkers for centuries. It deals with age-old theological questions such as: Does God decide every individual's fate and destiny *before* one is born? Is there a pre-determined collective or individual destiny for mankind? Can an individual, or a group, change its destiny? If one's fate is preordained and inescapable, what are the implications for the question of 'reward and punishment'? And how does all of this affect humankind's freedom of choice and free will?

Parwez has ably explained these and other related puzzles in everyday language for the average reader and has successfully removed the confusion that has surrounded this subject for the better part of the last millennium and a half. What is more important from an academic perspective is that the author has dealt with this topic in light of the Quran itself.

Translated by Khalid Sayyed, UK.

QUR'ANIC LAWS

Qur'anic Laws was written to meet pressing demands. It provides the code of laws for an Islamic state, and as such it may be considered a precursor of *Tabweeb-ul-Qur'an* – a grand, magnificent, and marvelous classification of the Qur'an by the late Ghulam Ahmad Parwez in three large volumes.

There is no denying that in this book, Parwez has given the purport of Qur'anic verses in prolific detail. In places he has also drawn some inferences of his own, though he acknowledges that these represent his own suggestions and that in practice this right belongs to the Legislative Assembly of an Islamic State.

Although this collection of Qur'anic laws shall be beneficial to all Muslims in general, it will be particularly useful to those involved in jurisprudence, i.e., judges, advocates, members of the legislature, the constituent assemblies, those working with other legal sections of the government, and those concerned with the media. The chapters of this book deal with topics such as state affairs, government agencies, justice, general injunctions for family life, inheritance and testament, protection of life and property. Other chapters pertain to economy and basic human rights, etc.

Translated by late Dr. Syed Abdul Wadud, Pakistan.

REASONS FOR THE DECLINE OF MUSLIMS

For the last two centuries or so, the Muslims have been emotionally and mentally preoccupied with their own rise and fall, and have lamented and wailed endlessly about their glorious past. Others have become disgusted at their present state to the extent that they now reject it altogether in the name of modernity. The Muslim world at large remains traumatised by events of the recent past: The disintegration of the Mughal Empire, leading to the dethronement of Bahadur Shah Zafar in the last century, followed by the self-destruction of the Ottomans and dethronement of Sultan Abdul Hamid II during and after the First World War.

Even a cursory glance over history makes it abundantly clear that the collapse of a civilisation does not happen suddenly. It is usually preceded by a prolonged phase of decay, with Nature watching, as if hoping against hope that humankind may yet see the edge of the precipice and turn back. In Qur'anic terms this is the 'period of respite'.

The fact remains that the decline of Muslims ocurred because, as with others before them, they had reached the point of no return. G.A. Parwez is one of the few who objectively and scientifically attempted an analysis of the causes of the fall of Muslim civilisation from the Qur'anic perspective of history. This little book is available in both Urdu (orginal title: *Asbaab-e-Zawal-e-Ummat*) and English.

Translated by late Ismail Atcha, UK.

LETTERS TO TAHIRA

Letters to Tahira is essentially a collection of letters written to a mature and inquisitive young lady. They represent the responses to queries the author had received from many female readers of his earlier book written for young men, *Letters to Saleem*.

These letters address the trials, tribulations and the vexing problems that the unfortunate and helpless girls of our society have to face today. Some letters highlight the maladies that are currently rampant amongst our modern educated class, and which have resulted from following Western cultural values blindly. The nation is gradually pushing towards destruction, and if the orthodox section of the society needs reform, then so do the liberal modernists. It is imperative that both extremes be brought to the middle path, in light of the Qur'an.

It is a stark fact that women can train, discipline and build a society more easily and effectively than men. The publishing of these letters will hopefully initiate the reformation process at home.

Translated by Surraya Alvi, USA.

www.ingramcontent.com/pod-product-compliance
Lightning Source LLC
Chambersburg PA
CBHW072112270326
41931CB00010B/1531